PSYCHED
Inner Views of Winning

by
Terry Orlick and
John Partington

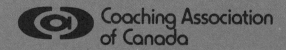 Coaching Association
of Canada

PUBLISHED BY

COACHING ASSOCIATION OF CANADA

333 RIVER ROAD, OTTAWA, ONTARIO
K1L 8H9 CANADA

Photographs courtesy of:

Athlete Information Bureau
Canadian Olympic Association
Canapress Photo Service

Photographers:

Ted Grant
Crombie McNeil
Jim Merrithew
Tim O'Lett

ISBN 0-920678-24-6

Printed by Johanns Graphics

The programs of this association
are financially supported
by **Sport Canada**

 Government of Canada
Fitness and Amateur Sport

Printed in Canada

PSYCHED
INNER VIEWS OF WINNING

INTRODUCTORY CHAPTERS

ATHLETE STORIES

FOREWORD

by Abby Hoffman

s is the case with virtually every current or former athlete, I can recount in vivid detail one significant performance which stands out above every other competition in a lengthy career. The performance stands out not just because the ultimate result was gratifying, but rather because the feeling leading up to, during and after the competition seemed to constitute one of those rare days in sport when everything seemed to be "just right".

And years later, when other competitions have receded into dim nostalgia requiring reference to diaries or newspaper clippings for re-creating, the reliving of that one performance seems effortless — the details and the feelings are so real it's as if the event concluded just a few moments ago.

In my own case, I can re-create my event in the 1972 Munich Olympics, as though a permanent video replay was stored in my mind. What was significant for me about that event was not that I accomplished my quadrennial objective of placing in the final 8 at the Olympics, nor even that I accomplished my lifetime objective of breaking the Olympic record (preceded unfortunately by the 7 other Olympic finalists!), but rather the focused energy which was applied to the three races during that Olympic competition. That is what stands out in my mind.

I remember the almost unnerving calm in my reaction as I stood in the warm-up tunnel at the Munich Olympic Stadium watching the first several heats of Round 1 competition in my event. Several outstanding runners recorded performances faster than my personal best in those early heats but fell by the wayside as the qualifying position of top 2 from each heat eluded them. The fear that fills many athletes faced with the prospect of recording a "best ever" performance just to survive the preliminary heats provided on this occasion a greater resolve rather than that oft-felt instinct to flee the stadium.

In each of the three races in which I competed I recall the visual focusing — only on the physical space spanned by the pack of runners — about 10 feet at most; the absolute silence — even in face of the din of 80,000 spectators cheering the home country favourite, national heroine and eventual gold medalist Hildegard Falck; and total concentration on each step, the split times (for the first time conveniently displayed for athletes to read on large stadium time clocks), and the placement and movements of every other runner.

I remember as well the irony associated with the fact that only the 5 non-medalists recorded personal best times — everyone went home happy! In my case the performance capped 10 years of international competition and a 6 month period of training — in the form of a rather self indulgent though necessarily singleminded and virtually solitary training "camp" at ideal locations in North America and Europe. This period of training was subsidized through a Sport Canada program titled, appropriately enough for that era of Canadian sport "Intensive care"!

It was only several years later at a sport conference at Esalen, California that I first heard people talking seriously about the psychological dimensions of sport performance. Focusing, centering, visualization, mental rehearsal, control of visual acuity and hearing, peak experience etc. are words which have entered sport parlance only in the last decade.

What we know now is that many athletes were able to achieve mental states extremely conducive to high performance achievement long before athletes or psychologists and coaches were able to put descriptors to those states.

What was frustrating to athletes of my era was that the "once in a lifetime" feeling was just that — it couldn't, seemingly, be re-created at will, and so despite apparent optimal physical preparation, the psychological predisposition which might have helped turn a good performance into a superior one simply never arrived. The athletes in this book seem to have been able to re-create optimal feelings on multiple occasions.

The athletes whose stories are recounted in this volume demonstrate that performance is dependent on the critical and correct combination of a variety of physical and psychological attributes and specific preparation. No amount of positive thinking or psychological manipulation can transform an under-prepared athlete or team into a champion.

The personal stories of successful Canadian Olympians you will read about in the pages which follow were originally gathered as part of a research project designed to survey and assess sport psychology practices and services in Canada. In addition to the formal data collected, which will serve as a guide for sport psychology activities in the current quadrennial and beyond, the commentary provided by the athletes themselves proved so insightful that their stories warranted verbatim publication. Many thanks are due to these athletes who have provided some insight into their inner life of sport for the benefit of the next generation of Canadian high performance athletes.

These "inner stories" document the delicate interplay of "state of body" and "state of mind". It is a sad reality that there are still many talented athletes in Canada today — including some nationally carded athletes — whose training conditions (facilities, regular access to top coaching, sport science, medical and para-medical services, financial means etc.) are less than optimal. Much of the effort and new resources for Canadian sport in recent years has been directed to improving these conditions — and, while the growth has often been incremental when more dramatic measures may have been required, these athletes demonstrate that conditions are sufficient for Canadians to excel in international terms. These stories demonstrate as well, that if we neglect the "mental side" of high performance, we will do so at our peril.

ACKNOWLEDGEMENTS

This book would have remained a dream, never to have been realized, without the help of John Bales, Abby Hoffman, Vic MacKenzie, and the Canadian Olympic athletes who agreed to talk with us and share their inner stories.

John Bales, Vice-President of the Coaching Association of Canada, provided unwavering support for this project from conception to the birth of this book. Abby Hoffman, Director General of Sport Canada, not only authorized funding for our documentation of athlete mental readiness for the 1984 Olympic Games through Sport Canada's Applied Sport Research Program, but also worked with us as a member of our small research committee. Vic MacKenzie, Publisher for the Coaching Association of Canada, was the person who put this book together, from cover design to last line. Canadian Olympic athletes provided their insights, their experiences, and their hard earned knowledge. On behalf of ourselves and the future Canadian athletes who will gain from your insights, we extend our most sincere thanks for your willingness to share your wisdom and your time.

We are delighted that Canada's Athlete Information Bureau allowed us to use all the photographs in this book and that Victor Davis and the Canadian Amateur Swimming Association permitted us to use the photograph on our cover. Nothing could better portray "Psyched" than his reaction to winning at the 1984 Los Angeles Olympic Games.

Our sincere appreciation is also extended to Nadeane McCaffrey for her excellent contribution in the marathon task of typing and retyping transcripts, Penny Werthner-Bales for research on athlete backgrounds, Anne Pitman-Davidson for her valuable editorial contributions, Sue MacKenzie for typing and retyping manuscripts with the highest level of enthusiasm, Joannie Halas, Karla Pulsifier, Ann Hyland and Mary Woods who helped with the proof reading process, and Sylvia Guy who guided the final phase of producing this book.

Only those who were directly involved with this book can fully appreciate the whirlwind of circumstances which brought this book to a successful conclusion. We thank you all for giving of yourselves to meet our time lines.

Terry Orlick and John Partington

To those who dared
and those who cared

Years of dedication and perfect teamwork paid off handsomely for kayakers Alwyn Morris, (left) and Hugh Fisher, (right) who paddled to a gold in the men's 1000 metre K-2 class and a bronze in the 500 metre K-2 competition.

Hungarian-born Alexandra Barré (left) and team veteran Sue Holloway made perfect waves together to win a silver medal in the women's K-2 500 metre competition.

The women's K-4 team— Alexandra Barré, Lucie Guay, Sue Holloway and Barb Olmstead—capped the most successful competition ever for the Canadian canoe team—six medals in all—to win a bronze medal in the 500 metre final.

At the first-ever Olympic synchronized swimming contest swimmers Sharon Hambrook (left) and Kelly Kryczka (right) show the exquisite form that won a silver medal in the duet.

Sylvie Bernier, in perfect form, upset the favoured divers from the U.S. and China to win the gold medal in the women's three-metre springboard competition.

Larry Cain pulled ahead early with smooth and powerful strokes to win the gold in the men's 500 metre C-1 canoe event and then added a silver medal the following day in the 1000 metre C-1 race.

Alex Baumann sparkled in the water, winning gold medals in the 200 metre and 400 metre individual medleys in world record times, to lead the Canadian swimming team to its finest performance in Olympic history.

Winning a gold in the women's 200 metre breaststroke, a silver in the 100 metre breaststroke and a bronze for her performance in the medley relay, Anne Ottenbrite became the first Canadian athlete in history to win a complete set of medals at an Olympic summer games.

Alex Baumann leads the Canadian Olympic team into the Los Angeles Coliseum on opening day, July 28, 1984, where over 7000 athletes from 142 countries have gathered for the XXIII Summer Olympic Games.

Brian Orser, master of the dazzling triple axel, surpassed all previous Canadian Olympic performances in men's figure skating to win the silver medal at Sarajevo.

Figure skaters Paul Martini and Barb Underhill won the gold medal in the pairs event at the 1984 World Championships in Ottawa.

In what has been called one of the most remarkable races Canadians have ever rowed, the men's eight with cox upset their American rivals for the gold medal. Crew members were: Pat Turner, Kevin Neufeld, Mark Evans, Grant Main, Paul Steele, Mike Evans, Dean Crawford, Blair Horn and Brian McMahon.

Laurie Graham, Canada's most experienced women's downhill skier came within a hairbreadth of winning the overall women's world downhill title in 1986.

Chris Speedie

Wrestler Bob Molle bounced back from a back operation just three weeks before the Games to win a silver medal in the superheavyweight freestyle class.

At Sarajevo, speedskater Gaetan Boucher became Canada's greatest Winter Olympian, winning two gold medals and a bronze while setting an example that will inspire Canadian athletes for generations to come.

Photographs courtesy of:

Athlete Information Bureau
Canadian Olympic Association
Canapress Photo Service

Photographers:

Ted Grant
Crombie McNeil
Jim Merrithew
Tim O'Lett

1
REACHING FOR THE TOP

The inner stories you are about to read come from great athletes, all Canadians, all raised within a Canadian context, all of whom have made it to the top and have broken some barrier in their sport. Their total commitment to excellence, and their persistence in developing and refining their own formula of mental and physical skills, can serve as a model to any of us interested in greater achievement.

When we watch world class performers on T.V., we see their outer performance. But we are left wondering about their inner performance. What goes through their minds at critical moments? How do they stay motivated? How do they focus? How did they get to be so good? We can now share that message with you.

For a year and a half following the 1984 Olympic Games we crisscrossed this country numerous times, interviewing seventy-five of our most accomplished Olympic athletes. One hundred and sixty-five others with whom we were unable to meet face-to-face, due to time, timing and budget restrictions, responded to our interview questions in writing. Each of these athletes had an important story to tell, from which we can all learn.

To conduct the interviews, one of us usually went to one area of the country while the other went to another. As soon as either one of us got back we would hurriedly call the other, and with excitement not even surpassed by young children, we would share some of the insights we had gained. A day rarely went by when we did not spend hours sharing our learning experiences with each other. It was a very exciting time in our lives. We met some very special people whom we had always wanted to meet. We sat with them for two or three hours and learned about their path to the top. And we did this with many athletes from many different sports.

We have not included entire transcripts of our interviews with each athlete. In many cases original transcripts were 60 or 70 pages long. In editing the transcripts we attempted to preserve the essence of what each athlete said, as well as the specific way in which it was expressed. We removed material which was repetitious, or less relevant to athletes and coaches reading this book.

After editing each transcript we sent it back to the athlete for feedback and to ensure that it was both accurate and acceptable for use in that form. The feedback we received from the athletes was that the transcripts were accurate accounts of their inner stories. After reading her edited transcript Sylvie Bernier called and said, "I can't believe how accurate it is, my whole life is in there, it's exactly the way it happened." Some athletes suggested that they re-write their stories in more formal prose. However, we urged them to preserve the spontaneity of their stories by leaving the style in its conversational form. Sometimes, an athlete chose to soften or eliminate a comment about another person to avoid hurting that person's feelings, even though it was an accurate statement. On one occasion we decided to eliminate a one sentence comment about a coach from a seventy page transcript, just in case it might put the athlete in an awkward position. We sent that edited transcript back to the athlete several months after the interview. She sent it back to us saying it was great, but that we must have missed a line. She re-inserted, from memory, word-for-word the comment that we had removed. This time we left it in.

We attempted to include a sufficient number of inner stories to give you a complete understanding of the mental approaches utilized by a representative sample of Canada's greatest athletes. We recognize that we have included the stories of only a small number of Canada's many great athletes. We have struggled with that. Due to our own restrictions on time, space, funding, and our desire for a concise flowing book, an all-inclusive presentation would have been an impossible task for us. However after having completed the project, we are confident that the inner stories of most great Canadian athletes not included here are housed within the stories that we have included, in spirit and substance.

In conducting these interviews, if one of us had previously worked with an athlete, the other did the interview. For the team and pairs events represented in these interviews, we were unable to include everyone involved, either because some athletes were unavailable, or because of budget constraints. In cases when more than one perspective was available, we included the interview which provided the most complete account of mental readiness factors, since that is the focus of this book. An exception to this editorial practice may be found in the story on the Men's 8 gold medal rowing team. Perspectives of coxswain and crew are provided because their roles and performance demands were so different; and two crew perspectives are given since these were obtained from the only joint interview in our survey.

The two hundred and forty Olympic athletes, who contributed their thoughts and experiences to this project, by interview or questionnaire, were assured confidentiality. We said at the outset that names would not be attached to any responses without written permission. We maintained that confidentiality throughout this project. There were times when we very much wanted to quote some of their comments to sport administrators so that they could make fully-informed decisions which were in the best interest of athletes. To protect the anonymity of individual athletes and respect the promise of confidentiality, we refrained from doing this.

Those athletes whose stories appear in this book were very much in favour of sharing their insights with fellow Canadians. The response of Paul Martini, 1984 World Champion in pairs skating, to our request to share his interview, was typical of other athletes in this book. "With pleasure! Any of the information in my interview is yours for however you see fit to use it. I hope that your findings are well received by everyone to whom you present, and that Canadian athletes benefit in the long run from this project." He went on to say that, "Until this interview, no one has come and said, 'Let me pick your brain.' We (Paul and partner Barbara Underhill) were both really perturbed about that. We wanted to put something back in, even though we turned pro. I don't think we use our best knowledge

2

and experience, in terms of putting something back, like you are doing here; asking for some feedback: what do we do differently, what can be learned from someone who has just taken an emotional roller coaster, from the low of Barb's fall at the Olympics to the high of winning the Worlds three weeks later, and who has gone through the system for 15 years."

The lessons we learned from the athletes, extended beyond the realm of sport. For example, on one bleak and rainy day we got out of the car for the long walk across campus. We turned what might have seemed like a wet and miserable chore, into a positive fun-filled challenge by leaping and bounding across campus with a clear goal in mind; to avoid puddles and yet keep going in a straight line. We both had a good laugh about that, but we also realized that some of those very positive ways of looking at things, so evident among our top athletes, were becoming more natural for us. Thinking about things in a more positive light or "cognitive restructuring" can become natural for anyone. I guess even old dogs can learn new tricks.

We are very excited about being able to share these stories with you because we sincerely believe they can make a difference in you and your performance. If you choose to act upon the lessons in these stories, they will bring you closer to your dreams, whatever those dreams may be.

2
SUCCESS ELEMENTS

hen you sit down and talk with so many great athletes in their homes and in training centres across the country you cannot help but be impressed by some of their common and yet unique qualities. We often compared notes on our impressions of these vibrant young Canadians who had already accomplished so much in their chosen field of excellence.

They were all highly committed individuals with clearly established success goals. They were open and receptive to us, to developing their mental strength, and to what their coaches had to offer. At the same time they were very selective in terms of drawing out what might work for them as unique individuals, when developing technical, physical or mental strengths. Perhaps most important, they reflected an experimental, "Let's try," attitude. They were willing to try, and to learn from those trials.

Total Commitment — Athletes who reach the top have an incredible commitment to excel in their sport. For a significant chunk of time everything in their entire life revolves around their training. Their athletic goal is the most important goal in their life. Family and friends are still important, but the central and most meaningful focus and goal is the pursuit of excellence in sport. They didn't begin sport with this total commitment. It grew as they began to recognize their own potential. Several years before becoming Olympic or world champions all of these athletes had very clearly established goals of reaching the top. The goal was to win an Olympic gold, to be world champion, to be the BEST in the world. Most "saw" themselves achieving that goal, in their minds, long before it became a reality.

Our questionnaire data from 165 Olympic athletes clearly shows that athletes who could best control and direct their focus before and during their performance had the best results. Moreover, the extent to which athletes could control their mental images and "feel" performance images from the "inside", as if doing it, was also directly related to performance outcomes at the Olympic Games.

A striking result from the interview portion of this study was the surprising consistency of certain success elements for virtually all of our best performers in all sports. An overview of each of these success elements follows under the headings, Quality Training and Mental Preparation for Competition. A more complete appreciation for what is meant by each element of success will be gained when you read the athletes' own stories in the remainder of this book.

I. Quality Training

The most common and probably the most important element of success was quality training. I know what you are thinking, "Of course you need quality training, that's obvious. I do that, doesn't everybody?" There were notable differences between what most of our athletes thought was "quality training" and the actual high quality training that has helped our best athletes get to the top. Several athletes put it this way, "Everybody thinks that practice makes perfect, but 'perfect practice makes perfect.'" The best athletes don't just go through the motions in training. They have discovered that the only way to establish the winning patterns they want to draw upon in the competition is to go through the motions with the highest degree of quality or with absolute intensity.

The best ones mentally prepare for training. They are thinking about what they want to accomplish the night before, the morning of, and even on the way to training. Before they arrive at training they have already committed themselves to their best effort in accomplishing those goals. They train with the highest quality of effort or the highest degree of intensity and they mentally prepare themselves to do this. They also rest well between training sessions so they can continue to give their best effort.

Simulation Training — The very best athletes use a lot of simulation training. They approach training runs or go through routines in practice as if it was the competition, wearing what they would wear, preparing like they would prepare. They take the time to mentally prepare to do it well.

Imagery Training — All the best athletes have very well-developed mental imagery skills and use them on a daily basis. They use imagery to prepare themselves to get what they want out of training, to perfect skills within the training sessions, and to "see" themselves being successful.

The refined imagery they have developed for running through skills and performances in their mind, is one which takes an "inside" view, as if actually doing the skill, and one which involves feeling the action and excitement, as if actually being there. Most of these athletes call up these inside images or perfect feelings before every attempt at executing a skill.

It is interesting to note that these athletes did not initially have good control over their mental imagery. It was through persistent daily practice that they perfected these skills.

Clear Daily Goals — The best athletes have clear and usually simple, targeted daily goals. They know what they want to accomplish each day, each workout, each sequence or interval. They are determined to accomplish these goals and focus on doing so, daily. They also maintain excellent year round conditioning.

II. Mental Preparation for Competition

The quality of effort in training, the simulation training, the imagery training and clear daily goals have moved these athletes along the path of excellence. But in addition to this quality training, the best athletes have developed very sound procedures for drawing upon their strengths in important competitions.

Pre-Competition Plan — The best athletes have a well-established and well-practised pre-competition procedure which they follow consistently. The pre-competition plan includes the use of mental imagery, a good physical warm-up, positive thoughts, and reminders to focus on what has worked. When an athlete arrives on-site she knows what she is going to do, and when she is going to do it. By following a well-developed and refined pre-competition plan, a constructive focus is maintained going into the event.

Competition Focus Plan — The best athletes have taken the time to discover what kind of focus works best for them in a competition. They have developed a refined plan to draw upon this focus during the competition. In almost all cases the best focus is one which keeps the athlete connected to what he is doing, his job. In contrast, the worst focus is one in which the athlete is connected to factors over which he has no control, such as competitors, final outcome, or other distractions.

Competition Evaluation — The best athletes pull out the important lessons from every competitive experience and adapt or refine their mental approach based upon these lessons. If the performance was excellent, they will note the mental factors or focus associated with that best performance. In this way, they integrate important lessons into their plan for subsequent competitions. If the performance was "off" they will try to assess why, paying particular attention to their mental state or focus, before and during the competition. They are extremely good at drawing out the important lessons and then letting the performance go, especially if it was less than their best. Many of the best athletes use their diaries, logs, or some other post-competition evaluation procedure to write down the lessons learned. Some go back to these notes to help direct their focus for subsequent competitions.

Distraction Control — For the success elements discussed thus far, virtually all of our great athletes have a common strength. However, in terms of mental skills for dealing with distractions or setbacks, which is extremely important for the consistency of high-level performance, there is greater variation. Some of the best athletes have excellent strategies for getting back on track quickly when things don't go well, or when faced with distractions. Others appear to need work in this area to improve the consistency of their high-level performance.

Learning the Elements of Success — It was clear from our study that great athletes did not begin their sports careers with all of these success elements. They learned quality training, simulation training, quality imagery, daily goal setting, pre-competition planning, competition focus planning, competition evaluation procedures and distraction control. These success elements are developed and refined through practice. Without practice these skills will not be learned, and without persistent use they may be forgotten.

As a result of listening to others and themselves, watching, talking, reading, experimenting, practicing, performing, thinking, experiencing, recording and evaluating, each athlete recognized the importance of these elements. Each then began to develop, implement and refine his or her own unique plans, sometimes in conjunction with a coach and sport psychology consultant.

Many of these highly successful athletes felt that they could have reached the top much earlier if they had worked on strengthening their mental skills earlier in their careers. Some mentioned that they had had the same technical and physical skills honed to perfection four years before becoming world champions, but they had not yet learned how to hold their best focus in important competitions. Once their focusing skills were refined, their dreams became a reality.

Finally, it is interesting to note that almost all of the athletes who performed to potential at the Olympic Games had a very close personal bond with their coaches. They worked out programs, problems and strategies together. These athletes respected their coaches, and their coaches respected them, to the point of being flexible enough to individualize training programs and feedback based upon the athlete's input. Creating an atmosphere of mutual trust, mutual respect, and a genuine concern for individual athletes, appears to be a necessary requirement for helping Canadian Olympians to achieve their highest level of excellence.

Every great athlete may not have possessed every single success element we have discussed in this chapter, but the more elements they had working for them, the higher the probability of performing to their potential on a consistent basis.

3

PERFORMANCE BLOCKS

W e have identified and described the success elements that helped many of our best athletes reach the top. In the remainder of this book some great athletes will share their own stories about pursuing their dreams and performing to capacity when it counted most. These are important lessons for anyone pursuing excellence in any domain.

Equally important are the lessons we drew from the athletes who performed far below their capacity in the Olympic Games. Many of the seventy-five athletes we interviewed, and the one hundred and sixty-five we surveyed, did not perform to potential at the Olympic Games, despite the fact that some of them had a very strong track record. They were expected to do well, wanted to do well, yet fell far short of the mark. Why?

We discovered three major blocks that interfered with athletes performances at the Olympic Games: 1) Changing patterns that work, 2) Late selection and, 3) Getting blown away by distractions.

Changing Patterns That Work

This was one of the greatest obstacles to performance, and yet, with good planning, one over which athletes and coaches could have almost complete control. Individuals and teams that failed to perform well often changed patterns that had been successful in the past.

Some of our athletes had done extremely well at the international level during the pre-Olympic year but dramatically increased their training load for the Olympic year. Some adopted totally foreign training programs, others doubled or tripled their mileage, and in some cases were still doing extremely heavy work immediately prior to the Games. This, combined with the overall stress of the Olympics, left many of them completely exhausted when the time came to go out and compete. They were physically drained, mentally fatigued and in some instances injured. The overload was introduced without considering what had worked for that athlete in the past and without a monitoring system to check for signals of overtraining. As one athlete put it, "It was like cramming for an exam, too much, too late". In retrospect, these athletes felt they should have followed training patterns that had previously worked, and attempted to make refined improvements in these familiar patterns. Instead, major shifts were undertaken to unfamiliar and incompatible patterns. Some very skilled athletes suffered as a result.

Athletes reported that various kinds of shifts away from familiar patterns affected their performance negatively. For example, one team had been very successful when the players were closely unified both off and on the playing surface. At the Olympics, contrary to what had worked at their previous successful tournaments, this sense of "team" was not felt, largely because the players were not together the way they had been in the past. They "ate and went their separate ways". The patterns that had helped this team gel as a unit for previous all-time best performances were not respected at the Olympic site.

Also last minute changes were sometimes made in game plans which resulted in putting athletes into unfamiliar patterns which were not as well practised. For example, one team had developed a very successful offensive style, but shortly prior to game time were told to shift to a defensive style.

In some instances coaches totally changed their pre-event input to athletes. They did not follow the constructive, supportive and task-oriented patterns that had worked well in the past. This created an unfamiliar and uncomfortable distraction for some athletes. In most cases the intent of the change was good but the results were often disastrous.

Late Selections

The mental and physical preparation of some of our athletes was directly affected because of late selection decisions by associations and/or coaches. Some athletes still did not know whether they were on the Olympic team one week prior to the Olympic Games. Instead, they were involved in several days of head-to-head competition at the Olympic site, the week before the Games. The ones who finally made the team were relieved that they would not be sent home, like their less fortunate teammates, but were emotionally drained. They "had nothing left" for the actual event and in certain cases "competed injured" due to the long and arduous process of late selection.

Sometimes, athletes who were selected for some teams at a reasonable time did not know whether they were actually going to compete until the last moment. One coach first informed an athlete that she would be playing, then during the warm-up told her that she would not be playing, and then moments before the start of the game told her she was playing! It is difficult for an athlete to prepare when she does not know what she is preparing for.

Late selections and late decisions, with respect to the role that an athlete is expected to play on the team, block proper mental preparation, create self-doubt, and often lead to emotional drainage. Our advice is to select early and wisely, with alternates in case of injury.

Blown Away By Distractions

A large percentage of athletes who did not perform to capacity at the Olympic Games, trained well, but were blown away by distractions at the Olympic site. The hype of the whole event; the Olympic Village, the ceremonies, the "star" athletes, the crowds, the media, and the overall expectation they had felt, took its toll.

These athletes were prepared for performing their physical skills but they were not prepared for the multitude of distractions. In the face of these distractions, many athletes "lost" their focus. They failed to remind themselves to follow the same pre-event procedures and competition focus that had worked so well for them in previous competitions. They did not direct and hold their focus on the task, on their "job". When they stepped out onto the deck or into the arena these athletes were often focused on the crowd, on the cameras, on the outcome, on self doubts, or on the strength of their competitors. Their focus was everywhere but where it should have been.

Athletes need a plan to deal with distractions when going into major international competitions like the Olympic Games. Prior experience in an Olympic setting certainly helps you know what to expect. However, with proper mental preparation, it is possible to enter that scene for the very first time and have an all time best performance. It is essential to have a clear understanding of what to expect, what you are there for, and what kind of focus leads to your best result. Once you know this, you can develop a plan to avoid expected distractions and to deal with those distractions which are unavoidable. The most successful athletes interviewed did have a plan that allowed them to hold a constructive focus. For the most part they were in control of their own thoughts. When they got to the line they were certainly capable of focusing on their own performance.

The first step in removing the performance blocks is for future Olympians to be aware that they exist. The second is for coaches, athletes and support persons, to work together to prepare athletes for what they will likely face, long before they face the ultimate test.

It is interesting to note that several of our Olympic and World Champions involved in high intensity sports did not perform to capacity in the year or two following the 1984 Olympics. Part of the pattern that had got them to the top was training hard, resting well, and focusing fully on their pursuit of excellence. On the way up, their lives had not been overloaded with additional demands. After the Olympics they changed this successful pattern. They still trained very hard, but they did not rest as much. In addition, because of their Olympic achievements, they were forced to deal with an abundance of additional distractions. For example, they took on additional responsibilities to agents and sponsors, and did extensive off-season travelling for speaking, promotion and media engagements. They did the bulk of this work at a time when they had previously rested and recuperated, while maintaining their solid conditioning base.

For two of these Olympic Champions, their best and only really excellent performance of the post-Olympic year came after a week or two of rest. Throughout the year they could call up the perfect performance image or "feel" in their heads, but their tired bodies were not sharp enough to act upon those perfect images. They were physically fatigued and mentally drained when the World Championships rolled around. The lesson they both drew from this experience was that they have to continue to train with the highest intensity, but that the resting part is equally important. Squeezing training between many other obligations and demands which require lots of energy is not the pattern that will keep you at the top. It certainly wasn't the pattern that had got them there in the first place.

We hope that the individual athlete stories which follow will help you to create your own conditions for success, and strengthen your ability to prevent performance blocks before they occur.

4
ALEX BAUMANN

1984 OLYMPIC DOUBLE GOLD MEDALIST — SWIMMING

ALEX BAUMANN SWIMMING

- Double Gold Medalist (200m & 400m Individual Medley — Olympic & World Records) at the 1984 Olympic Games
- Male Athlete of the Year — 1984
- 1983 World University Games — Double Gold Medalist — 200m & 400m Individual Medley Silver Medalist — Triple Bronze Medalist
- 1982 Commonwealth Games — Double Gold Medalist — 200m & 400m Individual Medley Bronze Medalist
- 1981 Canada/USSR/West German Meet — 1st — 200m & 400m Individual Medley

My first goal for the Olympics was to win two gold medals in both my events, the 200 and 400 I.M. The secondary goal was the world record, to show that I was the best in the world, mainly because the Eastern Bloc was not there. But I did not really worry about a world record, all I wanted to do was win because twenty years down the road, nobody will remember if I had broken the record or not.

I felt physically ready for the Olympics. The training, and taper, and the times I was swimming indicated that I was ready. I was also ready mentally. I knew I was ready, but there are always doubts before a race. There is always that question of whether I can do it or not. In the first race I think if I had loosened up, not being as tense, maybe I could have gone faster. For the second race, everything was fine, everything was ready and I do not think I could have been better. After I won the gold medal, I had accomplished one goal, and it was very easy, in essence the pressure was off.

There was a tremendous amount of pressure on me, especially in the first event, because everybody expected me to win, and everybody expected me to break the world record. That was a lot of additional pressure which I did not really need. But then it was the Olym-

Working at being consistent has helped me. The thing that marks a true champion is consistency. I've definitely worked on that, day in and day out.

pics so obviously you are going to have a lot of pressure. The pressure came from Canada in general, and then from the whole Canadian team. They expected me to win, just because I had the world record, and I had qualified first, going into the final, breaking the existing Olympic record.

I felt really good in the morning, and my split times in the training and warm-up just before the 400 I.M. were really good. I did not swim hard in the morning, and of course I was 5 seconds off my best time. My heart was pounding because of the pressure and I was unable to sleep between heats and finals. Then at night, I felt terrible in the water. I thought, "Here goes eleven years of work, and here I come and get a silver medal." I really wondered if I could ever win feeling that bad.

I knew that I could win if everything went well, but I felt terrible going into the warm-up. That's a terrible feeling because you feel off and your warm-up times show it. You do a couple of 50's and they are half a second slower than in the morning. I think that really scared me. I didn't really mention anything, but my coach knew. I received a rubdown and went in the water again in an outside practice pool on our way back, about 20 minutes before my race. I tried to work on stroke technique. I just had to loosen up. I was tense because there was a lot of pressure and I could not sleep in the afternoon. I felt much better after loosening up in the water, and my confidence returned.

The day of the 400 IM was not the best day for me, even though I did break my world record and won a gold medal. In retrospect I do not think that I could have done better than I did on that given day. Now I look back at the tapes, I have seen them 20 times, and I criticize them a little bit more, because I have to, because I want to get better. I think I can go faster.

Sometimes in the past I've felt terrible but on those occasions I've told myself, "If I can do well and beat those people when I feel bad, imagine how well I will do if I'm feeling good." I try to perform the best I can even under the worst conditions.

Working at being consistent has helped me. The thing that marks a true champion is consistency. I've definitely worked on that, day in and day out. No matter how I feel, I try to put in one hundred percent. That has helped me over the years. It is not very often I go off my best time when I am tapered and shaved. Tapered means that I am totally rested, coming down from seventeen km per day to about 3 km per day, right before the meet. Shaved means that my whole body is shaved in order to have greater sensitivity to the water.

Confidence is very important in swimming. Once you lose your confidence it is very hard to perform well. You get into the race and you swim the first fifty metres, and then somebody takes off on you, and you say, "Well, that is it, I cannot catch up." You develop confidence by training well, doing well at meets, improving your times and by winning. You just have to feel good about yourself, and feel that what you have done is a big accomplishment. Normally I am always confident, and I feel that I can do whatever split times I have set out to do.

I think I train quite differently from other Canadian swimmers. My coach, Jeno Tihanyi, has a very scientific approach to training

14

that has helped me a lot in the past 10 years that I have been with him. To keep pushing through all that training, what works for me is setting small goals for myself. Rather than focusing on a long-range goal, like winning the Olympics, I set my goals on trying to improve a time, or trying to improve a part of the race. I concentrate on improving in small ways, rather than improving by large amounts. After attaining each goal, I feel totally satisfied and I can go on to another goal. Some swimmers have a problem with this. For example, in 1978 they may be looking only at the 1984 Games. You can't do that, because you have so much time. Those six years of training for one big goal can lead to a lack of satisfaction and a lot of frustration. Setting small, short-term goals, has really helped me. I just take it one day at a time rather than saying, I have to train another 20,000 metres tomorrow and after that, and after that. You just have to take it one day at a time and think about that.

I always have a certain performance goal to strive for. My coach and I are always putting together split times for the race, and we try to go for that. You have to be realistic about your times and what you want to do. You can't set goals for yourself which are totally ridiculous. I think knowing that I can do those splits has helped me a lot.

My coach helped me gain the confidence to do certain times. He writes up the splits and asks me if I can do them. I say, "Yes, maybe I can." Breaking up the race into splits helps me a lot. He pushes me a lot, and I think I need that to reach my one hundred percent potential. He is never over-reaching. He always puts down splits that he believes I can do. They are not far out of my reach.

The best way I have learned to prepare mentally for competitions is to visualize the race in my mind, and to put down a split time. The splits I use in my imagery are determined by my coach and myself, for each part of the race. For example, in the 200 individual medley, splits are made up for each 50m because after 50 metres the stroke changes. These splits are based on training times and what we feel I'm capable of doing. In my imagery I concentrate on attaining the splits I have set out to do. About 15 minutes before the race I always visualize the race in my mind and "see" how it will go. I see where everybody else is, and then I really focus on myself. I do not worry about anybody else. I think about my own race and nothing else. I try to get those splits in my mind, and after that I am ready to go. I think a lot of swimmers don't visualize a race, and don't visualize what they really want to do.

I started visualizing in 1978. My visualization has been refined more and more as the years go on. That is what really got me the world record and the Olympic medals. I see myself swimming the race before the race really happens, and I try to be on the splits. You really know if you are on the splits by that time because you have spent so much time training on different kinds of strategies, so you know what time you are actually going, without the clock being there. You are really swimming the race. You are visualizing it from behind the block. In my mind, I go up and down the pool, rehearsing all parts of the race, visualizing how I actually feel in the water.

In 1979 I trained with Graham Smith, then world record holder in the 200 IM. That experience helped me because he was the world's best. Obviously what he was doing must be right. I think that a lot of

The best way I have learned to prepare mentally for competitions is to visualize the race in my mind, and to put down a split time.

15

young swimmers can learn a great deal from the experience of top Canadian swimmers.

A big thing that helped me deal with a lot of pressure at the Olympics, with Canada expecting me to win, was asking myself, "Who am I doing this for?" I answered, "I am doing this for myself because I put in one hundred percent for 6 hours a day. So I am just going out there to do my best. That is all I can do. I am not going to worry about anything else." Before I asked myself that question I had started to think, "This is the Olympics but this is crazy." From that point on I was really focused in on what I had to do. I did not look at anybody else; I did not want to look at anybody else. A lot of athletes have a problem because we are put in a tent, with 8 finalists. Everybody is trying to psych each other; they are staring at each other. I keep away from that. I do not like looking at people. I just keep to myself and I think of the race that I'm going to race. Of course the adrenalin is starting to pump now and there is a lot of tension and I am feeling nervous, but that is to be expected. The best thing for me is not to look at anybody else. I just try to generate a lot of confidence for myself, and say, "You can do it," rather than looking at somebody and wondering what he is going to do.

Some people screen out unwanted things by listening to music. I just block into myself, block out everything around me, and just concentrate on what I have to do.

During the event I focus on my race and my pace. The 400 is a strategic race; if you go out too fast you may lose because you do not have enough strength left towards the end. You have to pace it very well. A lot of mistakes are made because somebody goes out too fast in the first 200. You can generally tell what kind of time you are doing. You know exactly what the other swimmers' splits are, so if you are ahead or a little behind, you know where you are going. Normally you can guess what you are doing. In the Olympics, I saw the time up on the board at the 200. It was 2:04.6. After that I knew I was on pace for a world record.

Between heats and finals I ate a big meal. Then I lay down and just rested and thought about what went wrong in the morning and what I could do better from the morning swim going into the night swim.

I try not to think about swimming 24 hours a day, but I have to think about it quite a bit. Once I have thought about what I should concentrate on doing, I can go to sleep and not worry for a while. When I get up I am thinking about the race, subconsciously or consciously.

One change that would help Canadian swimmers would be to gain the confidence that they can do it. I think a lot of Canadian athletes feel inferior to the U.S., the East Germans, the Russians or whoever. To win, I think they just have to feel confident. We have not had that confidence for a long time. 1984 was the first time we thought we could win, and we did win. Canadian athletes had a lot more confidence within themselves. They didn't get up on the starting block and look to one side and see an American and say, "Oh gee, he is going to beat me again." I think we are now getting up on the block and saying, "I can win." That can make all the difference.

After the Olympics, it was very anticlimatic. Where do you go after two Olympic golds and two new world records? When I was getting

16

up at 5:30 a.m. to go to the pool to do 10,000 metres, I was saying, "Why am I doing this, I really cannot do anything more?" It took a long time, about 4 months, to reassess my goals and get back into swimming. I want to compete in the World Championships in 1986 and try to win there. That is my next goal. I know a number of other athletes who had a problem getting back into it. It is just that the Olympics are the ultimate competition, and there is nothing else which compares to them. At times it is very hard to adjust. It is a once in a lifetime experience.

1984 was the first time we thought we could win, and we did win. Canadian athletes had a lot more confidence within themselves.

5

SYLVIE BERNIER

1984 OLYMPIC CHAMPION — SPRINGBOARD DIVING

Five days before my event, I felt that I was ready to compete. I wanted the event to be the next day, and I still had 4 more days to wait. I was so ready to go on the board and dive. I knew it was going to go well.

The day before the Olympic final I went out with my parents. My Dad knows a lot about diving but he's really quiet. He never talks about diving with me in case he gets me nervous. I remember talking to my Dad and I said, "You know what? It's not going to be that hard to win." My Dad just smiled and said, "I know you can win." So that was it, I knew I was going for the gold. That was the first time I said to the media that I was going for the gold. Before that I just said, I am diving well, I think I can do well, but I never said I was going for the gold. At that time it was right for me. I had done everything I could, I had trained so hard, and I really knew this was going to be my competition.

Everything was great. I felt great. Everything was going perfect. My parents were there. Two of my best friends came down. I called my best friend in Quebec. She's a swimmer and she told me, "We're planning a big party and we've got lots of champagne." Everything was planned for me to win. No one really said anything negative. In

The lady came to the pool and gave me two books. The books said, if you really want to do something, just see yourself doing it and you'll do it.

19

I read his corrections every day, before every workout. I set a goal to change something on that piece of paper every day.

my presence they were all saying that I was going to win. So you get to the point where you think you are going to win.

My parents had an important effect. My mother always put a little note in my baggage when I went to competitions. One time I found it in my shoe. The note said, "You are our champion, no matter what happens." Then it said, "Bring me home some chocolates." I laughed and cried ... but this helped keep things in perspective.

My parents, being there at the Olympics, were probably the best thing for me. If I wanted to get out of the village just to be by myself, and many times I wanted to get out, I went with my parents. I went to a private house for two days just to get away from the village and get away from everyone. It was really good for me. It was about an hour and a half drive from Los Angeles, right in the middle of the forest. I would just walk there and be by myself. It was great.

Everything was planned and everything worked. Usually I talk to the American divers and I feel inferior to them, but at the Olympics I felt they were afraid of me. I felt I was better than them, and that I was going to beat them, and I was in their country. It was the first time that had happened to me.

Everything was planned for the day of the event. A year before that day I knew I was going to dive finals on the 6th of August. I was going to dive at 4 o'clock in the afternoon. There were going to be twelve thousand people in the stands. I knew everything and everything was planned for that day. What am I going to do if it is raining? There was an answer. What am I doing to do if I hurt my hand or if my coach is late? There was something for that. I had thought about everything and had an answer for everything. I had an answer for everything, so nothing could really bother me that day. I was prepared to face almost anything. I was going to go in the pool. I wasn't going to talk to anyone except my coach. A 7 o'clock in the morning I would go to the pool and train a little bit. No one would be there. I knew I would come back, sleep for an hour and a half, go back, have a cup of coffee, cereal, go to my room. Everything was planned. I knew how to handle everything that day.

I read about some things that other top athletes did to have good performances at big competitions, like writing everything down, and being prepared for everything that could happen to you the day or the day before, or week before, and the kind of preparation I could do. I was really interested in every aspect of my sport, and everything about my preparation. For example, I went to see different experts and asked if it was better for me to do this or that sort of training. In the end I knew, I was just so sure, that I was doing the right training. Even if other people said it was wrong, my coach and I knew it was the right thing for me. You have to do whatever is good for you. It was very important for me to be able to set my own goals.

I read some books that helped with my mental preparation. A coach gave me one book, and a lady in Montreal gave me two other books for my birthday in 1983. At that time I was pretty depressed. I was sick all the time and I was in a bad mood. The lady came to the pool and gave me two books. The books said, if you really want to do something, just see yourself doing it and you'll do it. Every time she came in the pool she looked at me and said, "Did you see yourself on the podium today?" I would say, "I can't see myself on the podium right now." She would just laugh and leave. One book was 'The Power of the Subconscious Mind'. I never told anyone about this. I just read it in my room. It helped me a lot.

I didn't even know that lady. She just came to the pool one day. She enjoyed watching me dive and knew I was working really hard. She had a little girl in diving. She did a lot of painting and she gave me one for a present once. It was just a girl by herself, and the girl was reading. The name of the painting was "La Solitude" (by yourself). She helped me although she didn't know it. I hope she feels really good now.

Six months after giving me the books she came up to me and said, "So, can you see yourself on the podium?" I said, "Yes, now I can see myself on the podium." As the Olympics approached I would see it a lot, like flashes all the time. Every day I would see myself walking down and getting the medal. When it actually happened it was like I had seen it before, I'd done it all before.

In 1984 I started diving in the pool only at the beginning of January. The other divers started board training in September 1983. Many people felt I wouldn't do well because I waited too long. But I knew that if I started board training too early I could get bored and go crazy going into the pool and doing the same things all the time. So I decided to wait. I stayed in great shape though. I did lots of trampoline and dryland training, and lots of specific exercises for diving. I knew that the Chinese did lots of training like that so I tried it. I knew it was going to work for me. When I did go into the pool, I was so ready to dive and try new things. I won the first competition I went into, and I had only been doing board diving for two weeks. Everyone said it wasn't the best way to train. But I knew, and my coach knew that it was the best thing for me.

The pre-Olympic year was a really tough year for me because I was so tired of training. I trained 6 hours a day. It was hard. I lived by myself in a small apartment. I went to the pool every morning, came back to my apartment, and wanted to rest all the time.

I didn't really do any other activities. I stayed by myself and rested between workouts. Then I went back to the pool at night. That was my biggest workout of the day, so I had to be really ready. Sometimes it was really hard.

I was sick in January and February. I had a very bad cold. Then I had problems with my shoulders. I was sore everywhere. That was from over-training. I knew it was going to happen because I had trained so hard for 2 or 3 months just getting into shape. I had planned to slow down, but before I did it was really tough. I remember one day being really depressed. I went to the pool and talked to my coach. He was good because he just listened without saying anything. He knew how I felt and I knew how he felt, so we worked really well together. I remember asking him, "What am I doing here? Why am I doing this?" I was in Montreal and Montreal wasn't really my place. My family was in Quebec. So I said, "Why am I not in Quebec like my friends?" He just said, "Because you're different. You want to be the best in the world." And that was it. That put me in line and I knew what I was there for. Since that day I always trained really hard and I never had any problems getting up in the mornings and going to the

If my coach wanted me to learn a new dive, and if I couldn't 'see' it, I couldn't do it.

pool. I knew what I was doing, I knew why I was doing it and I had a great time doing it.

Right after the Commonwealth Games, when I went home to Quebec, I decided that I was going to win the Olympics. I called this coach in Montreal and said to him, "I'd like you to coach me. I think you would be the best person for me. I know you can help me win that medal." He was a little apprehensive, because I was the top diver in Canada and among the top seven in the world. Taking on the responsibility for training me was a big decision for him. He talked to me and first asked, "Why don't you go to the States?" I said, "I'm sorry, I'm going to Montreal, I'd like you to take me." The next day, in December, 1982 I went to Montreal, and from that day I trained for the Olympics, only for that.

My mental preparation for the Olympics was really different from the preparation of other athletes in my sport. That year I didn't dive as much as everybody else. I didn't train 6 hours a day in the pool. I probably did 2 hours a day on the boards. So I had to work on my mental preparation a lot.

My coach wrote up every single one of my dives on a piece of paper, all the bad things about my dive and all the good things about my dive. It was about 18 pages long. The first time he gave it to me, it was hard, because all the bad points were on the paper. Just to read it and to say I have to correct all of this before that day, the 6th of August was tough. I read his corrections every day, before every workout. I set a goal to change something on that piece of paper every day. My coach kept telling me, "Okay, this one's a lot better, now we have to work on this one.'

Even if part of the dive was bad, I knew something was better. That's why it wasn't boring for me to do the same dive 100 times, because each time I looked at it in a different way. One time I focused on my hands, then my head, my feet, etc. I think the other divers worked in a more global way, looking at the whole dive. The dive is good or change it. For me, the dive is good, but there's always something to improve.

In the beginning it was hard because my coach was kind of negative all the time. He says it's being realistic, not negative. Anyway he would constantly say, "This is bad, don't do this, you didn't do that." Most athletes don't like that. It makes them feel like they never improve. But it pushed me a lot, he made me feel like I had a lot of talent, and also made it clear that I had to work really hard to be the best in the world. He asked a lot from me because I could give a lot. I was always positive in training. I knew he was really interested in helping me and I needed that technical input to improve, so it was okay. I was able to say, "That's the way he is when he coaches" (negative) and still remain positive myself. He was very devoted to helping me in any way, any time, any place and he was also very adaptable to my input. When we got closer to the meet, my coach was more positive.

I did my dives in my head all the time. At night, before going to sleep, I always did my dives. Ten dives. I started with a front dive, the first one that I had to do at the Olympics, and I did everything as if I was actually there. I saw myself on the board with the same bathing suit. Everything was the same. I saw myself in the pool at the

22

Olympics doing my dives. If the dive was wrong, I went back and started over again. It takes a good hour to do perfect imagery of all my dives but for me it was better than a workout. I felt like I was on the board. Sometimes I would take the weekend off and do imagery five times a day. It felt like I was on the board and I did each dive so many times in my mind.

It took me a long time to control my images and perfect my imagery, maybe a year, doing it everyday. At first I couldn't see myself, I always saw everyone else, or I would see my dives wrong all the time. I would get an image of hurting myself, or tripping on the board, or I would "see" something done really bad. As I continued to work at it I got to the point where I could see myself doing a perfect dive and the crowd yelling at the Olympics. But it took me a long time.

When my coach gave me those sheets, I read everything I had to do and I knew my dive by heart. Then I started to see myself on the board doing my perfect dive. But some days I couldn't see it, or it was a bad dive in my head. I worked at it so much it got to the point that I could do all my dives easily. Sometimes I would even be in the middle of a conversation with someone and I would think of one of my dives and "see" it.

If my coach wanted me to learn a new dive, and if I couldn't "see" it, I couldn't do it. Sometimes I told him, "I can't do this dive, I can't see it." He then had to tell me every single element of the dive so I could really understand the dive. Then I could "see" it in my mind and do it.

I'm very serious in training and I hated to train with hundreds of people around me. Even in competitions I was well known for that. I often trained during lunchtimes when no-one else was there. In Montreal I trained early in the morning and in the afternoon when no-one was there. I was alone with my coach. He would say, "Okay, do a back two and a half." I would imagine the dive and then do it, but I wouldn't think about it. Whatever he told me to do I would first "see" in my mind and then do it. The moment he told me to do it I would "see" it. When I was on the board I'd see it again and then go. When I "see," I feel it. I see it and I feel it. If I do a front 2½, I can see how it is going to feel. I know if I can see it, I can do it. I do lots of my diving by intuition. I'm good at that. I would go on the board and try something new and it would be good. Some people are really mechanical. I wasn't like that. But first I had to see everything I was going to do or I would get confused. Before going to sleep I would "see" my dives with my eyes open or closed. On site it was always with my eyes open.

I first started working on my mental imagery after listening to a sport psychologist and after reading a lot about best performances in sport. I also talked to athletes. I was really interested in that because I had some problems in meets. I was great in practice. Everyone expected me to win, but I was always second or third, always missing one dive, and I didn't know why. Every time I went into a big meet I missed something. I wondered why. In big competitions like the World Student Games I was third, Pan-Ams I was third, and I could have easily won. It really hurt me all the time.

In 1982 a sport psychologist told us that if we have a problem with the dive, to write down the details of doing that dive, so I wrote down

I started saying, "I won't miss anything. If I do everything great, I will win. If I miss some it's not their fault, it's my fault." That's why at the Olympics I was really focused on my diving instead of on other divers.

everything I knew about the dive from the beginning to the end and I gave it to my coach. My coach said, "That's not how you're supposed to do that dive." That's when I found out that the way I was thinking I had to do that dive was wrong. That's why I couldn't do it. So my coach wrote down what I was supposed to do and gave it back to me. I read it over very carefully before I went to the pool that afternoon. My diving went so well that day! I felt like I had done the dive so many times before but that was the first time I ever did it right. That's the day I found out that mental preparation is really important because you have to be really concentrating on the right things to do your dive well.

I didn't like writing down all the details of each dive, so instead of doing that I started doing it in my imagery. I would talk to my coach about the right way to do each dive or look at films and then do it in my imagery. Later I started doing the whole process by myself. I didn't need anyone any more. I just did it myself.

I was in Edmonton for a training camp in 1983 and I talked to a coach from Ottawa who told me that I should go to Los Angeles in March just to see the pool. That was a good idea for me because I don't like to dive in a new pool when I don't know what it looks like. I like to see it first, to get the feel of it. That coach also told me that I should start to get ready mentally for the Olympics, and I agreed but at that time I didn't really know how. I did know that I didn't like to look at my score or the score of other divers when I dove because it got me nervous. At lots of the pools I couldn't get away from scores. For example, if I dove last, they showed the score of everyone and I had to look at it, and that got me really nervous. That was really bad for me. So I told him, "If the scoreboard is right in front of me, I'm dead. What am I going to do?" That was a year and a half before the Olympics. He said, "What you have to do is go there and look." He showed me a picture of the pool and said, "The scoreboard is going to be there," and I said, "That is great because it is far away and if I don't turn around I won't see it." So that was the day I really started to mentally prepare for the Olympics. "Okay the pool's going to be like this. I want to be in this place after the prelims, so that way I won't dive last. I won't look at the score." And everything worked like I planned.

I went in a competition in March. I was in third place, but for me it was great because I just looked at the pool all the time. I walked in there prepared. Beforehand I thought, "Okay, people are going to be standing there, the scoreboard is going to be there, the judges are going to be there, the sun is going to be there, and the wind there. Everything was prepared. When I practised on-site I knew I didn't have to look at the scoreboard. I planned to stay at a certain spot during my event. Everything was prepared.

I started that shift away from the scoreboard a year and a half before the Olympics because I knew that every time I looked at the scoreboard, my heart went crazy. I couldn't control it. I knew that I dove better if I concentrated on my diving instead of concentrating on everyone else. It was harder to get ready for ten dives than for one dive so I decided to stop looking at everyone else, just be myself and focus on preparing for my next dive. I decided not to talk to my coach on deck because that was the best way for me to concentrate on

When I needed Donald, he was around and when I needed Elizabeth, she was around. It was real teamwork. I think it's good to dive with different coaches. You can learn from all of them.

24

my event. I thought, "I'm ready, and if I'm not, then it is my problem."

Between dives at a meet I thought that using a Walkman was the best way of shutting out everything. In the prelims, my Walkman batteries ran out. I went really far away into the locker room. I couldn't hear anything in there.

A couple of months before the Olympics at a competition in Ft. Lauderdale, I felt just great. You have to feel great in your skin to compete well. I was feeling like I was on holiday and I was having a great time. Everything was going easy, and I knew that everyone was looking at me, and they knew I was going to be a tough competitor at the Olympics. I won easily and I did really well. I didn't miss anything. I was trying to get the same feeling from Ft. Lauderdale for the Los Angeles Games. So my parents came, and my friends came, and it was like I was at home. I went out, had some pancakes with my friends, had a good time. I didn't stay in my room and get really tight and talk to all the athletes. I wanted to get out all the time. I didn't want to stay with all the athletes. That really worked in Ft. Lauderdale. I didn't want to talk to the Americans or the Chinese before the event because I knew that it was not really very good for my performance.

My last bad competition was at the World Championships in 1982. I was just starting to be good so I can't say it was a really bad performance. I was 7th in the world. It was the best time for me to place 7th because I could learn from it. I had a lot of work to do before the Olympics. At that time I wanted to win instead of wanting to dive well. It was my first big competition. I could have won but I didn't approach it the right way. Following that day, everything changed.

I started doing imagery six months after that and in the good competitions I had, I was realistic with myself. I knew I could win, but I had to dive well. I had to feel confident in myself. I stopped saying, "This diver's doing this, so she's going to miss this one, or if she misses one, I'm going to win." I started saying, "I won't miss anything. If I do everything great, I will win. If I miss some, it's not their fault, it's my fault." That's why at the Olympics I was really focused on my diving instead of on other divers.

That was the biggest change in those two years. Before that I used to just watch the event and watch the Chinese, and think, "Oh, how can she do that? She's a great diver." Even my coach was always showing me Americans and Chinese and talking about them. One day I thought, "What about me? I'm good too!" That made me more determined. The next competition I won by a clear margin with the Americans and Chinese and all! I discovered that I didn't like my coach talking about them when I was as good as they were. I thought, "I'm as good as anyone else, so let's stop talking about them." That was an important step in my career because that day I realized I was as good as anyone else. Since that day, I never wanted to see a film about the Chinese or the American divers and I didn't want to hear about them. They were good friends but I didn't want to watch them in the pool because they had different techniques. My technique worked for me and I didn't want to see anybody else.

My coach was there all the time. If I had a physical problem he called the doctor. If there was a problem with my apartment or car, he was there. He was really with me for the last two years. It's really important to feel that your coach is going through what you are going through. If you're really nervous, your coach is nervous too. He felt exactly like me. I would go in the pool and feel really tired that day. He would understand and say, "Okay, today we'll do this." He adapted to me. I would choose what I wanted to do. We worked it out together all the time.

He never looked for the glory, he just wanted me to do well. He really cared about me. That's why he understood when I asked if Elizabeth Jack could be the on-deck coach at the Olympics. He wanted the best for me. He said, "Well, if that's what you need to win, go for it." I really appreciated that. But I really wanted him to be there too, because he was the one who put me there and I wanted him to feel how I felt the day I won. Donald was my coach. Elizabeth helped me on site. He understood that. He was the first one I went to see after getting the medal.

For two years I competed in Ft. Lauderdale and Mexico, in a tour called Can-Am-Mex. Every year I dove there I won every single meet and Elizabeth Jack was my coach there. I won with her because she was so relaxed. We'd go to the beach, or we'd have a drink somewhere. She was like a sister to me. That was good for me because I didn't need to train at meets. When I go to a competition I know I'm ready because I wouldn't go if I wasn't. She just says general things like, good dive, bad dive, and that's what I need. At that time I didn't need someone giving technical feedback. My coach is so technical. Everything has to be right. It would be hard to tell him, "Just tell me good or bad," and even if he did I would feel bad because it's not him. So I talked to Elizabeth Jack about three months before the Olympics and asked her if she would mind coaching me there, and she said, "No. The only problem is Donald, how is he going to take it?" I said not to worry about him, I was sure he would understand. That decision was probably the most difficult of my life. I felt I had to go for what was best for me but I didn't want to hurt my coach's feelings. So I talked to him one day and he said, "Sure, if that's what you want." I felt great because he didn't tell me, "I've been coaching you for two years and you're asking me to let you go with someone else." But they get along really well. I said to him, I want to dive with you there, at the training camp, but starting 3 days before the event I would prefer to come to you only when I need something. At that point I did not want a lot of technical input. That's what I told him, but even the day before my event I went to see him and asked him some questions. After every workout I'd go to see him.

Liz and Donald worked and talked together. Donald was always there in the gallery when I trained. He filmed everything. He would tell Liz some things and Liz would tell me, but at that time I didn't know it was coming from him. Hearing it from her was better for me at that time because she was so relaxed. She would tell me at night before we went to sleep, instead of telling me in the pool when there were hundreds of people around. We talked a lot at nights and she really calmed me down. She was great for me. When I needed Donald, he was around and when I needed Elizabeth, she was around. It was real teamwork. I think it's good to dive with different coaches. You can learn from all of them.

I did my imagery about fifteen minutes before the event, and listened to the Walkman and started getting warm. I went through the whole imagery sequence in ten minutes. Everything was perfect, the dives were great.

26

At the Olympics, there was a practice time scheduled for every country, and once we couldn't dive at our allotted time. I got upset really fast. That's because it was planned in my head; no Americans, no Chinese, and then I got there and there would be 50 people on the board. I got very upset, really shaky. But Elizabeth Jack, my on-site coach, was there at the time, and she knows how I am, so she planned everything and she went to the pool before me to see if everything was on schedule. I really ask a lot in meets. I want my room to be really dark and no-one to make noise. I ask a lot of my coach, but when it works there are no problems.

I slept really well the night before the finals at the Olympics. I wasn't really nervous. I didn't talk very much. I went to a singing show the night before. I didn't really socialize with anyone, but my boyfriend was there. He knows me really well and I talked with him.

I trained the morning of the competition, like I do at every competition. I went back for breakfast. Then I went into my room, listened to the Walkman by myself and read. I didn't talk to anyone. Then I went to the pool for the finals.

I was really psyched, I had so much energy. I warmed up in the room. My coach came in and said there was no-one on the boards. That means I can go. It was time to train because no-one was there to see. So I walked out and went in the pool and trained a little bit. I saw two friends who I hadn't seen before. After half an hour I got dressed and went to see my parents and friends. They talked to me a little bit. My Mom just told me, "Whatever happens, you're our champion. We know you're the best, we don't even want to see this event." I laughed with them. They had a huge flag. It was just relaxing. I wasn't even nervous, I was just talking to them like it was a small event. The stands were packed. Everyone was worrying, and I was just there walking around and talking to everyone, so it seemed like it was really my competition. My parents were nervous. I walked back to the pool deck and all the guards were after me because I wasn't supposed to go in the stands but I had sneaked in. So I went back into the pool area.

I talked to my coach then because I never really talk to my coach during the event. She just wished me luck. I went behind to my small place and I started thinking about my dives. I did my imagery about fifteen minutes before the event, and listened to the Walkman and started getting warm. I went through the whole imagery sequence in ten minutes. Everything was perfect, the dives were great.

I could see the water polo team there yelling like crazy, a big Canadian flag, as if it was my country we were competing in. I was in my place and I could see my parents up there. Then I started to get nervous, so I walked away and I got ready. Every dive was great. It was like a practice for me.

Before each dive they announce my name, I go on the board, I focus on my dive instead of listening to the crowd. I'm thinking of one thing, I "see" the dive and I just go. If you look at the Olympic video you'll see I don't move, I don't smile ... I focus and go.

Between dives my coach says "Good" or with movements what was wrong with it. I go back, I listen to the Walkman. Usually I look at my dive in slow motion on the TV. I keep warm, walk for about ten minutes and then come back and jog just to stay warm until I have to go. Then I do my exercises and think about my dive at the same time. Then I take off my clothes and just walk. Sometimes I would walk past some of the other divers but I didn't pay attention to them.

After my 8th dive, I was leading. I didn't know I was leading. One American started talking to me. I don't know what she said but I said, "I'm sorry," and I left. In competition I prefer to stay away from other divers because I have learned from past experience that they could psych me out. During the competition I want to focus only on what I am doing and not on what competitors are saying or doing. During the event they are competitors but right after the competition they are good friends.

I carried my Walkman on my last two dives right up to the ladder and left it on the table. I was so nervous then. I went on the board. The crowd yelled. I thought of my dive. When I think of my dive, there's always an image, even today if I think of a dive I "see" it. It's like walking for me now, it's part of me.

I always listened to the same thing on my Walkman — "Take your passion, make it happen", from Flashdance. I don't know why this song. Maybe because my best friend gave it to me just before I left. She said, "Listen to this song and make it happen for real." It was in me, and I listened to it all the time.

I think the biggest problem facing athletes today is the lack of good mental preparation. For the first ten years I was a great diver, but I wasn't the best. I could have been the best a lot earlier than I was but at that time I wasn't clear on how to improve the mental aspect. Why was I nervous? Why did I miss that dive? After every single competition I would come back and ask, "What happened? Why did I miss that dive when I should have got an 8 or 9?" Most divers just train physically, instead of taking a day off and thinking about what they're doing. I hope the kids are going to start doing more mental training because they don't do it right now. They do lots of diving instead of doing focusing exercises in the pool or simulating things on the board or looking in the mirror, or "seeing" in their minds what they're doing.

The problem with Canadian athletes is that they don't believe they can be better than the Chinese or Russians. But we can be as good as anyone if we just believe it.

Sometimes I miss competition, the feeling of being on the board and feeling that you're great. No-one can beat you, you're in your field, no-one can touch you at that. It's a great feeling to know that you are the very best in something and that you are in complete control. What I miss about diving now and then is the power of perfection. I've been diving for most of my life and sometimes I miss that, but I know that I'm never going to lose the mental preparation I did. I know I'm going to lose the physical skills, but what I did to get there, I'm never going to forget that. I will never forget those lessons.

When I was diving, sometimes I couldn't do something, I couldn't do a dive, or I couldn't "see" it. Sometimes it also happens in life. I am asked to do something. I think, "I can't do that. Don't ask me to do that." I sit down and think, "I said that before in diving, and yet I could do it, and my coach told me I could do it." I start to think about it. Sometimes if I have a meeting or a conference somewhere that I'm not used to, and I'm really nervous, I sit down and listen to music, or

In competition I prefer to stay away from other divers because I have learned from past experience that they could psych me out.

28

just concentrate on what I have to do. That's what I did in diving when I was nervous. I went off by myself and tried to relax and focus on what I had to do. It works in life too.

6

GAETAN BOUCHER

1984 OLYMPIC DOUBLE GOLD MEDALIST — SPEED SKATING

GAETAN BOUCHER SPEEDSKATING

- 1985 World Championships — 1st — 500m, 3rd 1500m
- Double Gold Medalist (1000 metres, 1500 metres) and Bronze Medalist (500 metres) at the 1984 Olympic Games
- Silver Medalist (1000 metres) at the 1980 Olympic Games
- Male Athlete of the Year — 1984
- 1984 World Sprint Championships — 1st All Around (Sprint)
- 1983 World Championships — 4th — 500 metres
- 1982 World Championships — 1st — 500 metres
- 1981 World Championships — 4th — 500 metres
- 1979, 1980, 1982, 1985 World Sprint Championships — 2nd — All Around (Sprint)

My goal was to win at least one gold at the 1984 Olympics. I knew I had a chance to win two or three medals, but my goal was to win at least one. My best chance was in the 1000 metres. Three weeks before the Olympics we had raced a 1000 metres against the Soviet and American skaters, who were the best in this distance, and I had beat them in 4 races. There was only one other guy who could beat me, a Japanese skater, and the week after that, I beat him. So I did not think I could lose. Also, in the tempo training we had done prior to the Olympics where we go maximum speed, I had skated my best time ever. So going into the Olympics I knew that I had beaten the Russian two weeks earlier and the Japanese the week before, and I was then skating a little bit faster than I was when I beat them.

When I got to the line I was ready. I was more ready for the 1000 metres because I had already won a bronze in the 500 and I knew that my 1000 metres is normally faster than my 500. If I could skate that well in the 500, then I felt I would have no problem in winning the 1000 metres, as long as I skated like I should skate.

On my way to the starting line, I was telling myself to relax and focus on the task. Because of my experience, I knew what to expect

31

On my way to the starting line, I was telling myself to relax and focus on the task. Because of my experience, I knew what to expect in a big race and have learned through experience to relax more and concentrate on the race.

in a big race and have learned through experience to relax more and concentrate on the race.

After I won the 1000 metres I knew I could win the 1500 too. I had what I wanted, the gold in the 1000. But I wanted to win the 1500 too. I was ready for the race, but the attitude was a little bit different. I was more relaxed in the 1500. I had everything to lose in the 1000 metres. I had nothing to lose in the 1500.

I had heard that no Canadian had ever won 3 medals at the same Olympics. I thought I had a chance to do that. I had never done a good 1500 in a big race, in a world championship. I had had the best 1500 time in the world for the last 3 or 4 years, but every time I got to a World Championship, the best I had placed was 4th. I wanted to show them that I could win.

At my first Olympics in 1976 I skated well, but nobody expected me to do anything. I was there to do as well as I could. I don't remember having any pressure. Nobody was telling me, "You have to do well." It was just, "Go out there and do the best you can do." That was my second year on the national team, but I had had 5 years of national-level skating and had competed in the North American Championships.

I guess you have goals and you have something that is over your head that you would like to do. After the 1976 Olympics I thought, well I have been to the Olympics, but just having been there was not enough. My improvement between 1975 and 1976 was so great, that I started to dream more. I decided I would make it slowly to the top in 1977 and 1978. Then I would win in the World Championships in 1979. My dream was to win 5 golds at the 1980 Olympics.

In a way that is what happened to Eric Heiden, except he won. In 1976 he was nobody. He was 7th in the 1500, I was 6th in the 1000. So nobody noticed him and nobody noticed me. The improvement I made in 1975 was probably equivalent to the improvement he made. People might have said that there was one Canadian and one American who were getting pretty good, but nothing else. Then he started winning. He won the 5 golds at the 1980 Olympics. I thought, "That is what I dreamed about when I was younger and he did it." I had not trained to win 5 golds but I had this dream, then I saw somebody else do exactly what I was dreaming about.

I was second in the world in 1979 and 1980. Heiden was first. I saw him train in the summer when I was with him for a week. He was the guy to beat. In 1979, when I was second in the World Championships I said, "Next year at the Olympic Games, I am going to win the 1000 metres and he will be second." I believed that the whole summer until I went and saw him training. Then I thought, "I cannot beat him, he is going to win," because his training was so much harder. I thought I was training as hard as I could, then I saw this guy train even harder. He started with a 10,000 metres warm-up of skating imitations, on a small 200 metre track. I had never seen skating imitations before. You run in a skating position (bent over). To do one lap of skating imitations is about the same as skating 400 metres on a track. If you skate a 27 second lap on a 400 metre track, at maximum speed, then you can do a 27 second lap at maximum speed on this track. Ten thousand metres on a 400 metre track is 25 laps so it is 25 laps on this track too. He was doing that just as a warm-up and he was going fast! I stopped after 20 laps. My legs were hurting, and that was just a warm-up. Then he did a 5000, 1500 and 1000 all at maximum speed, just like a race. We took 5 to 10 minutes of rest after the 10,000 metres to recover a little bit and he said okay, I am doing a 5000. So I followed him and I stopped after 3000 metres. After that he did the 1500, fast. This time I did the whole 1500 metres, but he was pulling ahead. Then the 1000. I saw him stagger and almost fall from exertion after the interval. It is all in the legs and it was hard. He said he had started the 5000 too fast, maybe because I was training with him. It was really fast. He was not keeping time. It was just the effort that was so impressive. The 1500 was maximum. The 1000 metres was maximum. Our team would do that same type of training and say, "Well, I have 5 or 10 laps to go, I'll go easier." He was doing the 5000 metres at that time at the same speed I would do a 1500 or 3000. So after that experience I knew that I could take more.

You never saw him hurting after a race, whether it was a 500 or a 10,000. He trains so hard and takes so much pain in the summer, he is probably used to it in the winter (for skating season). The only time I saw him almost fall was in the training session, just because his legs were too shaky to stand. So that gave me the idea that I could go beyond. I think you have to go harder and suffer more in the summer than in the winter.

A 1500 metre race hurts most because it is almost all maximum. Heiden got ready for that pain through his preparation. We never used to do that. He even put the pain in his imagery for his mental run through. He would think that it would hurt, and he would be ready to accept the pain, just so he knew he could do it. When I race a 1500 now, I think about that. I go to the line and think that it is going to hurt and I am prepared for it. You have to be mentally prepared to accept the pain.

After my visit with Heiden it was not my training itself that changed, but my thoughts on how much I could take when I do train. I train alone, so it is hard. I would do a 2 minute interval, for instance, which is supposed to be maximum and I know it is going to hurt. So I would think I was going maximum, but I could have taken more. So I changed my understanding of what I had to do to go maximum.

I thought I was training as hard as I could, then I saw this guy train even harder.

Everybody on our team now trains about the same on ice, when we are in Europe. There is nothing else to do so we train hard. But the attitude that some people had was that summer training was not that important. They didn't seem to realize that it is what helps you through the season, especially at the end and the World Championships. That is where I train a bit differently from the other guys. My training method itself was not different, but the intensity I brought to year-round training might have been different.

To push in training, I think about winning races. I think about going to the Olympics and trying to win. I think about how nice it would be to win those gold medals again. I think that I really want to win, and all I have to do is change, get ready and go out. The main thing is to get out the door. I think about my goals while I am changing to help me get going.

You need special goals. I think about winning the three golds in 1988. I was on the plane coming back from Calgary two days ago and I had nothing else to do, so I just thought about that goal. I thought about everything that had happened to me. In a way you see yourself as a hero and I want to be one. So I use that every time I train. When I do not feel like training in the summer that is one thing that makes it even easier.

I can't understand people who train and make a team and do not really want to win. Some people make the national team and their goal is to be in the top 10. I don't mean the top 10 the first year, but I mean their eventual goal. You read comments from people who you have heard about for 6 or 7 years and they say, "I was 14th and I'm very satisfied and happy to be here in the Olympics." I used to think, "Why do they do it? Why do they train?" I would not be able to train and not think about winning. It depends on what you want.

I thought and dreamed about winning a lot. At first you think about winning but you may not believe that you can win. You may need somebody to help make you believe it. But it comes naturally too. Maybe at the beginning I was like these people with low goals too, except then you see an improvement or you start winning. In a way you know what it is to win. Maybe that is what makes the difference. It can't be the gold to start with but it can be the goal eventually. At least you have to hold on to the possibility of winning. If you want to achieve something big, you have to feel that possibility.

At the beginning of each season I write down my best times and personal records in the 500, 1000 and 1500 on a board. I also write down the best time I skated the year before and the Canadian record, which are the same as my best times. Then I write down the times I want to skate in the coming year, and my goals in terms of finishes at the World Championships or Olympic Games. I also look back at previous years. I look at what my goals were and the times I skated. Sometimes I surpass my time goals. In 1985 I improved my times at three distances but did not reach some of my other goals.

To help prepare psychologically, I mentally run through all my races that I skate. I did it for the 500, 1000 and the 1500 metres at the Olympics. I often do it the night before when I go to bed. I picture myself going to the line just like I am racing. The skaters get ready, the starter raises the gun, and then I skate the whole race. The night before we know which lanes we are in, so I skate (mentally) in the lane that I will skate in. In the 1000 metres, I might not do the whole race but I will do the first 200 as well as I can technically.

From the moment I change on the ice, when I take my warm-ups off, I always do the same thing. When I go from the warm-up bench to the starting line, I go to the same spot, inflex a couple of times, make the hole for my blades where I start, get in position and picture the way I will skate. I try to get inside myself, instead of having a video view. The video view is more visual. You see yourself. If I am inside myself, it is really me that is skating and I do not see myself going around the corner like a video. I am trying to picture from the inside but sometimes I cannot. I usually see myself start the race from the back and then it is like I get closer and follow right behind. Then I see the turn from the side. But then I move back inside myself and I come around the turn, seeing the turn coming. Then I see the same corner from the front. When you have cameras on the track, the picture you see begins with the 500 start and then the picture you get is the start from behind. Then they switch and you get a picture from the front. I have seen that so many times. That is probably why I see that view when I do my race in imagery.

When I did imagery for my 1984 Olympic preparation I imagined the actual course that I would compete on at the Olympics: the place where you change, where you stand, and even the seat was the same in imagery. I follow my exact race plan in imagery and if something is not exactly what I want, I start again. For example, I start again if I see the person in the next lane. I do not want to look at the other guys because I have to race my own race. If I am thinking about another skater I start again. I try to see just myself. I want to go to the starting line and concentrate only on my own race.

Sometimes the other skater is in my image because of the difference in inner and outer lanes. If I have the first outer (lane) and he has the first inner (lane), then he will be ahead. Even though it is natural to be behind if you start in the outside lane, you have to be as close as possible to have a good race. Sometimes what I want to do is get close enough so I do not get any wind. So I try to picture the race that way, except I won't see the guy until I am getting to the straight away.

I have been doing imagery for at least 6 or 7 years. I get better and better. In the beginning I didn't even get a picture, or anything, but I thought about the race and how it should be. I didn't really see myself skate, not the same way I do now. It was more like being inside without even doing the movements. It was like I was on the ice and I was skating but I didn't feel myself moving around the track. Now I "see" it and I "feel" it. If I do it for a short period, like the first 100 metres, I can feel it better, but that is what I want to do, feel it.

I remember my first year on the national team, I didn't know anything about imagery. I asked one guy who was on the team what he did before the race, and he said he did the race in imagery. I had been told when I was younger not to think about the race beforehand. They said, "You'll get too nervous." So I had never done it. I was surprised to hear that he was imagining the race. I started doing it just to see. Sometimes I would forget. After I had had a bad race, I realized I had forgotten to do the imagery. Then I tried to do it all the time.

I start preparing the night before by doing my race in my mind. Then I go to sleep. In Sarajevo, we were racing at 10 a.m. so I ate breakfast at 7 a.m. and at breakfast I started thinking through the race. Half an hour before leaving for the track when I was still in my room, I did the race in imagery again. I do it once or twice and when I am satisfied I get up and do something else. I am ready.

Once I arrive on site I am busy. I always know exactly what I will do. I do a specific warm-up and I am busy sharpening my skates. When I have ten minutes left before my race I do the start in my mind but I don't do the whole race again.

I usually spend about thirty minutes on the ice and then warm-up again for another twenty minutes before going on the ice to race. I work backwards from my starting time so I know when to go to the track, and I leave ten or fifteen minutes before, just in case. The

I thought and dreamed about winning a lot. At first you think about winning but you may not believe that you can win. You may need somebody to help make you believe it.

35

active warm-up plan goes up to the time I have to put my skates on for the race, which leaves about ten minutes. Then I just try to relax. I might do the start again (in imagery), while I am on the ice just before the start, but it is just a flash to make sure I still have it.

When it is an important race, and I am nervous, I sometimes think, "What I am doing here? I could be in the stands, watching and having fun, instead of being here and having all this pressure." It only happens while I am waiting, like while the two pairs before are skating their last lap, because I know I am next. Once I start taking my warm-ups off, I shift focus. I think, "I am ready, let's go for it." I think about the way I have been skating in the last few weeks, which gives me confidence. On the way to the line I say, "I should win," or, "I should not lose," or, "I should be 3rd," if it is the 500, which i do not win as much as a 1000 metres. Then I think, the only way to do that is to skate my own race. I go to the line, think "relax", and make sure I concentrate on the start.

When the gun goes, it's, "Let's go!" I focus on my first few steps. I can feel when it is a good start and I just keep going up until maximum speed. Then I have to line up the corners in the 500 and 1000 metres, because if you don't then the inside corner is really hard to take because of the speed. So you have to be prepared; you see the corner approaching and you get ready so you can make it around the turn. A lot of people have problems on that last turn. If you go right in on the line you save distance. I used to go into the corner right on the line but if you go in too tight it makes it too hard. So at that point in the race I am thinking go straight, don't go on the line too fast, go progressively. The rest will come naturally. When you skate corners it is natural that you lean and you will lean because of the speed.

What makes you skate well is thinking about sitting down and pushing with the heel so you bring your weight over at the right moment. Every skater has a slightly different technique. If you are chasing the other guy you won't be thinking about what you are doing. You will just be doing more steps or rushing. Sometimes you get in a race which is really tight and you forget to skate your own race: you panic, instead of just letting him go and skating your own race. It can happen in the first 30 or 40 metres. I have a slow start the first 5 metres, so I tend to be behind for the first 10 metres. This is what I did in the Worlds (in 1985). I panicked.

My all-time best performance was one in Switzerland at the end of January 1985. The ice was really good. I wanted the world record and I knew the only way I could do that was to skate well technically. I knew that I was physically strong enough to do it, so I thought, "I am going to go for it," but first, "Do not rush anything and skate your own race."

After 600 metres, which is one lap to go, I heard my coach call the split, so that I knew what kind of race I was having. When I heard the 600 metres split I calculated what time I needed to skate on the last lap: I know that I can skate a 29.4, 29.3, 29.5 and that should give it to me. It does not take long to calculate. When you hear the splits you know almost instantly what kind of race you are having. There were only a few hundred metres to go. I knew I was getting tired, but everybody is in the last 300-400 metres of a race. So I said, "All right,

When I did imagery for my 1984 preparation I imagined the actual course that I would compete on at the Olympics: The place where you change, where you stand, and even the seat was the same in imagery.

36

you are getting tired, so think more of technique and try to push to a maximum."

To push your maximum towards the end of the race you have to stay low and push with the heel. It is the same as the beginning, we have to avoid leaning forward too much. Once you bring your shoulders down, which is not good, then you start pushing with your toes. So you must think about sitting down and lifting your shoulders and you won't lose so much speed, even though you are tired. Everything is always based on technique. You do well if you are skating well technically. I have had enough races to know how to focus to skate well.

At the Olympics every race is one race and that is it. At the 1984 Olympics I finally believed that I could do well in the 1500. It started last year at the beginning of the season, just by having good results. I had been skating well since 1978 or 1979. You have to do well to be in the top 3 in the world. I had 2 world records in 1981, and I got to the World Championships and thought, "Well the Russians were not at that meet where I set the world records. Maybe they would have been better." That is the way I was thinking. Then I started to shift my thinking. "I skated a fast time. Nobody can skate that time on very fast ice." I finally believed I had a good 1500 and I was able to show it at the Olympics.

Another thing helped me know I could win the 1500. When I got on the ice in the morning before the Olympic 1500 I knew the sprinter who had won the silver in the 1000 metres had beaten everybody else in the 1500, and I had beaten him in the 1000. I knew the time he had skated was not that fast, so that was something else that made me believe I could do it.

When I was younger it was Sylvia Burka who really helped me start to believe in myself, even though it took a while. She was not a coach. She was another skater on the team and she helped me a lot technically and mentally. If I came second in a race and I was happy she would say, "What is wrong with you? You won two weeks ago and the guy who you beat there skated a faster time than the guy who won today. You should have beaten him here. You're second and that is not good enough." She did that kind of thing every meet, even when I won.

A meet is 4 races. Sometimes I'd start the meet with an average race which would put me in second, third or fourth place. Then the second day I was much better and I would win the race. So Sylvia would say, "See, you could have won 4 races. You were able to win. Nobody should beat you", and things like that. Sylvia and I were on the same team from 1975 until 1980. It took a while for me to believe in myself, but slowly it came, and by 1979 I was second in the world in the sprints. Sometimes when I go to a World Championship I still say, "It will be hard." But some people on the team say, "What are you saying? You will win, no way you should lose," and things like that. It helps to have that kind of support.

I started recording my racing reflections in 1976. At the beginning there was not much information. I would just write in my time and not even the winning or placing time. Then slowly from year to year I started putting down more information. Now it is very detailed and very useful.

At the 1984 Olympics I finally believed that I could do well in the 1500.

37

After every race I write down the critical information. I write the date, the race, the distance, what lane I was in, the time I skated, the position I finished, who was second or who was first if I was not first, the ice conditions, if I made any mistakes and why, how I felt, it there were any problems technically and how I skated. After each race, I also rate my race out of 10. I never get a 10 but I was as ready as I could be at the 1984 Olympics. I rated it a 9 plus.

I write my reflections when I go back to the hotel, the same day of the race. It only takes a couple of minutes for each race. One book is only for races. I do not put my training reflections in the same book. I have 10 years of racing reflections in that book. Sometimes if I have problems I will go back and look at the same date last year and see that I was skating slower. I look and see that the conditions were about the same and I think, "Well, I might be having problems but I am going half a second faster than last year." At the end of the season I list all the races, and the time I skate in each race, as well as my best times. I do that every year for the 500, 1000, 3000, 5000 and 10,000. I also write the track records I set and I write about the World Championships; how I did, how many medals, the place I finished and things like that.

I also look back at my racing book when I am skating very well. This year, for instance, I had six 500 metre races under thirty-eight seconds. When I had four I looked to see what was the best I had done before. I looked at the end of the book where I have all the times and I said, "Well I am doing much better than last year." So I look at things like that. For instance, for that 1000 metres I skated in Switzerland this year, I looked back at the splits, the lap times. I knew it was a very good race but what kind of lap times did I do compared to when I skated the world record in 1981? I looked back and saw that my lap time was much faster, so I think I am much stronger. On worse ice I went slower at the beginning and I was able to finish with a much better time. So that gives me more confidence. I know that I am physically much better. I can look in the book, read the time I skated and sometimes even "see" a race that I skated 4 or 5 years ago in my mind. I remember the race, I know what happened. It is a lot of fun. I even remember who my partner was.

I have another book or diary for training. It is mostly to write what the program is and how I feel. I have three ratings, good, fair and bad. I write in my mood, my appetite, (if the appetite is good, fair or bad), my pulse, the weather conditions, and I write what the training program was, and the laps we did. There are very rarely any technical things in that book.

Sometimes I go back to that book to see how many kilometres we had skated the same date last year, or the year before and what kind of programs we were doing, and how fast that program was. One thing has changed a lot. We used to do a twenty times 400 metres with 400 metres rest, and the fastest we used to do them was in about thirty-five seconds at a pulse rate of one hundred and sixty. On very fast ice, we were doing them in 31, 31.5. seconds. Now we do them at 31.5 on average ice. It is not because we have become so much better, it is just because in the last 3 years we have had a physiologist working with us who has said to do less, maybe fifteen intervals at a pulse of about one hundred and eighty. So we have started going faster.

I write my reflections when I go back to the hotel, the same day of the race. It only takes a couple of minutes for each race.

38

Since the 1984 Olympics I have received a lot more attention. As far as training is concerned I have not changed anything. I was a little bit afraid last year because I had so many involvements in March and April. I wondered, "What will I do?" We had to start training twice a day. We refused more and more invitations. I gave my agent the training schedule.

Sometimes the extra demands get on your nerves, when there are demands all the time; dinners and speaking and everything. You look forward to training. When you go on a trip to Calgary or Vancouver, you do not know if you should be training or resting. You do not know if you can afford to miss that training session, or what would benefit you the most. So that was a problem, but I had the time to train.

In dealing with the media, one thing I remember, is that the one who is asking the question is not really the one who needs the answer. It is for the people. He might be asking a stupid question and you might think the guy is stupid. But the answer is not for him, it is for the people. That is one thing a reporter told me when I was a lot younger. He said, "The question might sound stupid but you have to remember, the average person does not know anything about speed skating." That helped me give a better answer instead of just getting mad at the reporter.

Getting ready is personal. It depends on how well you want to do. Athletes could gain from more information on how to set goals. There was one guy who was last in his event at the Olympics. He came home after and was interviewed by reporters. He said that next year he wanted to beat me. He had had a bad season and he wanted to do better next year, which is good. But if his goal is to beat me next year I would say that this is impossible. I won the 2 golds at the Olympics. He should have a more realistic goal. He should start with, "I want to be in the top ten next year." Sometimes people set their goals too high. And this skater had been telling that to all the reporters. If you tell reporters that your goal is to be in the top 5, you put too much pressure on yourself. They start to believe it is easy, that you should be in the top 5. That is a hard goal.

A lot of people change their preparation patterns a lot from a normal race to a big race. In a way they do not know what to do. They say, "I've got to do something different; it is World Championships or the qualifications for the World Championship team." One guy left for the track two hours earlier than usual. He never did that before when he raced well. It is a big race, so they change their strategy. They probably get in their own way. They get mixed up, they put too much pressure on themselves. You should not change what you were doing before. That would be one service sport psychology consultants could offer; helping athletes have a plan they can use on a regular basis. They could also teach athletes how to relax.

Last year, at the Olympics, we had a physiologist with us who took blood samples. I did it every day. He could tell us how high our stress level was. The people who had no experience with Olympic Games or World Championships were really high. He had to tell one guy to sit down and relax and do something else, but I do not think the guy knew how to relax. It was his first Olympic games and his first race. He asked me if I was nervous. Of course, I was really nervous. But

Getting ready is personal. It depends on how well you want to do. Athletes could gain from more information on how to set goals.

39

even the morning before the 1000 metres race for the gold medal, my stress level had hardly moved. I would wind up a little bit which is normal, but the thing is that I could control things. That is one thing people could be helped with.

7
LARRY CAIN

1984 OLYMPIC CHAMPION — CANOEING

LARRY CAIN CANOEING

- Gold Medalist (C-1, 500 metres) and Silver Medalist (C-1, 1,000 metres) at 1984 Olympic Games
- Double Gold Medalist (C-1, 500 metres, C-1, 1,000 metres) at the 1981 Junior World Championships
- 1983 Pre-Olympic Regatta — 3rd — C-1, 500 metres and C-1, 1,000 metres
- 1983 World Championships — 7th — C-1, 500 metres and C-1, 1,000 metres
- 1982 World Championships — 4th — C-1, 500 metres and C-1, 1,000 metres
- 1981 World Championships — 5th — C-1, 500 metres
- 1980 Pan American Championships — 1st — C-1, 1,000 metres and 2nd — C-1, 500 metres

I felt one hundred percent ready for the Olympic 500 metre final. About twenty-five minutes before the start of my race I went out with Peter Koschanow, who was a spare on the team and my training partner here in Oakville. We did a six minute piece, three one minute pieces at one hundred percent, and then a few starts. When it was time to start the race, it felt like I was in the middle of a workout. I felt very, very sharp. I had a very positive attitude. I couldn't wait to get on the starting line. I couldn't wait to get going and have a chance to race. I had been waiting for it for so long, the opportunity was finally there, and I was going after it.

The night before, we went out to a cheap pizza place and just pigged out. Without trying, my coach sort of "put his foot in his mouth" in an incident involving a girl at the salad bar. We were all laughing so hard that I was crying. It was a really loose, low-key kind of evening.

We raced at 8:30 the next morning, so there wasn't the usual day of getting prepared and having the tension build. We woke up, got ready and it was over. I woke up at 5:30, got up and ran for about twenty minutes down the beach. We were staying right on the beach in Ventura. I ran fairly hard. I didn't want my legs to be tired for the rest of the day, but I ran at a fairly good pace. I got the nice feel of fresh sea air in my lungs, and everything felt great. It was a great

41

morning. I came back to the hotel and had a few dishes of cereal, said "Hi" to a few people, listened to some music on my Walkman, and got my stuff together. A little later, we got in the van, and went to the site. My coach said he would get my boat ready. All I had to do was make sure I was there in time to get on the water to do those warm-ups. I did a really intense warm-up.

Doing a few arm circles gets a little bit of the blood flowing, but you want to warm up to something specific to what you are doing. So the best way to warm-up is to go out and paddle. I start by paddling slowly. The reason I did those one hundred percent bursts, is so I would feel I was in the middle of a workout, where you have worked up a really good sweat. I also wanted to feel what it feels like to go all out, before the race. Then you don't have to search for that feeling when you get into the race; you've already felt it. What I had discovered through experience was that when I do 250's ten times, or "minute" intervals ten times, I usually feel best on the fourth to the sixth one. The first three are really good, but the fourth to the sixth are even better. I seem to be a little sharper. At that point I'm into it a little bit more, then I start to get tired. So that day I went out during my warm-up and I did three, to get me to that point where I know from experience that I'm at my finest. Quite often, in the past, I'd just paddle up nice and slow, stretch out and everything, then turn around and start a piece. Essentially a few bursts, then I'd start a race. I have discovered that it's better to go out and actually do part of my favourite work-out. That really gets me into a groove. Rather than go out and do a couple of this and a couple of that, which another athlete might do, I like to do something which is personal to me. I've thought about it, and thought, why not pick my best, my favourite workout and go as far into that as I usually do until I feel really, really good, really strong, really super, then I'll stop and be ready to race. That worked well.

One reason I thought it was really important to do this in L.A. was because from the time we left Sacramento, where we were training, to the time we raced, I wasn't feeling that sharp. I felt just fantastic three weeks before the Olympic final, when I was in Sacramento. But the last week we were in Sacramento, I started to feel less sharp. We were doing less work because we were trying to come up physically for the Olympics. When we got to L.A. I still didn't feel that sharp. Then I had a very good workout on Thursday, the day before the final, when I didn't race. We had a day off because I had already qualified for the 1000 metre final.

The workout that I did on Thursday included those minute pieces. That convinced me I should do that workout again, because boy, I felt good when I finally got into it. I hadn't felt really sharp for about a week before that. In the heats, I felt good; I was paddling well, but I wasn't sharp. So I planned that the next morning: "I'll get up and go for a little jog just to feel like I've been awake for awhile, and when I get to the course, I'll get Peter to go out with me and we'll do '1 times 6 minutes' to warm up, and then we'll go 'three times 250', we'll make them perfect." I talked to Peter and he was more than happy to do it. We did it, and boy, did it ever work.

I think it served two purposes: one, it got me ready to go, it got me to that point in the workout, where I'm physically at my best; it also

42

settled me down, relaxed me, made me feel like I was home, made me feel like I was just on the river. I think that was a very good thing to do.

I was lucky that the spare was Peter, who I train with all year round. We did all our workouts together from the beginning of the summer in 1983, right through until the Olympics, and we are still training together. We know each other very well on the water. It is his favourite workout as much as it is my favourite workout. I didn't feel awkward, or out of place, or unsettled or anything, by asking him to come out and do that with me. He was more than happy to come out and do it with me, and when we were doing it together, it was even more comfortable. I felt like I was right on the river at home.

If I treat the race like a practice, like a familiar place, I go in knowing I can just fly, like on my river. If I can duplicate that feeling for a race, I can go even faster because it is a race situation. It's the Olympics, there's an extra bit of adrenalin there too. The familiar feelings take some of the worry out of being there. If you are aware that you are in some strange place, it is very easy to become a little bit nervous. If you make the time leading up to the race seem like nothing special, it just goes by in a blur. Before you know it, you are ready to race, and because it is what it is, you are ready to go and give it that effort that's going to win you the race.

I can remember that the K-1 (Kayak singles) went first. Then we had 20 minutes before we go. We did our stuff. Then the starter says, "Five minutes to start." So I'm paddling around with Peter and I'm really relaxed now. It is like I'm taking my four minute rest, which I do in that 10 times 250 workout, or that 10 times "minute" workout. Except I'm taking five minutes rest. I'm giving myself that extra minute to recover. I can remember paddling along, making a joke with Peter, and him paddling off. As I'm getting ready to pull into my lane, he just turns off the course and says "good luck", and he's off, and now I'm shaking.

Then I remember coming up to the box (start) and exhaling, and feeling very big and strong in the boat, and very powerful. People were coming into my river to play with me. When people come to paddle at Oakville, that's my turf. That's what I felt like. They were guests in my turf. I don't know what I must have looked like, but I felt like when you see weightlifters, when they're ready to go. That's the way I felt on the starting line. I was just really ready to go, exhaling, just like a coiled spring. I was ready to snap when the starter started the race. And sure enough, just when the gun went, I got out very well, and it wasn't just a temporary feeling of aggressiveness that I had when I was in the starting blocks. It just carried me through the whole race.

What I felt in the race was what I felt in warm-up, and what I feel during that workout at home. When we do the ten times a minute workout, we go quite a bit beyond that 250, which is half the 500 race, in the first minute. That's faster than you might want to go in a 500 metre pace. It's just an intense workout. You get more out of your body and you go faster than in any other workout that we do. It is very intense, not only mentally, but there is a tremendous amount of flow that your body feels. It is just a great feeling. I got out fast

It's the Olympics, there's an extra bit of adrenalin there too. The familiar feelings take some of the worry out of being there.

43

with that kind of feeling. Although we only do it for a minute in the workout, when there is that extra little bit on the line, that extra bit of adrenalin going, it is very very easy to carry that feeling and that speed another 250 metres. That's really all I did. It was comparable to doing that workout. We get very explosive in that workout and very prepared. You feel very big in the boat, very strong at the start. It was really the same kind of feeling, when it came time to race, except I was a little bit more aggressive. There's a little bit more energy, because it was the big race. I don't remember thinking much to myself other than, "these guys are in trouble". It was just like it is at home, a fantastic feeling.

During the race, I knew I got off fast; there is a certain amount you can catch with your peripheral vision. I knew I got off fast because I had a sense of being out alone with water all around me on either side, not boats. I didn't really look, until we got near the 250, then I took a look, and wow, I'm doing pretty good here. Usually I don't hear too much of the crowd, but I can remember it was like a static background, a fuzzy background, kind of quiet really, then all of a sudden I hit the 250, and I hear the 'whirr' of the crowd. With no American in the race, maybe I was a crowd favourite. My family was there and I had friends there. My mom said, sure enough, when I hit the 250, there was a roar. When they announced I was in the lead, I sort of heard that out of nowhere. I can remember thinking "this is great".

The last 150 metres, I was just thinking about bringing it in, being smart and bringing it in with control. Quite often, if I'm in heats or in qualifying races, if I have a clear lead, I'll slow the stroke rate down. In the Olympic final I kept the stroke rate high, but I just eased off in the pull a little bit. If the stroke is fairly fast, you can always put more power on it. If you slow it down it's hard all of a sudden to get going again. I kept the stroke high, and I just sort of let it come through by itself, instead of trying too hard by really cranking it through, just so I didn't make any mistakes. Until 350, the feeling was, "go and get it". From 150 out it was "you've got it, don't let it go". I knew I had a lot of control and my focus was to maintain that controlled stroke.

My goal in L.A. was to win two gold medals. I achieved half that goal. It was my goal before the boycott. It was realistic before the boycott, but it would have been very, very tough to do. After the boycott it became much more realistic. Certainly if I didn't win one gold medal, I would've been very disappointed. The competitors know each other's strengths and weaknesses and you know what to expect when you line up on a starting line. I knew that there would be a couple of strong competitors in each race, but if I hadn't won either race it would have really been a sub-par performance each race.

The belief that I can beat people is based on racing them time and time again; they beat you, you beat them. It is quite close. It also comes from the training I do, repeating regular workouts, to measure my improvement. I know how fast I can cover 250, and I know how fast I can cover 500 on an accurate course in calm conditions. I know if I can do that, I can beat everyone else. It comes from the training and the racing.

I definitely think that I train differently from most of the other canoe partners, and definitely different from the other paddlers.

Then I remember coming up to the box (start) and exhaling, and feeling very big and strong in the boat, and very powerful. People were coming into my river to play with me. When people come to paddle at Oakville, that's my turf. That's what I felt like. They were guests in my turf.

44

My programs tend to be very simple. We don't have a lot of exotic intervals in each workout. We tend to focus on one component each workout and have relatively straight forward pieces: like 5 times 500 metres, or work on race pacing, race distance work; or ten times one minute at one hundred percent, with lots of recovery time, on speed and speed endurance. I know that a lot of other people have had a mish-mash of distances within one workout. They might work on the speed component, and then change it to a long tempo endurance component in the same workout. My programs are the same workouts on the same days, from a week-to-week basis. It repeats all the time. A lot of people find that boring. Well I find having to do different workouts all the time boring, because you have no way to measure your improvement. That's the exciting part about training and competing: your own improvement, and looking at your times. Though in our sport, times are not always an absolute measurement, because there are outside conditions to slow you down. But you can look at how far a distance you covered in given wind conditions, with a certain stroke rate and maintaining your technique. When you are doing the same workouts on a week-to-week basis, it becomes very easy to measure your improvement. That contributes greatly to my confidence. I've done other programs for a short period of time, where there is no real repetition. You never really hit one workout more than once. You sort of wonder how you are doing. It is very nice to go along on a regular program for the whole summer, where you keep hitting the same workouts over and over again. It gives you something to get motivated for in practice. I can go down to the club, and not really be looking forward to going out and beating my head against the wall. But when you get out there, say the workout is 10 times a minute — "all out", I know that usually I cover 255-260 metres in a minute on the river. Even if I feel kind of unmotivated, which is rare for me, I very rapidly become motivated when I start doing it. If it is Monday, I'm usually already looking forward to this one workout on Thursday. You get really charged up in what you are doing. And it gives you confidence in what you are doing. The whole idea is to improve. Also you need a confident approach to racing. I think that type of training is the best for me.

My coach, Jim Reardon, writes the training program, and I go out and do it. He's the one with the Physical Education degree and quite a bit of practical experience in paddling, and also in coaching. He's the one who worries about the program, and he'll adjust it if I feel bad. I've got some input. I can express some concern about an upcoming competition, for example, that I don't want to be tired for it, or that I haven't felt good lately, that I've been tired. He'll adjust the program for me, so I feel ready for that competition.

My coach works with Peter and I, and basically that's it. He only works with the two of us on the Olympic team, on a year-round basis. That's just the approach we like. We let him do the worrying, we just go out and do the hard work. It seems to me some athletes are too worried about what their coaches are doing, and about having input into the program. They are not focused enough on what they themselves are doing. And really it is no secret. It is just hard work that leads to success.

I don't remember thinking much to myself other than, "These guys are in trouble." It was just like it is at home, a fantastic feeling.

45

I think I'm a little more canoeing-oriented in everything I do than some other people. If you look around our house, everything is canoeing. So everything I do, whether it is weights, or running, or the normal training things, or the leisure activities I do, it is all geared toward how it's going to affect my paddling. Everything I do is measured with respect to how it is going to affect my paddling: Everything is opportunity/cost. If I go out and go to a movie instead of going hiking as my leisure activity, what is the cost of that? If I go to the movies instead of a hike, does that help or hurt my paddling? I've got to judge that. I've always thought this way. Ever since I saw John Wood win a silver medal, I wondered: does he dream all the time about being the best in the world? I have always dreamed about doing that. Maybe that's different from other people.

When we talked, John told me what it was like for him. I can see a lot of similarities, and he does too. That's kind of fun to realize. Our basic philosophies are similar: keep the work simple, don't worry about making things too complicated, because you seem to get lost and you don't get clear feedback. Keep things simple and just work hard. It seems to be what he used, and it seems to be working for us. We are very fortunate that John has been training with us two or three times a week. He's preparing for the "World Master's Games". He paddles down at the club at Oakville, so we see him quite a bit. He's got an awful lot of experience. He can help me and everyone else in training.

Another way my training differs, is that we always do our workouts "head-to-head", two or three canoes at a time. We often get a little bit of a race situation created in our practices. Others tend to do a lot of work on their own, them against the stop watch. That's fine, but in all honesty, I couldn't care if I won a race in a time of three minutes, or with a time of one minute fifty. As long as you win. That's the important thing. So in a sport where we are racing head-to-head, where they don't keep world records, and where so much depends on the conditions, time is important, but it is not so much a factor as beating the other people in the race. So we do all our workouts together, we all line up together, we all go together. And it is sort of "dog-eat-dog". Somebody might get washed out, or cut off, or something, but when it is happening, you learn to fight to stay ahead.

You develop small skills, like learning how to "ride someone's wash", but more important than that, you learn to get the most out of yourself with other people around you. Quite often people who go out and do a workout alone may be very in-tune with their own body; they may know exactly what pace they are on, and everything like that, but when it comes to a race with other boats around them, they don't race to what the race dictates.

You want to race your own race, but you also want to win. And in racing your own race, if the pace you set is too slow to win, there's something wrong. You have to race the race. You have to race the eight other competitors in the race. If you can stick to a race plan you've devised, then that's great. But you have to feel comfortable with other boats around.

That's something that we've developed, and that's something I've worked on by just picturing other boats around me. I guess because I'm always thinking about canoeing, I concentrate on canoeing, even when I'm relaxed. So maybe that's a psychological tool that I've developed. It is always there, it is always in the back of my mind. When it comes time to actually go out and race, or go out and do a practice, I can draw from that base level of concentration on canoeing that I already have, and add to it. Maybe I'm getting that much more focus on what I'm doing than someone else. If you eliminate distractions, in day-to-day life, maybe you learn to focus better and maybe the distractions are less likely to haunt you when it comes time to race. This doesn't mean you can't go out and have a good time, but you use some good judgement and a little bit of common sense. It seems that these things pay off.

Ever since I can remember I've always pictured myself crossing the finish line first. When I was thirteen years old, it was crossing the finish line first at the local regatta. As I improved and reached that goal, things changed and the image became crossing the finish line at the Canadian Championships, then crossing the finish line first at the World Championships.

It starts in imagery. I'm piling along in the boat alone in the fall, during a long distance workout and I picture myself in a race. Before I really know what's happening, the stroke picks up and then I pick a point in the river that's a finish line and I'm gone, I'm racing. Sort of pretending, sort of play, or make-believe. It works. I can envision boats around me and it helps me prepare for situations that arise in the race, where there are boats around.

At international competitions, usually I'm incredibly bored through everything until I come to the final. I think that's a healthy attitude. You don't waste any psyching up on the unimportant stuff. You are saving it all for the final, the big race.

If the semi-finals go well, I can hardly wait to get into the starting line, to get the chance to win. I usually try and eat lunch early, so it is already digested when it is time to get out for the final. I listen to some music on the Walkman, I'm usually too excited to read. I remember in 1981, at the World Junior Championships, we had 4 or 5 hours to wait for the final. My coach and I were in the same room. To fill time in a focused way, we dropped rotten peaches out of the hotel window from the 11th floor. We timed them to see how long they took to hit. We were figuring out how high we were with simple physics. We did things like that. Then we would do a projectile motion, throw it out and try to figure how far out we threw it.

I think it might be a good idea to do something even more physical than that. I hate sitting around if it is down to the last 6 hours. I'd much rather get out and play touch football or something, because that's what we do in Oakville. We've got a big parking lot down there, and before a big workout, we'll play road hockey; it is a lot of fun. We're active, we are athletes, and we are used to doing physical things. When it comes down to the big competition, and you are on a reduced workload the last two weeks, you are able to handle activity before your final. A game of road hockey or something isn't going to exhaust you for your race. It makes you feel more at home. It makes me feel more relaxed when I'm doing things. If it is before something important, I know all the preparation is done. It is time to get your mind off it, think about something else. I don't like studying the last five to six hours before an exam. I'll go out and go for a walk,

If you eliminate distractions, in day-to-day life, maybe you learn to focus better and maybe the distractions are less likely to haunt you when it comes time to race.

47

quite often I'll go for a paddle, I'll go for a run or something, then come back and go and write the exam. It just takes your mind off the importance of what is coming up.

Another part of my mental preparation is to stay wide awake those last hours before the competition. Sometimes I've made a mistake by going back and sleeping, just waiting for the final. Incredibly enough I have been able to sleep soundly. But then when I wake up I'm really tired. Then I've got to splash water on my face but I still don't feel wide awake. I'm yawning, so that's no good either. I learned in L.A. that it is really good to be as wide awake as you can be, because when you are wide awake you tend to take charge of things. When you take charge of things you are going to be racing better. My "turf, territorial" feeling.

Another thing that has affected my mental readiness is that I've always been a fighter. I always used to try to develop a little bit of anger, in order to have more explosiveness on the starting line. It started to happen a lot in 1979. I started to pick individual people, and say, "I'm going to beat this guy. This is Canada, and I'm going to beat him". I wouldn't sleep peacefully at night until I had beaten this person. At times there was a lot of intense hate for the person. I would still get along with the person, but I couldn't sit down and talk to them, or have a beer with them, and feel completely relaxed with them, because I was always a little bit on edge, because he was the enemy. It would be like Reagan sitting down with the Russians. He could sit down and be diplomatic, but inside he would have no trust for the person, no good feelings about the person. You don't want to come off hating anyone, or eliminating possible friendships, but at the same time, that's something I was doing: picking a person and saying, "I won't sleep at night until I beat this person". I'm doing that now to a much lesser extent, because I've found some other effective tools that I can use to help me get around hating the person all the time. I think too, that as I become more confident solely in my abilities, I don't need to use as many of those little gimmicks.

One of the attitudes I can use now is, "Who the hell cares about the other people? I know what I'm doing; I don't have to worry about anybody else but myself; let them worry about me; come and get me guys". I can use this attitude because I'm at a level now that on any day I can be untouchable.

That's a good plan when things are going well, but every once in a while someone comes up and shocks you. I hate losing. I've always hated losing. I picture losing as an embarrassment. I hate being embarrassed. If I came 5th the weekend before, for whatever reasons, then I'd go into the race and say, "I'm not going to live until I get you back". It's almost like revenge. But there have been summers when I've had a string of races where I've done really well, and in the middle of that string I'm just cruising along saying, "Come on, come and knock me off, I feel so good right now, you're not going to get me", that type of thing. So there are two sides to it.

Those are things that I've learned by myself. That aggressiveness or competitiveness is part of me, part of my personality, so the fine psychological tools, like drawing a race plan, using cue words and things like that are tied into that part of me.

One of the attitudes I can use now is, "Who the hell cares about the other people? I know what I'm doing; I don't have to worry about anybody else but myself; let them worry about me; come and get me guys."

48

But I've not always been as mentally ready as I was for the Olympic 500. For example, my first competition that year at the Moscow regatta, I didn't make the final. I hadn't been racing since the last big competition and I had forgotten the tricks of how to prepare mentally. That hurt. It showed me the importance of being in touch with all the little tricks and mental things in order to get the most out of my body.

The second race of the year at a regatta in East Germany, I was more ready to race physically; but I got so hyped, so excited, so aggressive that I went out too fast in the first 250 and ended up coming in fourth. It wasn't an exceptionally smart race. If I had slowed my stroke down and had become a little more focused on what I was doing, I would probably have been more efficient and been able to hold that race the whole way. That was a case of being too explosive, too "nuts", and not being in touch with the fine body movements I was making.

For the 1000 metre Olympic final, where I got a silver medal, I went through the same kind of preparation except I didn't do three of those fast 250 warm-ups. I did two because it was a longer race. I would have been foolish to expect to go off in the pace I use for my favourite workout, and maintain it for the 1000 metres. But there were some things that bothered me before this race.

I was a little drained both physically and emotionally from the first day when I won the 500 metre. I went for a run that morning, but I didn't feel as awake once I got down to the course. Half a day of excitement is enough, but there had been a whole day. The 500 was over in the morning, but if you had taken my heart rate at 5.00 pm it was still, boom, boom, boom, fast. In the past, I've been able to bounce back and repeat a performance the second day. I guess it was the scale of the competition, and the fact that I wasn't the only person who was excited about my win. Usually I can channel my excitement, turn it off, and concentrate on the next day's task. But it's a little harder when there are a lot of other people around too: family, friends and everybody is excited.

Terry, our sport psychologist, tried to help us prepare for the fuss that would be created over us down there. He tried to devise a set of sample questions that we might have to deal with from the press. We sat down with Terry, a small group of us with the coaches, and devised a press policy, that we would only grant interviews at such a time, so that we could concentrate completely on what we were doing. I don't think he dealt enough with preparing for what comes after winning. It was really hard. I guess prior to the Olympics it seemed a little premature, to work on what you are going to do after you win. That's something we should work on; be a little bit more aggressive, expect to win races instead of focusing solely on how we can get there to the top.

I've had experience in winning one day and having to go out and win again the next day. I did that at the World Junior Championships. But the scope of that competiton was far from the scope of the Olympics. No one seemed to care at the Juniors. I was the only one it really meant anything to. At the Olympics, that's a completely different story.

It wasn't just press and relatives, it was something inside yourself. Even though it was a boycott Olympics, you've won; you've stood there, and you've got your Olympic medal. It is something eternal. It is an incredible feeling of satisfaction, but the job isn't over. Try as you might to put that behind you, there's still some excitement, some satisfaction. And I'm sure that drains you a little bit for the next day. We can learn how to set a policy where the press doesn't bother us, and relatives don't bother us that much, but we are going to have to learn to deal with ourselves, after a performance like that, so we are ready to come back the next day. That's just about the only circumstance that arose in L.A. that we weren't fully prepared for. Next time, when we go back, we'll be prepared for that.

The night before the 1000 metre final, my coach and I went out to a classy restaurant to celebrate the 500 victory. I don't know what it is about expensive restaurants, but I always feel a little out of place. The room is dark, candle-lit, and it takes forever to get your meal. I always get sleepy in those places. You just can't act loose when you get to a dark fancy restaurant. I have a feeling that something as simple as how you spend the night before, has an effect on what happens the next morning. The night before the 500, when we had gone out for pizza and beer, it was like home, fooling around with the guys.

The more you can make the situation familiar, and take away the things that make it different from everyday life, the more adapted you are going to be. The more adapted you are, the more likely you are to go out and give the kind of performance that you need to win.

Another thing that might have hindered my performance, was the lane draw in the 1000 metre race. I knew that the competition was going to come from the Romanian and the West German, who ended up winning. I didn't really count on the Danish paddler. I was in lane 1 and the West German was in lane 2. My race strategy has always been to jump out a long way and take command, then get that flowing feel, and then hang on. When things go well, I'm always able to do that, no problem.

In L.A. after we saw the line draw we adjusted my race plan for the fact that the West German was beside me. His strongest way to race is to start off fairly slow and build as the race continues. I'm a fast starter and he's a slow starter. We felt we could give away too much to him if I jumped out too fast, because with him being in the lane beside me, he could ride my wash, which is, in effect, surfing on a small wave. He could position his boat so that it is riding slightly downhill on that small wash. The wash pulls you along, you are paddling downhill and it makes the 1000 metres a lot easier. He was already strong in the second half, so I didn't feel I could afford to give him any kind of free ride in the first half. So we thought that it would probably be better to race a little bit more his kind of race, even though that's not my strength. Ideally what I had hoped to do was get about a half boat advantage in the first half, like I always had, and then try and break him when he was going for his move.

That's where I didn't have the steam to do it. I think if I'd been able to zip off the start, like I usually do, I might have been in a lot better shape, later on. It was really kind of a strange race, maybe just a little too tactical for me. My strength is just going out full power.

50

The two differences between my gold and silver races were that in the silver I modified my race plan because of the lanes, and I didn't feel quite as sharp, as awake and in control as I did the day before for the gold. It had nothing to do with the fact that I don't feel as comfortable in the 1000, because until that weekend I was doing better in the 1000.

My coach, Jim Reardon, was very good for my mental preparation, because he would go out and watch my workout before the race. I'd trust his opinion, because he sees me all the time. He'd say, "Gee, you look good". That positive feedback was very encouraging and helped build up the confidence. During the whole preparation stage, the program he designed was just essential in order to be confident when the time came.

The head coach, Frank Garner, went out of his way to do things to accommodate what I felt I needed. I didn't ask for a lot. I can blend in with the rest of the team. He did everything he could to see that I felt comfortable. In fact that is why Jim was able to go to the Olympics. Frank recognized the fact that the best thing he could do for me was to see that Jim worked with me as much as possible. He got Jim to come to Florida, to Europe, to Los Angeles. Jim is not a full-time coach, he's a manager of an Insurance Adjusting Branch, he has a family; he just doesn't have time. Yet Frank saw to it that the funds were made available so that he could get to the important places.

Another thing Frank did was let me out of going to Sacramento (training camp) for three weeks. I had just been in Europe for nine weeks and I would have had only a week at home. Instead I got two and a half weeks at home which did wonders for me really. I got to train on the river I know best. I got to spend some time relaxing. So just by listening, and saying, "What can I do for you?", then by doing his best to see if it could be accommodated, Frank made a significant contribution to my performance, and I think to the performance of the entire team.

Frank made sure that the whole team felt comfortable. That's why we stayed in the hotel 20 minutes from the course, when the alternative was staying in the Olympic village which was 70 minutes away from the course. A big advantage. That's why we had our own truck with our crest on the side of it and our own fleet of boats - because that made us feel we were in complete control. That's why he told the manager to have a buffet at dinner with a choice of two or three things to eat for supper. That's why he didn't get too upset if we split, and did our own thing at night. He knew that we were goal-oriented. The things he did for the team put us in a comfortable situation, a much more "homelike" situation, than any of the other teams there. By creating a homelike, comfortable atmosphere for everybody, he contributed significantly to the performance of the whole team.

Additionally, you could talk with the guy, he didn't seem to carry a big air of superiority over the athletes. He is very approachable. It is very relaxing when you can go out with the guy who is in charge, three weeks before the Olympics and have a beer with him. He is very approachable, very relaxed, and it was nice to have him in charge of the group. He's not going to be with us this year (1985). As a team, we are really going to miss him. I think it is going to be tough to replace him.

We had a good sense of team harmony, especially in Los Angeles. We had our own boats, our own truck, everything the other people didn't have. We stayed in our own hotel, and we all got along well because of the effort Terry, our sport psychologist, made. He did everything possible to make sure that everyone could fit together as a unit.

Unfortunately, at one point we had a staff member associated with the team who was a bit defeating to what Frank and Terry had tried to achieve. He seemed to have the opinion that he knew, better than us, what was good for us. Instead of asking where people wanted to eat or giving us ten bucks and letting us go where we wanted, he'd pick the restaurant. Once he picked Mexican food. If I eat that, it upsets me for a week. For me to feel in control, I should be allowed to make those decisions. The other thing is that although I like everyone on the team, people start to wear thin at the end of the year. That's the time you think of yourself and get selfish. You want to think about your own race. When everyone starts thinking that way, it's better to get away on your own.

Instead of helping us to get that space we needed, this guy would say, "I don't want to give you the van so that you can go out tonight, because we want you to stick around the hotel. We don't want you to get tired". How the hell does he know what is going to tire me out? Sitting around the hotel might exhaust me mentally; I'd be bored as hell. It is better for me to get out and do something. No-one is going to go out and get pissed drunk, and come back at three in the morning. I mean these people are here for a reason. They have spent so much time preparing for it, they are not going to throw it all away at the last second. If anything, they want to get out and do something, because they think it is going to help them tomorrow. Like I said, every decision I make is based on how it will affect my paddling. He seemed to have the attitude, "No, no, you can't do that, because it is not the best thing for you". Responsible adults don't have to be told, they don't have to have little strings tied around their wrists joining them all together. They should be allowed to do what they want.

At the very, very end, individuals should be able to take charge. We may all have to travel at the same place at the same time, that's fine. We may all have to check into our rooms at the same time - that's fine. That's realistic, and it would be unreasonable to expect to be able to do otherwise. But if there is a van sitting in the parking lot, which is quite often the case in Europe, with no-one driving it, and you want to go out and they say, "No, you can't" – that's arbitrary. There is something wrong there that should be eliminated. By doing that, I think he tended to ruin some of the harmony that was there.

Frank Garner brought Terry in to work with the team three years before the Olympics. The first time I talked with him was at a Florida training camp. He said he had heard some things from the coaches about the way I prepared and he was interested in talking to me. We had a little informal chat about sport, paddling, preparing for a race, and basic philosophy about training and things like that. Obviously the first time wasn't a heavy discussion on preparing for anything. Very rapidly he became a friend to everyone on the team.

At first, Terry worked with us as a group. He got us to learn how to relax and let the little hassles go by without bothering you. I think

At the very, very end, individuals should be able to take charge.

52

that is what saved me a lot of times when I was getting pissed off at one of our staff members. When you think of what you are there for, the fact that he's in your mind should have no significance whatsoever. That's what saved me a lot of the time, when I was getting frustrated: the fact that Terry had got us together to relax, and focus on the real goal and let everything else ride.

He played us some relaxation and concentration tapes. That was great. We would all go over to the adult education centre in Florida and lie down on the floor and relax. I'd never tried that before. If I had to sleep, I could use it to fall asleep. Then he suggested using your own tapes that you find relaxing. When you get into a situation where there's a hassle, you can put them on your Walkman. He encouraged us to find things that make us relax, so when things got bad, we could shut them out. He talked with us about different techniques for doing that. I think the way he did it was very effective.

He also lead discussions about dealing with conflicts. This became very useful for creating a sense of team harmony, because many times hassles do arise from conflicts between athlete and coach, or coach and manager, or athlete and manager. To put the petty things aside and arise above all that was something he tried to get the whole team to work at.

Terry worked with us both during training camps and European trips. He would usually come over to the World Championships, and to one of the big European regattas, for about a week. In that time he would do a number of group sessions, and also in that time he would see each person individually. Plus he is always there for consultation. Like I would come off the water and he would be standing there. I would go over and chat with him. He was aware of what we were working on in a race plan and he'd say, "Well, how did it feel"? I would say, "Well, it felt pretty good. I'm really pleased with it". And he'd say, "Well, it really looked good, it looks like it is coming together". Just that much is a big plus sometimes.

He really helped the K-4 in 1983 at the World Championships. One day they did just awful and the next day they came fifth in the world. He can't take all the credit, it's the athletes that take the credit, but he helped steer them in the right direction. He helped turn them around from a dismal performance, to something that was very, very good. Basically, the only time we ever use him, is when the whole team is together.

Terry is an easy-going guy, he is a friend of everyone on the team. He is also a funny guy. Like at the training camp in Florida, when everyone goes out after the whole week of training is over: quite often, there will be a bit of a release in one of the local bars. He'll get into the action too, but quite often you'll see him just sit back, he's observing. I see him looking around the room, and I always have to laugh. I wonder what he is thinking when he is looking around, not just at us, but at everyone in the whole place. I don't feel that he's passing judgements. He's very open, and you never have any reason to suspect that he is hiding anything from you.

I like knowing he is on our side, he's there checking the whole place out. You don't have to worry about what other people are doing, because I feel like he's taking care of that. When he gets to a big international competition, he checks out the other tables, you don't have to do it. Who cares? Eat your food. Terry's looking at them. He's learning a lot by watching them, just by the atmosphere at the table, when they sit down and eat their dinner at night. A certain atmosphere is related to the success that they have. He's been able to try and instill that in us, and get our table thinking the same way. So it is great to have him there, because he does all the worrying about other people and you worry about yourself.

He's everybody's friend on the team, and he's very easy to talk to, and he's genuinely concerned and interested. You know if he's going to say something, he's saying it for a reason, he wants to help. My philosophy is you can always listen to somebody, and if you don't like what they are saying, you don't have to do it, but you can always listen to them with an open mind. I listened to Terry and what he was saying made good sense. He made it very easy for us because he gave us planning forms, race evaluation forms and things like that. It just became very easy, and made very good sense to sit down and try and look at each race more closely.

At the end of each race I'd fill out a race evaluation form and I'd look at it. Part of the thing about filling out a form is it just gets you to think about the race. Often I gave it to Terry and he would go over it, and if he saw anything that struck him as strange, e.g., "I felt shaky at a certain point in the race", he would come back to me with a suggestion. He's become more effective as he's gotten to know the sport better too. He's seen an awful lot of races and he can relate to what's happening at each point in the race. Before, he was more an outside observer. He had the psychological tools to give us, but he didn't have the knowledge of our sport. Now he is more effective.

Quite often after your last race, if things go well, the first thing you want to do is hit the party. You don't really have time to sit down and fill out an assessment form. But it is good to do it while the race is still fresh in your mind, because you are not filling it out for anyone but yourself. If you think you are filling it out for anybody else, don't bother doing it. Terry doesn't care if he's got to look at one more sheet of paper or not. Some athletes may think that Terry's forms are stupid. But in the long run it helps you. If you don't study every stroke, you're missing something that could be helping you. Those forms are for the athletes. If somebody doesn't want Terry's help, well that's one less person for him to talk to. No one is forcing sport psychologists on anybody. The evaluation forms are a useful tool to help the athlete look at his or her own race.

He's given us two sheets. On the first one you comment on your state of physical and mental preparation: did anything hassle you before the race, did you have to re-focus at any point in the race, what was your "activation", as he calls it, how ready to go were you? You just circle on a scale from 0 to 10. Then you can look at them. You can put five of these sheets down in front of you during the year and say, well, there's an obvious relationship between activation, energy and performance. But it may not necessarily be that an activation energy level of what you call "10", is the best thing for your performance. You might have been too hyper, and you might not have focused enough on exactly what you were doing. You can see things like that. It is going to be different for each individual. A different sort of blend. He can look at them and see how well you are doing.

54

And obviously, if you just aren't getting motivated, then he can come back to you with some suggestions on how to get prepared.

There is another form that breaks the race down into 100 metre sections. Within those sections you can get as explicit as you want. Sometimes I fill it out and go by 100 metre sections and sometimes I try to do it on a stroke to stroke basis. What happens in stroke 10 and what happens in stroke 11 may not mean that much to Terry, but it should mean a lot to the paddler. Those are especially for the athlete. The idea is you try and recall exactly what happened in the race and gain from it.

I'll sit back now after a race and I'll analyze it with a fine tooth comb, whereas before I might have said, "damn it, I lost". I would have just figured that I softened up at the half-way point. "Well next time I'm not going to soften up," I'd say. I wouldn't be sleeping peacefully at night until I'd made up for it. But now I can sit down and go over the race with a fine tooth comb, and I can pick a stroke here and there that may have affected the outcome of the race. When I do that, and I find out I missed the fifth stroke off the line, or the stroke was still short and it should be long, or my transition wasn't as good as it should be, I can go back and work on that phase of my race and get the kinks out. I think it is very valuable to do that.

Before I would be very aggressive, but I didn't have a base of perfection. I could be thinking, "Come on you guys, come and get me, you're not going to touch me, I'm going to show you," or, I could be thinking, "I'm going to beat you, and I'm not going to sleep peacefully until I do." But by analyzing my race, stroke for stroke, figuring out what I did wrong, I can put together a more perfect race as a base. Then depending on what kind of psychological frame of mind I'm in, I can build upon that base. Before I would be very aggressive but I didn't have a base of perfection.

I've always been strong technically, but I haven't always strived for technical perfection the whole way through. In the past, when it came time for a race, it seemed like it was time to get out and go nuts. But now, there is a little bit more thought that goes into every race, a little bit more planning. I'm always repeating the plan in practice, and working on certain points that I can identify as screw-ups in a previous race. There's a base through the whole race that's close to perfection. That's what you are looking for.

I can still go nuts, and quite often I do, but I can also be aware of exactly what each part of my body is doing at all times during the race. That has been really helpful, especially in a longer race, to take that mental energy and everything else you've always had, and add to it that base of perfection that you have developed by analyzing the race.

In the last three years since Terry has been working with us it has become more important to identify as closely as possible where I've screwed up, and then to work on that in practice to make sure it doesn't happen again. I also use cue words more explicitly now. I sit down and look at a race plan before I go out and use a certain point in the race, within five metres, as a point of kicking in, and really charging in the last 150 metres. I have cue words for this. I try to pick out a few alternatives in case a section of the race doesn't go well. I also have tried some of the procedures for relaxing before a race.

55

Of course, you can't control everything. Sometimes we are at the mercy of the weather. Chances are if you race in the World Championships and you are in the worst lane, you're not going to win. But you can still turn in a performance that is satisfying to some extent, if you keep in mind that you are going to fight the conditions and you're not going to give up. That's the other thing we have to learn to deal with. You have got to see you are conquering the conditions of the race too, not just the other competitors. It is not very satisfying if you quit the race. You may as well go as hard as you can the whole way, even if you know you don't have a hope. I've learned that through experience.

I have had some bad luck. It is something you don't like, but when it happens, you have to be prepared to face it, and go out and give it your best. You still have the rest of the year. Even if it was the big regatta at the end of the year, you have next year.

I'm concerned by the fact that a high percentage of the athletes on our team distrust the selection committee. Quite often the athletes feel that the selection committee doesn't like giving an athlete the time of day. The committee seems to think the athletes are dog meat, sort of thing. If so and so steps out of line, they can replace him with someone else. You don't know where you stand. The committee has never come out and made themselves seem approachable. We get to the trials and they are always up in the finish line tower. We all call it "the ivory tower," because they are all up in their own little world. As a result of that, quite often they don't know what the circumstances are out on the water. We are very subject to wind conditions. But you really have to be out on the water, or standing on shore, to feel exactly what the situation is. If they are up in the tower they can't tell what the situation is.

The whole thing sort of stinks of a separation between them and us. The higher ups and the peasants. I think they should open up a little more, and mingle with the paddlers a little bit. So what if they pick the team? So what if they have the power that says, "You stay home and you go on the trip"? There are more suspicions being raised by the fact that they are always behind closed doors, than they would be if they were out in the open, like your average person.

I'm concerned about that, but not so much for myself. One of my basic philosophies is to settle things out on the water. If I'm going to control things, I have to go out and win. I am concerned about changes going on in the coaching, and the attitude of the selection committee, but I'm just going to make my waves in the water.

One of my basic philosophies is to settle things out on the water. If I'm going to control things, I have to go out and win.

56

8
LORI FUNG

1984 OLYMPIC CHAMPION — RHYTHMIC GYMNASTICS

LORI FUNG RHYTHMIC GYMNASTICS

- Gold Medalist (All-Round) at 1984 Olympic Games.
- 1984 Four Continent Championships — 1st (All-Round)
- 1983 World Championships — 9th (Ribbon)
- 1982 Four Continent Championships — 2nd (All-Round)

I love training, I love competing, and I love performing even more. For me, it's my job to come into the gym. Everyone else has their job to go to from nine to five. My job happens to be in the gym, but the difference is, I just love it. I train twice a day, a lot more training hours than the other girls in Canada. I'm pretty well going at it full time.

I train differently than most athletes in my sport. I've trained in eastern Europe three times and I've picked up a lot of their training methods. But what has helped me a great deal is not just to try to get to where the Bulgarians were, but to kind of think of where they are going and try to get there before they do. By doing that you are pushing ahead. That is what artistic gymnastics has to do. So we have tried really interesting choreography. We may lose a lot of points because we are trying something totally new, but then if it works, we are going to be that much closer to them. Slowly and surely we are closing the gap.

Everything has to come from within myself because I don't have a coach to push me; to make sure I'm in the gym at nine o'clock. Recently I did work with a coach and I just grasped at every bit of information that she gave me because I appreciated it so much. It was novel for me to have someone helping me. She really enjoyed

What I've learned to do is, if I'm going to take the energy and go out on the floor to do a routine, it's got to count and so I'd be better off to go out and do four perfect routines than to do twenty that are just mediocre.

Sometimes you look at it from a camera view but most of the time I look at it as what I see from within, because that's the way it's going to be in competition.

working with me, and she gave me more time than she did her own girls because I appreciated it so much more, whereas they took it for granted.

I've seen a lot of girls train, and I've seen them think of practice as only practice. They go out on the floor and do repetition after repetition, you know, "Oh well, it's only practice, it doesn't matter." What I've learned to do is, if I'm going to take the energy and go out on the floor to do a routine, it's got to count, and so I'd be better off to go out and do four perfect routines than to do 20 that are just mediocre. It's quality not quantity. When I walk out around the floor in practice that's what I would do at a competition. At a competition, I wouldn't just sort of drag myself onto the floor, get into position, wait around, talk and then go. Once I decide to do my routine, I set the mood exactly, as closely as it could be to competition. I train here in the UBC gym — you can see there are so many basketball players and volleyball players all around. If I can block them out I can block out anything. Here, we are working under the hardest conditions, so anything better is great, and if it's the same, no problem, we can handle it.

I don't have any trouble training hard all the time. If you give in to every little ache and pain, then you're never going to get anywhere. Yesterday I worked really hard. When I went home I was just exhausted and very, very sore; my muscles were just feeling terrible, but my piano player said, "Well, maybe you're working too hard", and I just keep remembering little sayings, "No pain, no gain." You know you've got to push through it and so that's what keeps me going and also having my piano player here. Also, when Trisha, my student, comes, I really want to set a good example for her. She's really very young and impressionable right now. She's going to develop habits now. If I give her the wrong impression, she's going to develop bad habits. That also keeps me going.

My mental preparation for competition has come through my training; I mean ninety percent is all mental imagery. I believe in it because for so many years I used to just go out and do a routine and I didn't think about it. I would just hope, and I'd miss lots of things. Now I've found that by thinking about it, I can produce so much better routines. That's proven to me. And so I do a lot of thinking. I try really hard not to just go out and do a routine for the sake of doing it. You have to go out, and you have to think about it, and you have to know what you're doing.

Your mind has to be totally aware of absolutely everything that's going on around you, but, at the same time, it has to be centred on what you're doing. And in rhythmic gymnastics it not only has to centre on your body, but it has to centre on the apparatus. For me, I'm aware of what's going on around me, but that's faded out, and everything else is within myself.

When I do my routine, sometimes I actually talk to myself; I tell myself, "Okay, take a deep breath here because the next part is very, very strenuous as far as cardiovascular goes, so you have to be prepared for it." In certain parts I'll actually say to myself, "Okay, breathe. All right, think about your free arm here. Think about the apparatus. Don't get too excited. Don't rush it." I talk to myself before I go out on the floor too.

58

Mental rehearsal comes to me naturally. I think about my routines a lot. I'll be driving along and I'll be thinking about certain parts, but that's just because I'm in the gym so much. I'm doing these routines so many times that it's natural for some things to remind me of them. But if I miss a practice, or I can't practise for some reason as much as I want to, then it's important to really sit down and try to think about it.

In mental imagery, you have to see how the apparatus is coming down. If the club is coming down this way, I would grab it this way in my imagery. Sometimes I would think about the last time I actually did it, "Why did I miss that one move? Okay, I know what happened, I pulled the body in too close to the apparatus and it knocked my shoulder and it went off. Okay, now how do I avoid that?" Then I try to see myself doing it correctly in imagery. I can actually see the apparatus coming down; I can see the stripe on the club as it rotates the same way you'd see it when you're doing the routine, that's the best way. Sometimes you look at it from a camera view, but most of the time I look at it as what I see from within, because that's the way it's going to be in competition. It is natural because I do the routines so many times that it's drilled into my head, what I see and how I do it. So if I think about a certain part of my club routine, or my ribbon routine, I think of it as the way I've done it so many times, and that's from within my body.

In my mental preparation for competition I try not to turn to superstitions, because sometimes you are not going to be able to do some sort of little ritual that you have always done. Then you are going to go into competition with a negative attitude. You are going to say, "Oh, I didn't do this. Oh no, I'm not going to do well." I used to be that way. I used to think, "Well, I wore a blue ribbon in my hair the time I won that competition." To prove to myself that those things don't matter I said, "Okay, I'm going to wear a red ribbon today." I won that competition.

There are certain things that matter. In training you've got to warm-up properly. I have a certain warm-up that I do prior to a competition, it's not quite the same as the one I do in the gym because you don't usually have as much time. Also, just making sure by checking over my apparatus gives me a sort of self-confidence.

My piano player's been travelling with me all the time and so we usually room together. When I wake up on the morning of a competition I like to hear everything really positive. Not like, "I had a terrible sleep last night", or, "Oh, this is terrible. The floor was terrible yesterday at practice." Everything is, "Wow, the sun's out, the flowers are. . .this is going to be a great day." And that develops a positive attitude. She knows that I need that. And I have to do the same to her, because when I'm on the floor, she's on the floor with me and so we're a team. It's not like Lori and her piano player, it's Lori and Donna out there competing. Donna works only with me. She knows me better than anyone else. I know what she's thinking and she knows what I'm thinking; it's almost like we're twins.

A coach once told me about another point concerning positive attitude and mental imagery. If you wake up, stretch and smile and then get out of bed, you're waking up with a positive attitude. I try to do that because it makes me laugh. I think to myself, "Boy, I must look

59

pretty stupid stretching and smiling," and then I get up and I'm laughing, because it's sort of funny, and then that puts me in the right tone of mind.

At competitions, immediately before each routine, I "see" myself do my routine, I look over at Donna at the piano and I get out there. Sometimes my first reaction is, "I'm scared and I don't want to do this," but I know I can't get out of it. The next reaction is, "Okay just get out there and start, you'll be so involved in the routine you won't think about it or anything else." It's like jumping into a cold pool, the initial reaction is you've got to jump first.

As soon as I start, I think, "Well, I'm in it. Okay go for it. Now concentrate." That is exactly what I think. I'll walk out on the floor and be thinking, "Oh no. Oh, no, I'm so nervous," and then I'll just say, "Okay, now, you've just got to do it, that's all there is to it. Go out, start it," and from then on it's great.

During the routine, what you have to think of is to release the apparatus a certain way. If you make a mistake, you have to tell yourself to pull back really quickly and don't let the mistake bother you.

Between routines there is just time to go and change and get warmed up for your next apparatus. If the routine was good it's hard not to reflect on it too much. You have basically three minutes to hug your piano player, hug your coach, jump around for joy, and then it's back to zero. You've got to get back to zero. And if you had a bad routine, you've got to get back to zero again. No matter what, you can't let one good or bad routine ride. You can't say, "Okay, I was great in that one. I'm going to do great in this one," because the chances are you won't. Or, "I did so bad." You just have to say, "Okay, that's forgotten. It's totally forgotten." That's it. Go out and do the next one and pretend that the next one is the first routine of the day and it is going to count. Otherwise, you are never going to pull back again. You're always going to be too involved in the other routines, and they're finished. You can't do anything about it. You can't do anything about the score you're getting. You can't do anything about why you dropped that one move or how great it was; it's over and done with. Sometimes it's really hard to make yourself forget it, but the more you try, then the better you're going to get at it in the future. Maybe it won't work this one time, but the next time it's going to help that much more.

Mental readiness is very important. Once I went to Japan for a major meet. I felt really exhausted and let that get to me. I was saying, "Well, I can't go out and perform properly because I'm tired!" I didn't say, "Well, I've got to push through it." I gave in to the tiredness and I didn't perform up to level. This was about three or four years ago. I realize now that I had gone out on that floor with a negative attitude and so I was destined not to do well. At the Olympics I was just as exhausted before the last routine but I said, "Well, that's it, I've got to do it. I've got to push through it," and that's what happened. There was one competition last year, I went to Poland. My first routine was disastrous, the ribbon got tangled into a knot and that lost me just a horrendous amount of points. My second routine was right on and I was really pleased that I had pulled myself up for the second routine. I ended up placing 12th overall and that was one of the highest places I'd ever had in an international meet, even with

60

that one terrible ribbon routine. What I think about now is how great that competition was, even though there was one really bad routine. It was because I managed to pull myself up, instead of letting it take me down with it. I just forgot about it and did the other three really well and that was important.

When I was just making my mark on the international scene I wasn't sure of myself. I would think to myself, "Gee, I don't belong in this crowd, these girls are really good." I was the only athlete from a western country in the finals. There were three Russians, three Bulgarians, a Czechoslovakian and me. But my coach put this attitude in my head that I deserved to be there, I'd worked hard and I'd given up so much that she said, "Never let yourself feel inferior to anyone. Even though they are the best in the world and they've won 50 titles, you're just as good. You deserve to be out on that floor as well." In that way I'd go out with a really positive attitude. The audience can feel that. I find a lot of times I get really good audience support when I'm at a competition, not because my routines are the best at the meet, but because I go out there and I try to enjoy myself, and I try to bring the people to enjoy them too.

I've read different sport psychology articles, but every person is different. I'm sure that sport psychologists can help a great deal, but you have got to learn for yourself. You have got to learn through trial and error. If it means learning from your bad experiences at competition, you have got to go through that. In the last year I've done really well at six international meets. Those meets are the result of all the bad meets that I've had in the past. You have to learn from those first.

Mental skills can be learned, but not all at once. For example, my student doesn't even know that she's learning these things because she's not at an international level. I want her routines to be much harder next year, but I decided to start off slowly so that she'd feel confident. If she does good routines and places 9th, she'll be happy she did good routines, and that's my first priority. That's what I told her. She doesn't realize things that she's learning. In practice I told her she had to have two perfect routines before she could leave that apparatus. So in her first routine she did well, but she had to do it six times before she got two perfect routines. Finally I said, "Look how much energy you're wasting trying to do two perfect routines." I said, "Think about it, prepare yourself and do the perfect routine," and she did it. Then I asked, "Okay, now, what's harder, doing a routine with mistakes or doing a routine that's perfect?" And she said, "Doing a routine with mistakes." I said, "Then why are you doing the one's with mistakes?" From then on she mentally prepared herself to do a good routine and she was a lot better. Just from that she's learned a little bit, and she doesn't even know it. It's going to carry on with her, and hopefully she'll be at a competition and she'll say, "Oh, I remember that time I thought about it and I could do the routine, and so if I think about it again ..." But I don't want to say, "You have to think about ... Now, this is important," because then it will overwhelm her, and she's not ready for that yet.

Deep down my goal for the Olympics was to win a medal. Realistically I knew that I could be in the top seven or eight, but I thought possibly a bronze medal was within my reach.

When I heard about the boycott, the first thing that most people said, including all the newspapers, was, "You can win a bronze, you're in third place." But I said, "You can't take results from one competition and put them into another. It's who's performing well on that particular day, at that particular moment. I know I'm considered ranked in third, but I'm just going to go and do my best routines, and hope to place very high." I never once said to anyone in the press, "Yes, I'm going to win a medal." I was very careful to keep myself totally clear, just saying, "What I want is my best performance, and I'll be happy with that regardless of where it places me." By doing that, no one could ever say, "Well, she said she was going to try and get a medal, and she didn't, or she did."

In all aspects I felt ready for the Olympics. We prepared very, very hard for it. I wasn't injured and I had been having very good practices.

We didn't go down to Los Angeles until the second week, the 4th of August, and then we competed on the 9th, 10th and 11th. All the other teams had arrived there at the opening ceremonies, so they were burned out because there was too much excitement going on, not because they were competing but because everyone else around them was. Instead, we stayed and trained here at the University of British Columbia. The weather was very hot and we were in the same time zone, so we were prepared for Los Angeles.

When I got to Los Angeles, it was great. I knew that I was out there to do my best routines, and I was capable of them. There are two different ways: you can go out hoping to do really good routines but deep down you know you're not quite ready to do them; or you can go out knowing that you can do them. I knew I could, because I had been succeeding in practice, so it was just a matter of bringing them to that level right at that particular moment.

For the first four routines in the preliminaries I just did each routine and saw my score: I was doing quite well, I was in fifth place after the first night. I did two really good routines then I was in third place. Then I just decided, I don't know why, just to go out to the finals and do my four routines, but not know my score; just do one routine after another, come out, get changed then go back out on the floor and not know how I did. So I did four clean routines.

The third routine happened to be ribbon, which I had trouble with the first time because of the air conditioning. I was really scared while I was waiting to go out. Everyone had been having trouble with their ribbons. The draught was unbearable. They had the air conditioning turned up really high and they wouldn't turn it down. The ribbon would get wrapped around the athlete's neck, around their hair, around their pony-tails, just terrible. I knew everyone was having trouble and so I said to myself, "Okay, I'm just going to go out. I hope I can do it!"

My coach came up to me, just before I went on, and she said, "Lori, they've just turned up the air conditioning even more because of the computers, they're getting overheated." And I thought, "Why? Why is she saying this to me now? Thank you!" It made me really nervous. It really made me mad; so I went out there and I fought with the ribbon. My arm was just ready to fall off at the end of the routine. I came off; it was a perfect ribbon routine, the best of the day. It

I find a lot of times I get really good audience support when I'm at a competition, not because my routines are the best at the meet, but because I go out there and I try to enjoy myself and I try to bring the people to enjoy them too.

62

turned out she had just said that to get me fired up for the ribbon routine, because she knew I was just going to go out there and just hope to glide through it. Instead she wanted me to fight through it, so that's what she said to me. She took a really big risk, but it worked!

9
LAURIE GRAHAM

WINNER OF 5 WORLD CUP RACES — ALPINE SKIING

**LAURIE GRAHAM
ALPINE SKIING**

● Winner of 5 World Cup Races
● 1986 Female Athlete of the Year
● 1986 World Cup Standing (Downhill) — 3rd
● 1985 World Cup Standing (Downhill) — 4th
● 1985 FIS Final Ranking (Downhill) — 3rd
● 1985 Canadian Champion (Downhill)
● 1984 Canadian Champion (Super G)
● Member of 1980 and 1984 Canadian Olympic Team

T he thing that is different at the Olympics is the media attention. All this energy is focused on the Olympics for that one week. The whole world is watching. This is a new experience for most athletes. I have been in two Olympics. The first was 1980 when I was twenty. That was when I had just come onto the scene and I just had my first top 3 result. So the whole time I said, "It is just another race, don't even listen to all this hype." It was in the States where it is total hype. It came and went and I am sort of sad I didn't let it have more of an impact.

Sarajevo was a great time. I enjoyed those Olympics more. The skiing part wasn't as good. My result was exactly the same, 11th. I didn't have good results in training or coming into the Olympics. In downhill you have 2 or 3 training runs and I was far off the pace. So that's why I say on the actual race day I improved a lot and came 11th. I was happy with my performance in terms of rising to the challenge and rising to the pressure. Still my actual result wasn't that good because I wasn't skiing that well. The good times I had at Sarajevo had to do with the other girls who were there, and really getting into the Olympics. Also with the delays we went and watched the hockey

If we make a mistake in our mind we rewind, go back and just see ourself doing it right from start to finish. Actually I don't watch myself, I visualize it as if I'm running the race; the course is coming at me.

games and other events and got to know our team mates from different sports. That really was great.

The 1984 season was the worst of my career due to equipment problems. I changed my ski boots and the foot beds were wrong. My basic stance was wrong, but I couldn't figure out how to fix it. It was a frustrating year, but Sarajevo was one of my better results of a frustrating year. I just lost the right feel and couldn't figure out why, and that caused me to have knee problems because the angles were wrong in the feet.

The boot problem almost caused me to retire. I was so fed up with playing with the fine tuning of my boots. I knew they weren't right and I couldn't get them right and I was just fed up. But finally, when we were down at a camp in Argentina, the Vancouver doctor travelling with us who specializes in Orthopaedics, and therefore footbeds and correctional things for runners, prescribed footbeds for my running shoes and my ski boots. I've never looked back since.

All of us use visualization a lot in our sport. You have to know the course one hundred percent; all the bumps, which way the turns go, what the terrain is like, what the snow is like, the optimum line you want to be on, and the optimum position. All that goes in and we watch ourselves in our minds run the course and run it well. If we make a mistake in our mind we rewind, go back and just see ourselves doing it right, from start to finish. Actually I don't watch myself, I visualize it as if I'm running the race; the course is coming at me.

There are different ways to visualize. You can go through the course just skiing the gates, so you know where the gates are. But then you have to ski through the course fast, feeling the way you want to ski. Currie Chapman, our coach, helped us with our imagery because in downhill we inspect in a group and we talk about the course and we name corners; usually the name fits the terrain, like the dive turn, or the "carousel" if it is a big long one. We would go over it as a team. We'd all be out there and he'd lead us through it. He's a great motivator and he'd get us going. He'd say, "You are going to skate here and tuck right here and blast this corner." That's how I sort of started getting into imagery.

I don't like to think about "don'ts" before a race, like "don't do this or don't go too straight." Instead of saying that, you say, "Stay on line but go fast." I like it put in a positive way, "Stay on line and go with the flow." We often corrected our coaches on that. We really found that don'ts came in as a negative. If when we first inspected the course the coach said, "Don't come in here too straight or this will happen," then, when we were going through it in our mind, we'd remember more what we were not supposed to do. Now we just try and start positive right from the beginning. "When you come in here, make sure you are high and come around the corner from behind." When you notice that you had a bad feeling on a course, or a bad run, you remember that there were a lot of "don'ts" involved instead of "do's."

When race day comes, I have done all the preparation and I've done all the training runs and I know where I stand; if I'm in the top 5, or whatever. So that I'm not nervous on race day, I just say, "You have got a job to do and just go out there and do it." It is very unemotional and matter of fact. Go out there and do it the way you know

66

how. That seems to help a lot. Don't let nerves get in the way, they're just a block. I get above nerves and be very concentrated on what I'm supposed to do. I think I got some of that from my father. That's the way he is, and that is the way he would tell me to do it. "There's a job to do and go out there and do it."

The night before a race I don't really do anything different. I just try to be normal. When I first go to bed I run through the course a few times in my mind, but not to the point of dwelling on it, because that gets you nervous. I do it distantly, not really attached, just to make sure and keep confident to remind myself that I know it. Then in the morning things start to pick up, not with tension but more excitement in anticipation. It's not a negative feeling.

On race days I don't like going up the lifts with people who really don't know what is going on. They ask me all the same questions, things that are obvious. I don't like the detail of this ho-hum stuff so I try to avoid going up with the tourists. Also, I don't like to be around people who are over-excited about the race. I try to stay calm.

My team mates are great and we just go up and warm-up with free skiing for about an hour and a half, where we just ski on an open hill, making fast turns, with our helmets on, getting the feeling of our feet. Then you go into the lodge for about half an hour before your final preparations, get my downhill suit on and the numbers, and warm our feet. That is fun too because it is getting a lot closer to the race time. Going up the lift I always have time. It takes 20 minutes or so, and I know the next time I'm down the hill it will be all over.

Going up the lift it is better for me to stay loose and relaxed and not think about the race, still stay distant. At the start area I do a lot of physical activity, warm-up, stretching and getting pumped up, and that is where I go over the course a few more times in my mind. That is what really finally gets you out there to do it.

Skiers start at one minute intervals. You see the next person go so you know you have a minute. That is when you do your final stuff: everything is ready. I get really picky, I want everything to be right, like my number on straight. By then I'm not thinking about what is ahead, I am thinking mostly about the start, and maybe just one other thing about how I have to approach this race. Say it is a windy day and the main comment that the coaches have called up the course is that you have to stay really compact. So I will be thinking, "Good start and just get as 'little' as you can get." That is all I think about, because the course is in there, the tape is running now. You don't methodically think of each section, it just unwinds in my head.

I'm getting really excited just thinking about it. I could go and race right now!

Once I push out at the start I am focused on where I am at the time. A lot of it is "line" in downhill. You don't go right at the gate, you've got the "line" that you have been running all week and you just say, "Okay, I've got to stay high here, I have to go direct here, I have to jump this jump," just so I am thinking of each obstacle as it comes.

If I make a small mistake, often it doesn't even register for me until the end, when I'm at the bottom. We talk about the run, and I say, "Oh yeah, I was low here too. Did you have problems in that turn?" That is when it all comes out. At the time you are still thinking, "for-

The night before a race I don't really do anything different. I just try to be normal.

You don't carry the mistake down the hill. It is shelved until later while you try and compensate.

67

ward, speed, momentum." You don't carry the mistake down the hill. It is shelved until later while you try and compensate.

Often those mistakes will mean just running them out, and it really won't cost you that much time if you don't panic, if you just let it turn out and get back on track. But if you make a really big mistake and you feel yourself slow down, then you know it, you just shake your head and say, "Well that is that."

I've won 2 World Cup races now in Canada, and those have been the most satisfying because I have shared them with everyone. I think I do better in Canada because I know all the organizers in the race and all the sponsors. I am related to them because they're Canadian. When you win you realize how happy you are making them too, and you are sharing the win. Maybe in Europe it feels like it is more "all mine". It's interesting because perhaps it is one of the reasons why I won more in Canada.

For me a good performance is when I have had 3 or 4 training runs, I'm running 4th or 5th in training and I improve that in the race. The last race of the year (the 1985 Husky World Downhill in Sunshine) was actually a double race, because a race had been cancelled previously. The first race day I was 3rd and that was an improvement from my training. That left me only 2 places to get better and on the 2nd day I won. The pressure didn't get to me. It helped my confidence. I was pretty detached about it all. I was just determined to run it the same way I had run it before, not try to cut any corners and not try and go any straighter. Sometimes you have to take time at the top of the turn to come around and if you are trying too hard to go too fast you'll hurt yourself in the long run. So that was my focus. Do it like yesterday. That day was windy as well, so I did have one change that I could focus on. I like to have one little trick to pull out that I can count on, that I know is going to speed me up a little bit. That day it was the wind and I focused on just being small. That helped and that was a little boost that was different. I often do that. On the last inspection, even though by this time I know the course and have been over it with a fine tooth comb, I still like to go over it again with the coach and really talk about how I felt here and there. It is amazing he can coach me because I'm the one running it and really, I should know. Yet he sees so many people go down that he knows too, practically as much as I do, and he can give me little hints like, "Maybe you came in too straight or maybe you didn't do this." I like to have one little correction that is not major. Those are on the good races. A bad race that really disappointed me this year was one where I had won the training run. This was in December in Italy and I ended up tenth in the race because I tried too hard. I knew I could win and I just wanted to blow them away. I went too straight at things and therefore didn't ski well.

In my good performances I was focusing on skiing, on the job, not on the result. In the last case, the bad race, I was thinking of blowing them away. Going into the "bad race" I had won the training runs, but I couldn't really accept that I was the favourite on this course. So on race day I felt pressured to really prove it, and so I tried even harder to go fast.

Overall I've had a great season. I was in the top ten almost every run. Over the season I've learned that I am a threat, and I am a little more confident that I know what I am doing. Ski my own race and not worry about everybody else. To focus on winning for me doesn't work. It is better to focus on the job at hand and just do the right thing and the result will come.

Currie, our coach, is a big motivator and confidence builder. He says, "I can't believe you guys need to be told. You know how good you are. I can't believe you still need to be told it." But we do because everyone else is really good out there too. They are the best in their country and we know we are in high level competition. It is nice to be told that he really thinks we can do it today. I admire coaches who have 4 or 5 girls in the top who can all win. They have to have a personal rapport with each one of those potential winners, and get each individual fired up; yet they are all competing against each other. He is like a juggler.

I like to have the coach watch us in the morning in warm-up and even give us a few tips if we are doing something wrong that can be easily corrected. Once the race has started they radio up how the course is running that particular day, if it is faster or slower than in training, and they remind us of last minute corrections. Walking through the course with the team and the coach a few days earlier, and naming the points helps in the imagery and kind of puts things together. It also helps for communication on the hill. "In the dive turn you have to come in a little higher today," and you know exactly what they are talking about. So it is very important for the coach to learn the names of the turns too. Currie often draws a map of the course and gives us each a copy. You have to learn the names so that we all know what everyone is talking about. The names are linked with landmarks that just happen to be close by, that we can remember and refer to, like "restaurant turn" if there is a restaurant there, "telephone turn" if there are cables going across, "valley view" if the course is coming out onto the flat and the horizon is in view there.

Terry Orlick, our sport psychologist, first came to one of our fall training camps 2 years ago. He had personal talks with each of us and helped set goals and discussed ways of approaching racing. We all went and people participated to different degrees. Some of the girls are younger and don't really know what they think, so Terry sort of had to drag it out of them. He and I always rambled on for hours. Initially I was skeptical as to just how much he could help because he really didn't know the sport, and he really didn't know the lifestyle. For an outsider to come in and tell us how to do it, there is a tendency to think, "I've been doing this for a long time." In the end, he has helped me largely with some re-affirmations. For instance, last year when I considered quitting, but chose to continue, we worked together on this issue of choice. He said, "Remember you are here because you want to be." This he kept stressing, that I had considered retiring and I knew I could make it in the outside world, and yet I had decided to come back because I wanted to finish what I'd started to do. He helped me establish that. It took a lot of the trapped feeling away.

I have kept the papers Terry gave me. I carry them with me all year, and the brief notes that he made. I read them. I look them over maybe 3 or 4 times a season just to remember. But his main contribu-

In my good performances I was focusing on skiing, on the job, not on the result.

To focus on winning for me doesn't work. It is better to focus on the job at hand and just do the right thing and the result will come.

69

tion was to help me see I wasn't trapped or locked into this thing. It was my decision to ski and I wanted to be here. That was a good one.

I learn from my races by going over them myself that same afternoon. I think about, "What went right and what went wrong." We also talk about it among ourselves, "Well how did it go?" "Not very well, I skied very badly." "Well, why do you think that?" We try to figure it out. I can tell if I was too upright or tried too hard. Usually I went too straight, which is a result of trying too hard, or there are physical things that just happen, like it froze up overnight and it was sheer ice. I'm not very good on ice. When it is something like that, beyond my control, then I just say it wasn't my fault basically. Whenever there is a mental thing involved I usually try to mark it down in my day book. I put it in my own words and use it to instruct myself, as a reminder for next time. I have never referred back to it but writing it down imprints it better. The race evaluation forms, devised by Terry and Currie, got us started, and it did help me to think about it, but then I found I could do it myself more quickly. Sometimes in the day book I don't go into much detail, but I always question what went right and wrong, and then drop it, because it isn't good to dwell on it.

At one point the team was having poor results, and morale was low. We decided that an over-kill on analysis was our problem. The whole atmosphere was very technical and analytical yet we wondered, "Why aren't we getting better? Why aren't we winning?" We were able to sit down as a team and figure out the reasons for what was going wrong. That's when we said, "Guys, we're dealing with too much detail. Let's get to what we are here for." Instead of receiving coaches' corrections after each run, we tried to think more for ourselves, and acquire our own feeling. We replaced the coaches' comments with timing equipment. We used this to experiment with ourselves to find which approach was actually faster. We focused on the feel and the speed. By doing this, things started to flow together and we were 'off and running'!

I learn from my races by going over them myself that same afternoon. I think about, what went right and what went wrong.

70

10
SUE HOLLOWAY

1984 OLYMPIC SILVER MEDALIST — PAIRS KAYAK

SUE HOLLOWAY CANOEING

- Silver Medalist (K-2, 500 metres) and Bronze Medalist (K-4, 500 metres) at 1984 Olympic Games
- Competitor in 1976 Winter Olympics (Cross Country Skiing) and 1976 Summer Olympics (Canoeing)
- 1983 Pre-Olympic Regatta — 5th — K-4, 500 metres and K-2, 500 metres
- 1983 World Championships — 7th — K-2, 500 metres, — 9th — K-4, 500 metres
- 1983 Pan American Championships — 1st — K-2, 500 metres and K-4, 500 metres
- 1982 World Championships — 5th — K-2, 500 metres and K-4, 500 metres
- 1981 World Championships — 6th — K-2, 500 metres and K-4, 500 metres
- 1976 Olympic Games — 8th — K-2, 500 metres

In 1976, I achieved my goal of making both the summer and winter Olympic teams. Then I had to decide what my next goal was. I had to re-assess, and I decided that being outstanding in one sport was my next goal. That's when my values changed. It wasn't just 'participating' that I wanted any more, it was 'excelling'. I wasn't particularly good at school, where other people were excelling, and I wanted to be special and I wanted to be good at something. Right away I did very well in canoeing. I was well accepted and I got a lot of positive strokes. That's when I decided that I wanted to be the best and that's when my focus changed. The training became more important, and it became more important to get to the goal.

1980 was a major crisis for me because I had trained so hard for the 1980 Games. I was 25, I'd come 5th in the world in singles the year before. I saw myself on the road to a medal and knew I could do it. I was very confident and I was really paddling well. I was just the right age and I had taken the year off school to train more intensely. I was really going for it, and then a boycott. I was devastated, to put it mildly. That was my whole life. Everything important to me was taken away. It was crushing, so it took a long time to re-adjust.

That's when I realized that my education was important. I started taking courses that meant something, instead of just taking something to pass. I started looking at my relationships and deciding where I wanted to go with those. I thought about what was important to me and where I wanted to go with my career. I started doing things outside of canoeing and they started to take on more importance, which took away from my training and performance for a couple of years.

Then I decided I had to make some sort of timetable because my results at the Worlds were kind of waffling along. I asked myself, "Am I really going for an Olympic medal in 1984?" If so, it requires more intensity and a better effort. I decided that was my goal and I felt that it was important to say it. There was not going to be any more 'next year'. It was going to be this year or never. Whatever I did I would have to live with for the rest of my life. When I did have doubts about what I was doing, I would just say, "This is the last shot, this is the last time I'm doing it, and I have to do the best I can, and then I can live with it whatever happens."

I felt ready for the 1984 Olympics for a long time, not just the day of the competition, but the days and months preceding. I definitely felt like I was on an edge. As we got closer and closer I felt like the edge was getting narrower. I felt like I was teetering, like I could fall off at any minute, but I made a very concerted effort to stay on top. I realized that if I did go over then I'd lose everything. I didn't want that to happen, so I made sure that I did stay on top of things. I can remember watching the Olympic competitions and awards ceremonies when we were in Sacramento at our final training camp, and I'd start to cry. I'd tell myself, "I can't watch this any more, it's just getting too emotional." I had all this tension and some fear; everything tied up together, and I just wanted to let it go, but I knew if I did then I wouldn't have it for the race.

My mother and father were in agony because they could see all the tension and anxiety, and they know what I'm like. They've been around when I've been very nervous, although most of the time it's when I'm away. I've been home for nationals and trials which are very anxious times for me, and my parents have had to deal with me at times like that. We had discussed it before we went to Los Angeles. In the spring, I said this is what it's going to be like, this is where you're going to be, this is where I'm going to be, this is what I'd like you to do and this is how I'm going to be feeling. I prepared them because I said I didn't want to talk about this in the heat of the moment. I said let's talk about it now so that you understand what I'm going through.

I didn't want to have to worry about them or feel they were worrying about me. I didn't want them making a big deal about anything, because the deal was big enough as it was and I didn't need any additional, "Is there anything we can do for you, dear?" If I wanted to talk to them, I wanted to be able to get hold of them, but I didn't want them hanging around just waiting for me to talk to them. So they went off on their own. But they said it was really difficult to sit there and watch me going through all this agony. They saw me wrestling with it, and my mom said she just wanted to take it away and do

72

it herself, but she said she knew there was nothing she could do, so she just had to watch.

I knew I could talk to my parents and I knew my parents would behave, because I've brought them up well! They're excellent sports parents. They don't interfere, but they direct and guide. They have a very clear idea of what their role is and they've been very helpful and supportive. They've stressed what they feel is important; their values about education, and if you're going to do something, do it well. We had a meeting of the elite paddlers in Florida. At that meeting we said that we wanted to make sure that all the parents were aware of what the athletes were going through, and what it was going to be like, and why we put restrictions on them coming to the hotels. For instance, we felt it wasn't fair for them to come into a room where their son or daughter might want to see them, but the roommate, who is not related, might not want them around. That was all discussed and rules were made that we all agreed to.

I had said I was going to retire after the Games no matter what. This was definitely the end. Happily, everything just happened the way it was supposed to happen. It was very planned, it was very orchestrated and I tried to see it happening only in the way I wanted it to.

My training for the 1984 Olympics was more intense than I had done before. I got a lot from Alexandra's (partner) intensity. I knew that she trained very hard and I used her intensity to raise my intensity level. When John Bales and I had gone through our planning sheet and review of the previous year, I noted what I had set out to do, what I had done wrong, and what I wanted to do next year. There were two major areas I wanted to work on, my intensity and my technique.

Before I even got on the water, I made the decision that for that whole year I would do anything and everything in order to do my best. Quite often before, I would make a decision based on whether I'd be close to my boyfriend, or have time to spend with my family. This year I said, I'm going to put all those things aside. Any decision I make is going to be based on whether it will make me better at the Games. That made things very easy. Before there'd been so many other things pulling, like thinking about school and where my boyfriend was. I decided that it was worth it to just go wherever I had to go and do whatever I had to do. So I went to B.C. for fall training, I made sure that Denis, my coach, and I were in close proximity in the spring so that I could consult with him regularly. Alexandra and I trained together because I knew she trained a lot harder than I did. She could push me especially when we were in the same boat. Right from day one, I just thought about working a little bit harder than felt comfortable, all the time. Everytime I went out on the water I'd try to keep the quality and the intensity.

I was going to be satisfied as long as I raced as hard as I could at the Olympics. Our realistic goal was a bronze. My dream goal was a gold. I felt the Romanians could beat us. But I also knew that if we went full out there was the possibility that we could beat the Swedes. We had beaten them in Denmark earlier in the year. Anything was possible. But I just wanted to get a medal. It had been a long time since I had surpassed a realistic goal.

I asked myself, am I really going for an Olympic medal in 1984? If so, it requires more intensity and a better effort. I decided that was my goal and I felt that it was important to say it.

73

I believed that we could win a medal because we'd raced against the exact same girls for years. We knew that everyone had trained hard for the Olympics. Many, like myself, had stayed on from 1980 and this was their last chance. We knew everyone had prepared to the maximum. We knew what people could do in certain circumstances, how they raced. We had everybody on video tape and we knew what they were like, what their mental attitude was. We've known them for years.

You have to do something very special to get ahead of what you thought you could do realistically. I think that our achieving beyond our realistic goal was because of the planning. Everything gelled, everything came together, and we knew it would. We knew that we couldn't afford to have anything out of place, and that included Alexandra and I getting along well, our boat, everybody being cool and not hassling each other, and having no interpersonal problems within the whole team. It had to be that everybody was getting along, and that happened in Sacramento.

It's hard to remember how everything developed in my mental preparation for the Olympics. It was not just at one time that I learned this or that; rather it was a little thing from here, and a little thing from there, and then it all developed into a big picture. I used things that Hugh (athlete) said, that Denis (Olympic coach) said, and that Terry (sport psychologist) said, and they all came together.

I'd try something and it would work, or it wouldn't work, and then I'd just keep trying until I found what did work. I ultimately got to the point where I was writing these things down so that I wouldn't forget them. Terry got us to do that. I didn't do it before. I'd just get the "feel" for it, but then I'd forget it. Before every year I'd start the season and say, "What did I do to mentally prepare before the start of a race last year?" This way, you just look back, in your log, and say "This is what we did." If you don't write it down you don't improve on it.

One year I was having a terrible time with starts, so Hugh helped me out. I improved them that year, but the next year I wished I had written down what he had said, because I was having trouble with them again. I think Hugh suggested bringing in a focus about what to think about right off the start; just concentrating on the power on the first stroke.

I think I've always used some imagery on my own but it was never done in a very organized way. When I consciously started doing it, after Terry introduced it to the team, I could already do it. I had no trouble producing images of my races. When I was skiing at the World Cross Country Ski Championships in 1974, a man with our team suggested that we go over the course in our mind so that we would know every turn, every hill, and where we can pick up time. At that time we all kind of looked at him! "What the hell's he talking about?" But I guess I kept it in mind.

John and I did some mental stuff too. We used to do things like trying to mentally feel the other person in the boat, and try to get timing from the feeling of being 'one.' I used to look out over my partner's paddle when I was in the back of the boat because I found that was the easiest way to keep in stroke with her. I could see a 'big

74

look' by looking beyond her paddle. When I did that, I would feel myself move into 'sync' with her.

Very early on I was the best in Canada. It would have been easy for me to just sit there and not improve. So, John would try to get me to push harder. I had to use some kind of incentive, because I didn't have anyone to push me within the country. I did a lot of fantasy and imagery.

We would pretend that there were other people on the course. We would pretend that the boys we trained with from the club were competitors. We would pretend that so-and-so from Germany or Hungary was beside us. It was helpful.

I used to deal with being tense by talking to people and moving about a lot. But it's not always good to depend on other people because they might say something that affects you negatively. So towards the end I got much more introverted. I knew what I wanted and I wouldn't depend on other people.

I also did some relaxation, because I get very tense and very hyped up about things. I used to get myself worked up about anything, a tendency I've had since I was very young! My mother noticed this so she taught me some relaxation breathing. My mom was in physical education so she has a very good understanding of the body. She had me lie down on my back on the floor, raise my feet, and then concentrate on breathing through my stomach with very long slow breaths. I also tried progressive muscle relaxation. I used those two methods for relaxation and to try and get to sleep because sometimes I would just get so worked up I couldn't sleep.

When Terry became involved, I already had a lot of the mental skills, but together we identified them. We could say, "Okay when this happens, then this is the coping response." Everything was much more systematic, much more planned. Now I knew what I was doing and why I was doing it. I felt I was being more consistent in my performances because I controlled more things. I knew what was happening. I'd prepared for it and I did what I wanted to do. The post performance analysis we did was invaluable. Without it, you can kind of just keep going and get into a rut, especially when you've been in the sport so long.

Every year you need to take a step back, analyze, and have a look at what you've done to make the push, otherwise you just stay where it is comfortable. I first took that step in 1977. John Bales, my coach at the time, went to France to do his M.B.A. degree. He was gone for twelve months and it meant I wouldn't be getting his phone call every Monday morning. He had tried very hard to make me independent. He explained theories, so that I could look after myself. But still I felt like he'd deserted me. I knew that it was important for me to have someone watching me, and keeping me under their thumb, because at that time I just didn't have what I felt was enough self-discipline. There was a girls' swim team starting up at the University and they needed bodies. I volunteered. I just said, okay, I need someone watching over me, I'll join this team. This will be appropriate training. We did weights and we swam. The training was tough for the kids that were swimmers, but it was that much harder for me because I'm a "sinker", and a much less experienced swimmer, so I had to work ten times harder than any of them did, just to keep up. It was

Before I even got on the water, I made the decision that for that whole year I would do anything and everything in order to do my best.

fantastic training. My performance improved. Every day I was exhausted. I just staggered home after each work-out and went to sleep. I had never trained that hard and it was a real enlightenment about what hard training was. It pushed me up to that next level. Then when I decided that 1984 was my last Olympics, the next push happened. I said, "Okay, we've got to take it to a new level, we're going to have to go harder and better." And my performance in canoeing improved a lot.

It just shows that we have to take from everyone to learn. You can't just be insular. We have to look to other sports to see what they're doing and how they're training, especially ones that have great successes like swimming. Because of his interest in coaching, John was always looking to other countries to see what kind of program they were following, and that's why I think we did well earlier on. My third year of paddling I made both the Junior World and Senior World teams. The year before, John had gone to the Olympics in Munich and then he'd travelled all over Europe, going to different canoe clubs and seeing what different countries did. He learned about all these different sports programs. The next summer John took four of us to Sweden because he liked the program there and he felt they had been successful. We started following a similar program. We went to little regattas there and got to race against the best juniors from Sweden.

We got a little bit of international exposure because we were preparing for the Junior Worlds that summer. That was all on our own money. My parents didn't want me to go because I had been away from high school all year skiing on the national team. Somehow John convinced them. We came back and all four of us made the Canadian team. It was going to Sweden that had prepared us. It gave us an idea of what we were up against. The girl that I had raced against in Sweden was also at the Junior Worlds, and I knew how I could do against her, so it gave me some kind of feel for what was going on at the Junior World level.

Looking back, the way to improve our sport for women is to treat women like they are winners, like they have potential and are important. That is what John did. In most countries women are second to men in terms of priority in sport, and it shows. That attitude used to be through all levels in canoeing. They were not thinking about the women. They didn't expect you to do anything. When you have those kinds of expectations around you, then you live up to them. We Canadian women in sport need leadership, and realistically high expectations. John had those expectations for us.

My worst race in international competition was in 1980 after the boycott. I hit a real low. It was just terrible. We were very angry about not going to the Olympics. We were in Poland, the food was bad, the accommodation was terrible, the water was awful, it was just before martial law was enforced. There wasn't a good atmosphere on the team, everyone was really negative. There were a lot of discipline problems within the team; people were not acting in a responsible manner. The place we were staying in was disgusting, the whole organization of the race was pretty shoddy and the site was awful. There was a big smokestack from a factory at the end of the lake. It was spitting out all these fumes with bits of coal or ash in them;

things that would get in your eyes. You couldn't even see to the end of the course. And then they had these army guys in motorboats going up and down creating all this wash.

I didn't have a lot of adaptability to water conditions. If the water was calm then I usually had a good race. But I didn't have a coping response for waves. My knees started to shake, my stomach would go into a ball, the boat started to shake, and I couldn't paddle. I just tensed up and that's it. That happened in Poland. In addition we hadn't really been training very intensely because we couldn't see any point to training. There were no World Championships or Olympics. There was no goal. We were just going through the motions. We would rather have just gone home, there was no reason to be there.

I think there are basic things you can put up with. I was in Poland my first year when I was at the Junior Worlds. We had no baths, no showers, we only had cold water in the room, but I still did really well. The actual water and paddling was going well and was all under control, and I was very excited about the whole thing. We were getting along well, everyone was having fun and it was a good atmosphere. The years when we've not had a very good team atmosphere, the results haven't been good. Even though you are not necessarily in the same boat, you still have to be around each other, and have respect for each other, and for each other's abilities. You get some guys who aren't taking the whole thing seriously, or aren't as intense as you are, and that can be really irritating. It can really throw you off. You're saying, "I'm putting this much into it, and you're not. What are you doing here if you're not trying?" It doesn't matter if they excel, or if they achieve the same way, but it's the attitude that they aren't putting as much effort into it as everyone else is. I don't think that we try to be primadonnas or anything, but you're there to do a job. If you're not there to do the job then you shouldn't be there. When we all had that same feeling we got along really well. That's why I thought our success at the 1984 Games was complete because everybody did what they were supposed to do. Although we're not really close and we don't depend on each other for anything, we're all part of the same team. We did what we set out to do, and we did it together. We could enjoy each other's success.

Several people played a major role in my mental preparation for the Olympics. First, there was John Bales, my former coach, confidante and friend. I look to him for advice on everything. Next to my parents, he's probably been the most influential person in my life because he's always been there. I go to him to talk about lots of things. He was at the Games. Twice he said something that really made a big impression on me. One occasion was when the 1984 boycott was announced. I realized that I wasn't feeling very motivated and I said to John, "I'm really depressed." He said, "Well, you've got to look at what's going on here. Now you've got to work even harder than before because it's your big opportunity. Whether the other nations are there or not makes no difference. Whoever goes the fastest on that day, gets the Olympic medal, and that's all there is to it. No one's going to remember down the road and it won't make the value of your medal any less whether there's a boycott or not, because it's whoever's fastest on that day." And so I said, "You're right." It just turned me around.

If you don't write it down you don't improve on it.

The post performance analysis we did was invaluable.

77

Then the second time was at the 1984 Games. We met almost every day because he was staying with my parents. He said, "Have you been watching the swimming?" I said, "A little bit." He said, "Have you seen Baumann and Davis in the starting blocks?" and I said, "Not that I can remember," and he said, "Well, watch them. Just look at the determination in their eyes. Look at how determined they are. That is what you have to capture. You have to be determined to go out and win your medal." So that's what I kept in mind. I couldn't settle for anything less. I wanted to go out there and race my hardest. John had that ability to just pick something, and I used everything, even that one little thing. It was a very important time for him to be there.

And the same goes for Denis Barré my Olympic coach. I know that he cares a lot about me as a person. They both do, and it's not that they're just doing it as their job, from a coaching standpoint. Denis could joke with me and was always supportive. When we were working on style at the beginning of the year in Florida he would sometimes stop the practice and say, "You're not very relaxed are you?" Then he'd say, "Let's go back," and we would take the time to do a few exercises that would get me more comfortable in the boat, work on my balance, and help me relax. Then he'd say, "Okay, let's try again." So we wouldn't try and fight the balance problem, we'd go back, get rid of all those jitters and fix them, and then we'd go on with the practice. That was great because later whenever I did have balance problems, I'd just say, "Okay, go back to the basics." In fact, we worked it into our warm-up so that I never got to the stage where I was jittery. He really wanted us to do well, and he exudes such an incredible amount of enthusiasm. He would tell us, "You girls can win a medal. . .you can win a gold medal, you're strong, you're the best."

It's important to have everyone around you believe that you can win. My parents believed that, John believed that, Denis believed that, and I felt our head coach, Frank Garner, believed that we could do well. Frank always made special arrangements for us and I think he felt we were special, and appreciated that we were trying hard.

One coach didn't believe that the girls could do anything, so I just cut him out. I didn't want that negative attitude around me, so I just didn't have anything to do with him.

And then there was Terry Orlick, our team sport psychologist. Most of Terry's work was done before the Olympics. He first started getting involved by helping a few canoers who were having some problems with their racing, and then Frank thought that we should involve more sports science people, so Terry got involved that way. The first time I met him I went and talked with him in his office at the University in the springtime, before I went to Florida. It was just to see how things were going and what we needed, because he didn't know canoeing at all. He wanted to get a feel for what it was like, what kind of things made me anxious, and what kind of things I wanted to work on, where I thought I could improve, what kind of things I did to cope with stress, and if I did any kind of mental preparation.

When Terry came to work with us at the Florida camp we'd meet with him on an individual basis. We'd have a group meeting too

Looking back, the way to improve our sport for women is to treat women like they are winners, like they have potential and are important.

where he'd introduce new material. The large group situation didn't work well for us, unless it was arranged just to give out information. For discussion our team did much better in small groups and one-to-one situations; the individual sessions were very good. We would talk individually, and then Terry would talk to Alexandra and I together sometimes, and sometimes the three of us with Denis. We'd discuss the things we'd want to try to do together.

Early on he introduced doing our race strategy. He gave me a 20-page race plan used by Graham Smith, the Butterflyer. A lot of stuff was helpful from that. So I started doing that after '80, then just kept working on my own race plan every year. Terry would go over it with you, or he'd pick out things you might have said that would be useful, and pick your brains for the cue words you used and what kind of feeling you wanted to achieve. He was someone to bounce things off. A lot of the time he'd just listen and you'd start to say things and realize that you hadn't verbalized them before. He would try to get you to write things down, and do the evaluation sheets which I think were really valuable, even after a bad performance. After the race we would sit down and say, "Okay, did this work? Did we do this? Or did we forget about it? How are we going to remember this?" We'd analyze the whole thing. Terry would always ask us if we'd done the evaluation and John would ask us, and Denis thought it was very important, so he'd always ask us if we'd done it. After the race before we went to a party or something, he'd say, "Let's have 5 minutes to sit by ourselves where no one can interrupt us and talk about the race." It was important to make sure that we evaluated our feelings because you can forget, or they can change after a few hours or a day. The evaluation was critical, but never in a personal sense. It was more like expressing, "I felt that the boat didn't move here or I felt the boat go down here, or I felt the boat really surge here." That made it very comfortable to do the analysis.

If you don't get something positive out of a negative experience then you may as well not have gone out at all. You should analyze the bad ones more carefully because quite obviously something went wrong and we want to avoid that. Perhaps we veterans got more out of the evaluations than the younger athletes.

I believe that you can only train physically to a certain level. Your body can do so much, and then there's a limit, and you're not going to improve. When you first start training, you improve very rapidly, but after you've been training for a long time, those gains are very small, so you start looking elsewhere for areas to improve. The rest of the training is now old hat, so you have more to put into and gain from mental training. I used it and I found it very beneficial. A lot of the things made such an incredible difference.

Your "head" is most of the race. People can generally do a lot better than they expect, if they have the right attitude. I try to impress that on the kids that I'm coaching now. They're receptive to it from me, but I have had other coaches tell me, "Well, I tried to tell them that and they don't believe me." As a coach, you have got to believe that it works. Terry's a very well respected sport psychologist, so you believe him; but he's also very non-threatening. He's prepared to give whatever you want to take. If you don't want to be part of it, well that's fine. He was very effective with me, I related well to him.

The years when we've not had a very good team atmosphere, the results haven't been good. Even though you are not necessarily in the same boat, you still have to be around each other, and have respect for each other, and for each other's abilities.

It's important to have everyone around you believe that you can win.

Three weeks prior to the Olympics, before going to Sacramento, we trained in British Columbia. Things started to fall apart there. Alexandra, my partner, just clammed up and I thought she was mad at me. Usually partners have each other for support, so if there is a problem you talk to your partner. I talked with our coach, Denis, because he and I are very close friends, and Alexandra and he are married. When we got to Sacramento she was fine, fun, and willing to do everything. I still don't know what happened, but it made a big difference to me, because if she hadn't been happy like that, then I don't know what I would have done because we were in it together.

I had been concerned about going to Sacramento for our final training camp. I thought that three weeks was going to be too long for us to be together. But it turned out great because of all the preparation. There was lots to do, lots of videos, lots of entertainment, lots of extra food, lots of vans. Everything that we wanted was taken care of. There were even these little high school cheerleaders coming in every week for camps. They were just hysterical! We could go shopping, we had our time to go out. On our day off some people went to Reno and some went to San Francisco. We got to see some of the area. The water was fine, and the people at the place where we kept our boats were so nice.

Your 'head' is most of the race. People can generally do a lot better than they expect, if they have the right attitude.

Frank Garner, our head coach, orchestrated the whole thing. That's what I think a head coach's job is: to orchestrate so that everything goes the way it should. They don't have to do the actual on-water, hands-on stuff; they're there to make sure that the people who are the best at doing that technical work are there. He got Denis for us.

Frank and I had a long talk in 1983 and I told him what I thought I needed. Denis had suggested that I write a list of all the things that were good, and all the things that hadn't been good about the year before, what we needed to change and what we needed to keep the same for next year. There was incredible preparation and planning, and I credit Frank with putting it all together. Hugh and Alwyn needed a coach to themselves so they got Rob, someone they could relate to, and they needed to go to these particular competitions in Europe. Larry also needed to go to these particular competitions, whereas it wasn't particularly good for us. So they went on their tour and we went on ours. One thing I needed was my own room at the Olympics. I needed that because I really needed a private space. I knew that was crucial to me doing well.

Anything we asked for, Frank did his best to get. Once you're in that kind of milieu, where it's a class operation, you can't help act in the best possible manner, because of all these things being done. You're just obligated to do your best because everyone else is doing their best. When we were travelling, I always felt that we were a class act, and you therefore conduct yourself accordingly.

The day of competition we had a routine. We had our day planned from the minute we woke up to the minute we finished the race. We knew exactly what we were going to be doing. About three years earlier, when Alexandra and I first started paddling together, we made a plan. Terry got us to write it down. I thought it was great. The day before the race, we would have a meeting, sometimes just the two of us; we didn't have to have a coach or Terry there. We would talk

80

about what we were going to do. We developed the plan over the years in practice as well as at races. We practised the plan in Sacramento, getting up, having breakfast, doing the warm-up and time controls on the days when we would be racing at the Olympics. When we were in training in Florida we did it too. We practised doing time controls every day for six days because the Olympics were six days where you could possibly have to race every day. We were always trying to get used to the six day thing which was what we faced at the Olympics. When we were in Sacramento, we got used to getting up early, because we had to get up very early to compete at the Olympics. For three weeks in Sacramento we were getting up at 6.30 a.m. So it was no big deal to get up that early at the Olympics.

We knew how long it would take us to get to the site, we knew how long it took us to eat our breakfast. We had practised that, to see what worked. The night before we told each other, "We're going to get up at this time, we'll meet at this time, we'll eat until this time, then we'll go back to our rooms, and get our stuff," whatever worked best. We'd meet our driver and tell him we'll be ready to go at this time. That was all decided the night before. You knew what would happen, and if Charlie (the driver) wasn't there, you knew where Tim, the manager, was as a backup. If there was a problem, you knew what to do. So Charlie would drive us and we'd listen on our Walkmans to pre-selected music. One for getting more psyched, another for calming down. We got to the course. We had a time frame put in for chatting, because we knew you can't just arrive and expect people to not talk to you, so we had time to go and get a drink from the cafeteria, and say hello to people. We knew what time we were going to get our boat together.

Something we weren't as prepared for was sitting around for four days between heats. This was very unusual. Usually we have heats, repêchages, semi-finals, finals. In four days I would usually have 6 to 8 races, for K-2 and K-4, and this time it was 6 days and we had three races so it was an extended period of time between races.

We had the heat on the Monday and then we didn't race again until the Friday. We had the easier of the two heats. We decided to use it as a practice race by pretending that the other tough competitors were there in the race, because we knew that no-one would be very close to us. We used the easy draw as a positive thing. We went out there and did a good time even though there was no-one to race against. We felt good, the boat felt good, and we felt strong.

When the men's rowing 8 won, we were out training. We couldn't watch the races but when the race ended, we paddled closer. I thought there were some guys in red on the podium but we couldn't really see them. Then the flags went up and we could hear the Canadian national anthem coming across the water. I was just sitting there going, "Oh God, this is great, oh this is so wonderful!" Another thing that got me was one day when we came to the course after rowing was over. We decided to walk by the boathouse where the rowers kept their boats. The four Canadian girls who had won a silver medal were there, and they were just oozing happiness, they were glowing! They had their flowers and they were just standing there, they didn't know what to do. So I went up to them and I congratulated them all. God they looked great! And I just thought, I want to feel just like

No one was saying anything, it was so quiet, everyone was serious. So I said, "God, I feel like I'm going down death row!"

81

them. The day of the race, we came to the course just in time to see Larry Cain win his gold medal and my knees just gave out. I started to cry, and I said, "Pull it together Sue, another hour and a half and you can just let it go!"

For the finals we got the outside lane assignment and everyone else was on the inside. We said, "Okay, because we're over here, there's no way we can know what they're doing, and let's not even bother. We'll just do what we have to do." That attitude worked out to be so crucial. I just felt like we couldn't do anything wrong. It was just up to us. I said, "There's nothing that's affecting us in a negative way, the only thing now is to do it, and we can do it. . .I just have to do my best."

All I had to think about now was doing it, and doing the best we could.

We were the last race of the day and the rest of the team had left the competitor's area because we try not to interfere with each other's preparations. They're very individual. We had identified through Terry that everyone wanted their space, and that we should just leave people alone before the race. The only people at the boathouses were the girls who were racing. It was practically deserted. So I was trying to add a little levity to the situation; that was part of my coping strategy. A lot of times, if things got too heavy, I'd just say, oh, it's just another race. So Terry and Frank were carrying our boat down, and we were following behind – very 'funeral'! No one was saying anything, it was so quiet, everyone was serious. So I said, "God, I feel like I'm going down death row!" But really, we felt very light, very easy, very good; and then we paddled over to the course.

The last thing Terry said to us was, "Let's go right off the scale." We used a 10 point scale on our evaluation sheets. At the bottom of the paper it says, "How do you feel you pushed in this race, did you give it one hundred percent, did you fully extend yourself?" The goal was to extend ourselves off the scale and go beyond it. That was a thing we used to say, and that's very visual. It's a good feeling. It's like you're lifting off, you're taking off, and once you get to the end of the scale, you just keep flying.

I wanted to feel the power, the boat coming up, lifting and going.

We have a set warm-up, we know exactly how much time it takes and exactly what things we're going to do. On the way to the start line we were paddling by the spectators and I heard, "Go Canada!" It was my dad! One voice came clearly across the lake, and I said, "That's my dad!" At previous Olympics, the enormity of the situation I was in would get me down. I'd say, "My God, here we are at the Olympics!" I didn't do that this time. I felt, we're just going to go and do it, we're going to give it our best. I kept talking to myself a lot, and trying to keep in sight what I was going to do. I wanted to keep in mind what I had to do, to paddle well. I knew that we could think about what it all meant in larger terms much later. All I had to think about now was doing it, and doing the best we could.

Immediately before the race I was thinking about trying to stay on that edge, just letting myself relax, and doing a lot of positive self-talk about what I was going to do. One thing I identified early on was that I was afraid of not doing well. I was afraid of racing because I had been in it so long and everyone wanted me to lose. When you've been winning a long time, people don't want you to win any more.

I felt I was in a 'no win' situation, because if I won I was only doing what was expected of me. I was having a lot of anxiety about racing because I couldn't prove anything. Before the race I was trying to get around that; I was telling myself that the only failure is not to try, and that I had to go out and really give it my best and I shouldn't care about what other people were thinking. I was thinking all kinds of positive things, like I could do well, I was going to be good, I was feeling strong, how Alexandra and I had worked so hard, and our boat was fast, and things like that; all positive, trying to feel like I wanted to feel. That was something we'd practised and had been in my race plan all the time. I concentrated on that a lot. I wanted to have that powerful feeling. I didn't want the race to be an effort, I wanted it to be very powerful, all my strength would be moving the boat. I knew that in order to have that power I had to be relaxed and I had to be very strong. You can be powerful but tense, and the boat won't go. You windmill and you stay on the spot and dig yourself into a hole. I wanted to feel the power, the boat coming up, lifting and going. The first part of the race, with the adrenalin, you feel so strong but I knew that the adrenalin would not last. When it ends, which is about 300 metres into the race, then I knew it was going to be hard, and I had to push, but I was good at that, I knew that was my strength, strong finishes, and that I had more at the end than anyone else had.

During the race I was thinking all the time, it certainly wasn't a blur, I didn't get out of myself. My focus was very concentrated throughout the race. We have a start plan, and in it I concentrate *only* on the first few strokes. I've found that if I concentrate beyond that, those first strokes won't be strong enough. Then I concentrate on the next little bit of the race. Then we come to the 250, and I say, "Poof!" and we put in an extra burst to get the boat up and moving again. Then it's getting to the end, we have to really push. I said, "I'm not going to die from this, I'm just going to have to go as hard as I can. This is the last time I'll ever race, I have to give it everything," and I also had to say, "But you have to be powerful, you've got to use everything." Almost every three seconds or so towards the end I'd have to say, "Relax" and I'd let my shoulders and my head relax, and I'd think about putting on the power, and then I'd feel the tension creeping up again so I'd think about relaxing again, then power, relax. . .

You can tell where you are during the race because there are flags and buoys. I don't look straight down at the water. I look ahead down the lane. The last 100 metres is marked with red buoys and I knew how many buoys ahead of that to start our finish, because we had practised on the course. When it was time for the very last part of the finish, we just go all out power forgetting style and everything else. Crossing the line, the thing I remember was just letting the emotion go, and being able to say, "That's it, it's over!" I just knew that we'd gone our very hardest.

"I'm not going to die from this, I'm just going to have to go as hard as I can. This is the last time I'll ever race, I have to give it everything."

11
KELLY KRYCZKA

1984 OLYMPIC SILVER MEDALIST — SYNCHRONIZED SWIMMING, DUET

**KELLY KRYCZKA
SYNCHRONIZED
SWIMMING**

- Silver Medalist (Duet, with partner Sharon Hambrook) at the 1984 Olympic Games
- 1983 Pan American Games — 1st (team), 3rd (figures) 2nd (duet)
- 1983 Pan Pacifics — 1st (team), 1st (duet)
- 1983 World Championships — 1st (team), 1st (duet), 2nd (solo)
- 1981 Pan Pacifics — 1st (team), 2nd (duet), 2nd (solo), 2nd (figures)
- 1979 Pan American Games — 1st (duet), 2nd (team)

I think we prepared ourselves as well as we could have at home. One week before the opening ceremony we went to San Diego. In San Diego it was a matter of getting used to swimming in an outdoor pool, the hot weather, the humidity. It also got us away from all the hassles of home. When you're down there, you know you are down there for a purpose. You just totally concentrate on that.

We went to the Olympic village in Los Angeles the day before the opening ceremonies. We actually competed a week later. We checked into our rooms, got all the business out of the way, the sex testing, and we saw most of our old buddies on the Canadian team. We saw the hype and the atmosphere, and we realized that we were part of it and what it was all about. We realized a day later when we were leaving to go back to San Diego that it was perfect that we were leaving. If you want to continue to train properly, and we felt we still had to before we competed, the village was no place to be as far as trying to concentrate.

Before the Olympics we did a lot of mental preparation. Our support psychology consultant was trying to prepare us for when we would actually swim. She would sit us down and say, "Picture the morning of the day when you get up, what it is going to be like. Pic-

Everything in the script happened exactly as we had imagined it.

85

ture the crowd, the audience, the whole scene of the village, how you are going to deal with it, how you are going to block it out, or how you are going to use it to your advantage." When we went back to San Diego after the opening ceremonies we knew exactly what the picture was. We knew what the dorms were like, we knew where the pool was and what it was like with all the crowds.

When we got back to San Diego we (Sharon Hambrook and I) wrote out our own mental imagery script using very descriptive words. It included everything that you feel, the water, the sun, the hotness, the crowd, the roar and the excitement. After we wrote that script, our psychologist got us to relax and then she ran through that with us. A lot of times when she started us going, we would branch out from her talking and we'd take it from there. That was not the first time she had done it. We worked on that before.

The scripted imagery was just for the day of the competition. It began with on-site warm-up (half an hour) and continued through the next hour and a half where we put make-up on and get ready before the actual competition started, right up to the medal presentation.

Sharon and I composed the script together. It was our own scene. Our consultant read it back to us about four days before the competition. From then on, I could lie there and just picture it. Earlier in the year, we would do things like that, thinking about any sort of competitive situation, and feeling your heart rate rise and the anxiety building up. Then you had to figure out how you were going to cope with it. So it wasn't like this was a new thing. It was just much more focused on the actual Olympic situation.

Everything in the script happened exactly as we had imagined it. We were positive the whole way through, and it was all right on, minus the part of hearing the marks and what they were, and standing up there on the podium, as #1, and seeing the Canadian flag, and hearing the national anthem (we were 2nd instead of the scripted 1st.) As far as feeling great in the water, and on top of it, and everything so synchronized, the audience appreciating you and the roar, it was all there. I think going through that imagery process definitely helped.

I think a lot of athletes were not prepared in that mental aspect. You have got to realize it is a pressure situation down there. There are a lot of distractions. We were not used to that many people. After our mental preparation, the distractions didn't even phase us. It was more toward the positive, "Wow, look at us, we practised fourteen years!" We wanted to go up there, we weren't even nervous, well maybe a little bit, but it wasn't a 'freaking-out' nervousness. So I think it definitely made a difference. The Olympics is the peak of any amateur athlete's career. You have to face all the athletes at the Olympics. Physically, they have all pretty much prepared the same way and they are obviously the most talented athletes in the world. So you have to start looking for better ways, besides drugs, to improve your performance. I guess that's where the mental aspect comes in.

In a mental preparation script you include anything that might bother you, or anything that you realize will be there. But you have to mention it positively. For example a lot of times it kind of shocks me when I jump in the water, especially when it is a hundred degrees outside, and the water is cold. Instead of saying, "The water is freezing," you say, "The water is cool, it is refreshing and it feels so light" and that sort of thing. It was good for Sharon and I both to put the script together. It was our own thing. It was what we thought the day would be like.

There was a part in it where we compared our competitors to some sort of animal. They were a penguin and a sea lion and we were graceful dolphins. So when you looked at them, you didn't think, "They're my competitors" and freak out. You would see this sea lion standing there and you would almost laugh, but no-one would have a clue what you were laughing about.

We had been to Los Angeles the previous year (1983) for a pre-Olympic meet, so we could picture what the pool was like. I was preparing myself all year for what it was going to be like. I could picture it. But to actually sit there and do a script and use all the positive images and words, you get pretty cocky. Even when we were swimming, flashes of that script were good to have.

When the consultant first suggested doing this I thought it was a pain. I don't like little formalities. I'm a "do it" type of person. I can usually figure it out as it happens. After we finished the script we definitely thought it was a good idea. I was just being lazy about not wanting to do it. It made sense. It was fun to do. We were both proud of it and it was part of our project together.

I can picture almost anything. But to sit down and write it makes you think that much more. You just feel much more prepared. You have gone through it together. There was the odd time where I couldn't think of a descriptive word, and Sharon would say, "What about. . ." "That's a good one," or vice versa. This way we were thinking more on the same wavelength. It got to the point where we would read the script over, each night ourselves. Then once we each got in bed, we'd do relaxation and run through it in our own minds. You knew that your partner was doing the same thing. You knew that your partner over there wasn't thinking of something totally different, and freaking out. You've got it under control.

There were times during the year when we were at different meets, or different Olympic trials, and we would be in the same room, each lying there in bed; the tension was pretty high and we were wound up. So we would play these little games where she would try and visualize something in her mind, like a figure in the duet and I would try and feel what she was feeling. Sharon says she would just try and let her images flow into mine. We became really good at it. Most of the time I could feel what she was visualizing, at least 3 out of 5 times, (she could choose to visualize any one of ten different elements.)

Sometimes we would lie there at night and one of us would say "go." What we would try to do was go through the whole routine in our heads and announce when we were done. Our real routine was about 4:06 minutes. Quite often we would finish the imagery within 4 or 5 seconds of each other.

There are times when you are swimming, in imagery, when you are thinking about it and your body twitches a little here and there because you can feel your muscles. You feel like you are doing it, but you can still picture the two of you doing it. You get to a hard part in

I can picture almost anything. But to sit down and write it makes you think that much more. You just feel much more prepared.

There are times when you are swimming in imagery, when you are thinking about it and your body twitches a little here and there because you can feel your muscles.

87

the routine, and you know what it feels like and you can just feel it. When we are swimming we never look at each other, but I'm always aware of what she is doing. I can tell if she does something wrong and vice versa. For us in our sport, that is important.

We did a lot of imagery during training sessions, especially as the competition approached. When we were doing compulsory figures in practice, a minute before doing certain ones the coaches would say, "Okay, you are going to do a 'best one'. You are going to do a whole compulsory figure." So before we went out there and did it we would sit on the edge of the pool and picture ourselves doing it, and how it feels. You picture yourself doing it "right on," perfectly. Then go out there and do it. There were times when Debbie, our coach, would tell us to do the same kind of imagery for our routine.

Doing a lot of imagery was the major difference in our preparation last year, not just the duet, but also the compulsory figures. About half an hour before we actually did a competition routine we would go through the routine once together on dry land doing the movements. The two of us would do the movements, moving our arms, and feeling the moves while the tape was playing our music. When you do that you can usually tell whether there are good vibes going through the two of you.

You need more mental imagery for figures. There are six groups of six figures. Thirty-six hours before the meet, they draw the six figures you are going to be doing. The night before we did our figures, Sharon and I would both take a tape recorder and one of us would be in the room and one of us would be in the bathroom. We would talk into the tape recorder like a script going through our movements, like now I'm in a back layout and I'm stretching from my head to my feet, or whatever. We just practised those figures after they were drawn, adding reminders that we wanted to remember. If I was always a little bit too far over on my face I'd say, "Make sure you press back to your nose." I wouldn't say, "Don't look down your face," nothing negative. When you are in the meet doing it, you are so busy thinking of what is next. The tape is in there. I always prefer to make the tape. Sharon sometimes made the tape and sometimes wrote it out. When you actually say it or write it down you remember it better. A lot of times I wouldn't have to play it back. Just by doing it, it is in there. Just by sitting down for ten seconds and thinking about the figure, it all comes to you.

I guess the final results were unforeseen. The politics and American hype that went on down there were unforeseen. We didn't take that into account. Sharon tells a story of her parents sitting up in the stands in the finals and this lady leans forward and says, "These Canadians are pretty good, huh? They might even beat the Americans!" She says her Mom just kind of went, "I don't believe it." We were the World Champions and they didn't even know it. We swam well in each of the three stages. We could never have swum better. We never gave up, we never lost our confidence, and we did our best.

Sharon and I performed the best when we weren't nervous, or when we were happy. We would always joke and get giddy before we competed, and fool around before the focus was on our routine. That got us into the right psych. I don't know whether we were ever

One area we could have been better prepared for was the media questions.

88

down before competitions. Then usually before doing the routine we got our heart rates the same before we started. Sharon is really hyper compared to me. Her pulse rate is usually over 80, and mine is usually under 60. I can speed mine up and she can bring hers down. If, when we first take our pulse, it's 20 beats apart, the second time we take it within fifteen seconds; it was usually within two beats.

We would decide on what pulse rate we wanted to aim for. There were very few times when we couldn't reach that pulse rate. The only time we both usually had the same pulse rates without mentally controlling it was when we were both tired. When she is tired her pulse rates comes down.

One area we could have been better prepared for was the media questions. After the preliminaries Sharon and I went to a press reception and all these people were asking us, "What do you think of (this competitor)" and they would read us a quote like from update brochures handed out weeks before the Olympics. Or they'd say, "In synchronized swimming the Americans are pretty much on top of the world, what do you think of that?" "Is that how you feel? Are you worried about them?" No wonder we were running into such problems with scores, it was almost like a brainwash. A lot of Americans came up to us and said, "I don't know where the judging was, but you were great," and not only Americans did that.

We believed we would achieve our goal from beginning to end. I think we accepted the results, because we swam our best. We couldn't swim any better and we know that we were the favourites of ninety percent of those watching. The other thing is, both Sharon and myself had been in the sport for so long and therefore exposed to the politics and judging. I think the first time judging problems ever happened to me was in 1980, at the Pan Pacifics here in Calgary. I just couldn't handle it, I couldn't deal with it. It also happened to us in Seoul in 1983. You have to take a "do your best attitude," because quite honestly our sport is a judged sport, and you have only got fifty percent of the control.

I knew we were good. I guess deep down I feel we would have come first if it wasn't for the judging. But then again I'm not going to sit around and brood over it. Like I said, half is what we do and half is what they do. If we worry about their half we are not going to get anywhere. I didn't ever think negatively at the Olympics. We thought it was possible to pull ahead even under those conditions. I think in all our hyping ourselves we overlooked how much American hype there would be down there and how it could affect the judging.

When we were down in Los Angeles in 1984, I knew that I was better than I ever was. We had covered everything. In 1982, we never did any mental preparation. We (Sharon and I) were battling against each other because of our solos, so we weren't really together. Last year we scrapped the solos, so that our destiny was what we both did as a combination. I would support her and she would support me. We knew that we had prepared ourselves in every area. We knew that our potential was much greater than the Americans. Even if they did progress over the year, so did we, by leaps and bounds. There was nothing more, we were confident. I think when you are confident you believe in yourself and you can do almost anything you think you can.

Last year we scrapped the solos, so that our destiny was what we both did as a combination. I would support her and she would support me.

We were so prepared! Our coach made us swim our routine over and over again so our endurance was great. And obviously, mentally we were strong. We also went on a really heavy weight program. We worked really hard on that for the Olympics. We even did weight training in the water. Until that time there had always been some fear in my mind, "What if I'm not feeling too good that day or if by three quarters of the way through my legs are numb?" At the Olympics there was never even the faintest doubt or negative thought in my mind. We knew we were ready, we had prepared for everything and anything.

The final performance and the compulsory figures at the Olympics were without a doubt our best ever performance. As we stepped out onto the deck we were confident. We knew a lot of Canadians were there to support us. We knew we had the attention of everybody there. We knew they loved our routine, we were proud to show it to them. We wanted to show it to them, we wanted to do our best. We were so aggressive. If you watched our program at the Olympics, before we started, we were just so heads up. We marched out there like we owned the place and that was how we were feeling.

In our pose just before jumping into the water we do this six second relaxation response. We breathe in and unfocus our eyes, and tell ourselves we are going to do it as we imagined it. Then away we go. You don't think of your opposition. You just feel your way through it. When I finished that routine I could hardly remember swimming any of it. My body was just going through the motions, same with Sharon. I mean, we weren't thinking of the hot deck, or the crowds of people. It was probably harder on my mum than me. We were right into it. Our script didn't say, "You look at all the thousands of people, you are aware of opponents behind you. . .," it doesn't say any of that. We just kind of acted out our script with no faults.

At the 1982 Worlds in Equador we weren't a unit. We weren't thinking the same way. We were worried about making it through the routine. Once you start worrying about anything, forget it. If you're thinking, "Gee, I don't know whether I am even going to make it through," there is no way you are going to make it through and come first.

For that competition I thought, "I'll save my energy for the hard part in the routine." Well, the hard part was two-thirds of the way through. That is no good if you want to give it your all. There was just no comparison. 1982 was a joke. I didn't enjoy 1982. I enjoyed the very end of the routine, even though my legs were numb, just because I'd just finished the hard part. But up to then it was, "How am I feeling now, yes, it is up with my legs now, okay, that's good, really let up a little bit here now," - too much technical evaluation.

I was also worried about whether we were synchronized. I was so busy worrying and thinking, "This has to go there and slow down a bit here and do that." Your body should just be flowing through it. I was tense, even the night before.

The input from Patricia Hill, our consultant, was really good initially. She got us thinking in a whole different realm, imagining our performance as an image rather than a thought. It put a different perspective on how we approached the sport. At our level our best

We marched out there like we owned the place and that was how we were feeling.

competitors have all pretty much the same physical skill. We needed an edge in some way. Sharon and I obviously aren't identical twins. Just to get out of Canada to compete internationally, we knew we had to be thinking more like identical twins. That is sort of what we wanted. Our aim was to think alike, act alike, to be as much on the same wavelength as we could.

We once had a sport psychology consultant who we didn't like on site. This consultant changed under pressure. She was constantly there at the pool and at the practices. She'd say, "I'd like to talk to you now," and she would take hours to talk to you. At the competition site when we were away from the pool, except for our preparation at night, or watching videos right after the practice, we wanted to forget about it. We just wanted to get away from it. She was there the whole time, and always the approach was, "Are you okay now? Is everything okay?" I started wondering, "Gee, how come she is asking me this, maybe everything isn't okay," and then I would start to worry. That made us nervous. Even our coach left us alone after practice.

At the Olympics Sharon and I stuck together. We did everything around the village together. We ate at the same time and we went to bed at the same time. We have a very close relationship with our coach. She knows how we are under pressure, and what we need. At the Olympics we were doing fine. All the preparation had been done. It was now our game. At the Olympics in the morning we stretched and warmed up together, as usual. Then we ran through the routine parts, Debbie said a few words, and then we got out. "You look good. Go get ready." So Sharon and I went and put up our hair together and put our make-up on. We came back an hour and a half later and went through our routine. We know exactly what ways we like to prepare. When we are stretching five minutes before we go on, we are in our own frame of mind and we don't want any outside input. It is too late at that time.

The mental game is now a fact of life if you are on the top, or if you ever want to get to the top. Plus a good coach of course, but I think Canada has quite a few good coaches. Athletes really need to know how to prepare themselves better mentally because there is such a fine line between being good and being the best. I think a good sport psychologist has got to be specific, explain the basics of how it works, always be positive and ask good questions. "Why did you do that and would you do it again?" A good sport psychologist changes your whole way of thinking.

Script : Duet Finals - LA 1984 - by Kelly Kryczka and Sharon Hambrook.

We are totally prepared for the duet competition. With our glamorous make-up on we look stunning and attractive. As we pin each other's hats on we feel the aura of each other's excitement. We feel confident and classy as we slip our lean and muscular bodies into our designer red-and-white suits. As we execute a land-drill in perfect synchronization, we feel as one! The Lean-Mean-Swim-Machine is totally ready! As we leave the locker room, we feel awesome in the eyes of the envious on-lookers. Stepping onto the deck we happen to notice a ridiculously lethargic, outward-looking penguin and sea lion. . .We look absolutely smashing! Walking out to our starting

Our aim was to think alike, act alike, to be as much on the same wavelength as we could.

position, we can feel the positive anticipation of the wildly applauding audience. We feel light, cool, and bouncy as our feet skim over the deck. As we address the audience, we take a deep breath and feel our jaws relax. We sparkle and captivate the audience with our smiles. As the whistle blows, we take our pose with confidence and determination. We are ready to begin! A burst of energy fills us as the music blares through the huge speakers. As we flip into the water with grace and athleticism, we feel enjoyably revived by the cool, refreshing water. We feel strong and powerful as we perform our first stunt with precision. The end boost explodes with energy. We feel powerful, sharp and effervescent as our stream-lined bodies move in unison through the water. With the bubbly change in the music, our energy continues to grow. Our expression is frisky and fun-loving and entices the audience and the judges to follow every move. We hear the overwhelming applause of the appreciative audience. We see their smiling, supportive faces. The piano begins - making us feel relaxed and seductive as we slither through the water in euphoria. Our eyes express our alluring feeling. We are in another world. . .We are even more graceful and fluid. We feel like we are walking on water. The audience is mesmerized. We feel as straight as arrows as we execute our spins perfectly and with perfect synchronization. We are revitalized by the electricity in the air. The judges are in awe. The music changes and everyone comes alive. We are frisky and happy as we swim energetically through the water. True "show-offs!" We sparkle as we bring everyone to their feet, including them in our fun! As we go under for the last boosts, we feel victorious. Once, twice, we come flying through the air! The crowd is standing and cheering wildly as we surface for the end paso. We are popular and admired. We are obviously "THE BEST!" We get out of the water and confidently await our final marks. The marks flash across the giant screen - a brilliant display of 9.9's. We hug each other in ecstacy. The Canadian on-lookers are going wild! We wave thankfully to the crowd. As we walk off and wait for the presentations, we know that we have won the Gold Medal! The Olympic theme blares for the medal ceremony. We walk out to the podium triumphantly. As they announce the gold medal winners, we hear our names. The audience goes berserk! The presentor slips the colorful ribbons over our heads. We feel the weight of our prize. The sparkling gold medals dangle from our necks for all the world to see. We wave victoriously to the standing, cheering crowd. We hear, "Ladies and gentlemen, please rise for the playing of the national anthem of CANADA!" We begin to sing proudly as we see our red and white flag being hoisted to the top. We feel proud to be Canadians and to know that our country is proud of us. As we parade around the deck, we stop to share our moment of glory with our Canadian supporters. Tears of joy fill our eyes as we realize what we have accomplished - we are the BEST SYNCHRONIZED SWIMMING DUET IN THE WORLD!

Athletes really need to know how to prepare themselves better mentally because there is such a fine line between being good and being the best.

12(a)
PAUL MARTINI

1984 WORLD CHAMPION — FIGURE SKATING PAIRS

We didn't believe in the quantity ideal: the more you do the better you get. Instead of coming in and saying, we're going to do three short programs, or we're going to do two longs, which gets you more into the mind set of, I've just got to get through it: we said, "We are going to do one of each, and they're going to be good," because that's all you do at the competition. You've only got one whack and you had better do it. We always used to think, let's just do it once and get it right that one time, as if it were a competition. I think that helped a lot. Every day we would run through the short and long program once. Our off-ice program was quite comparable to what everyone else in the sport was doing. The quality we brought to our practice performance was the major difference.

We didn't have coaches to stand over us and beat us. Sandra and Lewis our coaches always felt, "You have only got to go through this once, but I want it to be the best you can do today." Knowing that you only had to do it once, whether or not you felt great, helped. You didn't have to think, "Oh God! And after this one, I've got to do another one, and that kind of thing." You only had to do it once, but to your utmost ability. It was easy to do once every day. Even if you

The quality we brought to our practice performance was the major difference.

didn't feel so hot you knew you only had to get through it once. You just make sure you gave it your one hundred percent.

We always had such a good time at the rink, between Barb, myself, Lewis and Sandra. If they came over, and said, "We'll work with you now", Barb and I could say, "No, not today we want to work on some things ourselves. We're not ready for you yet, we are still working a few things out". This was great because they were flexible. Up until the 1984 Olympics I can't remember a day that I ever went into the rink, at least on a regular basis, where it wasn't fun. We were up, very keen, really enjoying it.

We had planned two years earlier, that after the 1984 Olympics, we would retire. That was definitely going to be our last year of competing. We just couldn't live with the fact that our last performance would be what people saw at the Olympics. We so badly wanted to do well at the Worlds following the Olympics. We would come in and just hate looking at each other some days, because it just wasn't working for us. But we still got out there. No one forced us, no one said come in and skate. Every day we would show up at the rink in those three weeks between Olympics and Worlds and look at each other and say, "God, this just isn't working, but I've got to do it." It wasn't until Barb got back into the old boots that things started clicking. Everyone thinks the boots are a joke, but it was no joke. As soon as she got back into those boots and felt comfortable again, we both felt comfortable again and things started to work. I think the reason we kept going was the fact that the performance at the Olympics was not what we wanted everyone in the skating world to remember us by.

Between the Olympics and Worlds, there were lots of days where it just wasn't fun anymore, when we dreaded going into the rink because we knew we weren't skating up to the potential that we had. At that time, it was really the only time in my life that I didn't want to skate, because I couldn't do as well as I knew I could.

It got to the point where we were seriously considering not going to the Worlds, because we just weren't skating the way we knew how. It was almost better to not go. Fade away! But as soon as she put the other boots on, you have no idea! It was incredible! She felt confident again.

Leading up to the Olympics we had not had a good year, Barb had a bad ankle at the beginning of January. She was very tentative about forcing that ankle, especially in a pair of skates that didn't feel right on her feet. She had separated her shoulder in August which set us back two or three weeks. We had scheduled our first competition to be Nationals. We had won every major international previously, so there was no point in risking. We were staying with the same long program. It had been a big success for us. The Canadians was going to be our first competition, and then when she blew her ankle out, we missed that, so that set us back again. It was a combination of a lot of problems. Looking back I think we coped really well.

That last week and a half before the Worlds, it was great! Everything was working. We didn't have to struggle to get through programs, everything worked. It was fun again. It was like someone had just turned the lights on. We had been struggling all year long, getting over injuries, never really being able to skate as well and as comfortably as we wanted to. That last week was a treat. We were so

I can't remember a day that I ever went into the rink, at least on a regular basis, where it wasn't fun. We were up, very keen, really enjoying it.

94

psyched up for the Worlds in Ottawa and we were ready to skate. We were having fun, and we couldn't have given a damn who was out there competing against us. We felt so good. We just wanted to show everyone, that whatever you saw at the Olympics, forget that! This is how we can really skate.

At the Olympics we felt good, but we were still struggling with some injuries. Barb's foot was still bad, and she was struggling with boots a little bit. But enough good things were happening to make us feel confident going into the Olympics. We looked back on the videotape and watched the first part of that short program at the Olympics before Barb's fall, and watched the first part at the Worlds, and it is really close in terms of how good it was, how we looked, how it was going. I would beg you to put them both on, if you couldn't see the boards, and tell me which one was the Olympics and which was the Worlds.

After going to the Olympics in 1980 we were far more prepared, we were ready for everything that happened. We had never been to Yugoslavia, but we had heard a lot. We knew what to expect and we had plenty of experience on a European ice surface. We knew how much of a media bazaar event it was. None of those factors came into play in 1984. We knew how to handle them. We look back and think maybe we shouldn't have done as much press as we did at the 1984 Olympics. When we came to Ottawa for Worlds we did one press conference and then cut them off. I don't know whether that was a key factor or not. Barb felt a lot better that we cut the press off. It didn't bother me that much.

Going into a competition, our attitude has never been, "Let's beat so and so, or we have to place here." It was always, "Let's skate our best and let everything fall where it may." It is not worth getting upset over who you beat or where you place in the long run because skating is a sport where you have so many other factors that you have no control over anyway. You just approached the sport remembering that you skate because you like it. You enjoy getting up there skating and performing.

I think we were very close to feeling that "up" feeling at the Worlds in Helsinki (1983). Things had been going well, we had had a good year. We won two internationals going into Helsinki. Everything was feeling good. We skated well.

We came off the ice and for the first time in our careers, we had skated clean short and clean long programs. That in itself was just the greatest feeling. Who cares where we placed. I went out there and did it twice. It was such a rush. That is how we have to approach the sport. A lot of times you will go out there and skate great, or what you thought was great, and what you thought was the best thing out there, and the judges will pull out marks that say you are second or third. People were saying, "Gee, they should have won, they were better than the other two teams." But it was just that aspect of old skaters being judged on past performances. So you really must make it a thing of personal satisfaction, more than anything else.

The media might ask questions about winning or competitors but we would always answer by talking about what we have to do. We have to go out there and skate well. They didn't really press the issue, "Are you going to beat so and so?"

Going into a competition, our attitude has never been, "Let's beat so-and-so, or we have to place here." It was always, "Let's skate our best and let everything fall where it may."

95

We had really hoped to win a medal at the 1984 Olympics, and we had every reason to believe that we would. After placing third in the 1983 Worlds in Helsinki, after having a lot of people in the skating world saying, "They are going to be the ones to beat next year at the Olympics." Yes, we hoped to win a medal and we had every reason to believe that we would, based on prior performances.

It took us four years of competing at a world level before I really began to realize what I had to do mentally, to put a successful program on the ice. We were getting rapped, and rightly so, for being inconsistent. We brought down one really hot program, and the next program had stupid little mistakes that cost us. I think I know what it boiled down to. In the cases where I was making the mistake or having the problem it was a concentration lapse. It was like, "Well, I'm almost finished, I'll just take a break now." I realized in the past two years, that I could never do that. I had to think about every arm movement, every head movement, every time I moved a foot, a skate, anything. I had to concentrate strictly on doing that. I had to stay totally connected to what I was doing. It took me four years to learn that. No-one sat down with us and said, "What do you really think about when you are out there? You made a mistake, why?" I was never forced to think about why I made a mistake, in terms of mental preparation things. I guess it really struck home at Copenhagen. I fell at a back cross-over with 30 seconds to go and a medal went out the window, just because I wasn't concentrating. I let myself get involved with the audience. It had been a really clean performance, we had done everything well and we only had 30 seconds to go. You could hear the audience behind us, and I let myself drift and start sucking that in, and down I went. I realized that I can't afford to do this. I have to be focusing every step of the way.

The last two years I started really concentrating on what I had to do. I didn't want to ever have to cope with the fact that I screwed up again. So I really started concentrating something wicked. This was before Olympics too. I just never wanted to ever have that hanging over me again. I forced myself to really concentrate, whether or not Barb was feeling great or bad. During that time, prior to the Olympics when she was having some problems, I would say, "Don't worry about that, it will be fine, we will keep working at it." But inside I was really just worrying about myself. I think that was good, because one of us remained consistent. It may sound a bit selfish, but I found that it was the only way I was going to get this job done successfully. Maybe some pairs can cope with worrying about how their partner is doing, and still do their job. I couldn't. I just had to concentrate on what I was doing. I was in touch, timing-wise, with what she was doing but otherwise it was all me. Whether or not she completed the element, or slipped up or something, that didn't connect.

In the last couple of years leading up to important competitions I really started to mentally funnel towards it, really concentrating on what has to be done. I started to block people out, be it parents, coaches, friends, even family and finances. Everyone just sort of started getting pushed aside a little bit as we approached the competition. I found myself thinking more and more about what was coming up, what I wanted to do, and how things were going in preparation for that competition. Driving to the rink, even before I got on

I had to stay totally connected to what I was doing. It took me four years to learn that.

Driving to the rink, even before I got on the ice, I was thinking about what we wanted to do today and what had to be done.

the ice, I was thinking about what we wanted to do today and what had to be done. In social situations I'd be sitting there and the conversation would be getting dull and I'd begin to drift away to my skating.

After falling on the back cross-over in Copenhagen, I said, "I can't believe I did that. Why?" I spent a lot of time trying to work out what I had done to foul up that process. And even now in the show (professional ice show) I realize it. We skate ten times a week. I have fallen maybe 3 times in this whole year, and each time I was in the 'Twilight Zone'. All of a sudden I am on my arse on the rink. "Paul, you are on the ice and I know it is a little bit boring some days, but would you pay attention." When I fall, 10 times out of 10 it is because I'm not concentrating on what I am doing. It may sound kind of strange for a world-level competitor to have that problem but I definitely know that's what it is. After Copenhagen, I don't think I had a fall in competition. I can remember some slips or a technical problem where I didn't have the ability to do the element, but nothing like a fall through lack of concentration.

Everyone coaches and analyzes technically. They look at the tapes and tell you what went wrong, technically, but not in terms of mind set. They don't sit down and say, "Why do you think you didn't do it, what was bothering you, what are you thinking about?" It is funny because now I think it should be a mandatory thing. And it is not. It was definitely a lack. I don't blame my coaches for it. For the longest time I think the coach viewed himself as someone to technically get the skater ready. Give them the skills to do it. How the athlete coped with the outside situation was 'to each his own'. I think a coach thinks that by the time you get to a world level, you know how to do that. I don't think ninety percent of the kids do.

Once I recognized that I had to concentrate on each move, I constantly practised concentrating. I knew then what I had to do. I knew what I had to be thinking. To put it into practice, during training sessions, and at the rink, I just forced myself to continually concentrate during practice and during run-throughs. In the last two years, for those two hours, I concentrated completely on what I was actually out there trying to do. I can feel it. I am very conscious of what my feet are doing. I am stepping through each and every step, and I feel each one. And the ones I don't feel, I usually fall down on. I find myself very much in contact with the body. I know exactly what I have to do. Mentally I am concentrating very much on what I am doing. I wish I had realized it five years ago. It made me mad that no one had sat me down and said, "Why? You were doing back cross-overs, why did you fall?" I had to do that myself. Everyone said, "The rest of the performance was great, you look super, you had a little fall." It wasn't until it cost me a medal, that I really realized. I often thought, god, why didn't someone take me aside and ask, "Why did I fall?" "Why do you think you are slipping up out there?"

We always went into the long program feeling very confident with everything we were doing. That was a good move on our coaches part because we always went in knowing that there wasn't anything in there that we couldn't do. So you went out there feeling really good about it.

Everyone coaches and analyzes technically. They look at the tapes and tell you what went wrong, technically, but not in terms of mind set.

97

Leading up to a competition we always gave ourselves a day or two each week to do complete simulation run throughs. The day before we would say, "Tomorrow we are going to warm-up and then we will do the program."

I never used to feel good on a warm-up at a competition. I felt my skates were on the wrong feet. I used to come off warm-ups and say, "God, I wish I hadn't even gone out there, because I don't feel any better." I got used to accepting that if I felt that way, it was okay, it was fine. "You are going to be all right." But for the first couple of years it was awful. Just awful. I would come off and feel just terrible and then worry about feeling terrible. I had to learn to plan my warm-ups and to accept the fact that less than perfect in warm-up was okay, it was fine. I could come off feeling like that and everything would be okay, once I started into my program.

For the last couple of years our warm-up was always totally pre-planned. We knew what we wanted to do. You have to find out what you want to do in the warm-up to feel good about yourself. So we always planned exactly what we wanted to do and we knew the order in which we wanted to do it. We knew that was what worked for us. We had learned that by experimenting, which is one reason why we went into so many competitions.

There is a definite pattern right up to the start. If you're the first skater, the warm-up ends, and there might be 10 seconds while the skaters get off the ice. "Ladies and gentlemen, our first competitor is. . ." and you go on. I used to like to get off the ice, but if we happened to be the first couple I'd think, it's good because you get to keep the feel of the ice. If we were the second, third or fourth skater, we'd get off the ice. We'd always make it a point to not watch the other competitors. We'd get in underneath and just walk and walk, keep moving, keep warm. I used that time to refresh myself on the things that I wanted to be sure I did right, things like lifts and throws with Barb. I tend to rush those things in a competition situation. I had to remember, "When you go into a throw or lift go with her timing, just relax, go with her." So I always made a mental note of reminding myself. I could "feel" those thoughts.

As I walked back and forth I would imagine a throw, a certain lift and I would feel my body doing it. For things that I was comfortable with and for those where I didn't feel that element of rushing, I didn't feel the need to do the timing in imagery before I went. As I was walking I would go through the program once. I'd be saying, "Open lift, that's fine, spins, that's fine. . .that's fine." I could feel myself doing it. I would say, "That's fine," knowing I felt good about it.

Shortly before the competition was a very anxious period, for both of us - walk, walk, walk. "Let me get out there. I want to do this." How do I feel when they call my name? Terror! There are just so many emotions, it was terror. Sometimes on the ice we'd be standing there and they'd call your name and I'd look down at Barb, "What am I doing this for?" You wanted to do it, but all those fears, all those things that could go wrong and the implications, just came like a train. "God, if this doesn't go." But then I would say, "No!" I'd instantly shift all of a sudden, I'd snap into this, "Let's go!" "Get your position." "Concentrate." That time frame!

I had to learn to plan my warm-ups and to accept the fact that less than perfect in warm-up was okay, it was fine. I could come off feeling like that and everything would be okay, once I started into my program.

98

Sometimes in a skating competition as soon as the skater before you has finished and they step off the ice, you can get on the ice. During that time, judges are getting their cards ready and you can get out and warm-up. There's the buzz of the crowd about the skater that has just finished, and maybe about you coming on. It is during that time when you are out there, that minute and 15 seconds, that your thoughts can drift to all the things that could go wrong. It is your turn. This is it, there's no other chance! It is a one shot deal. This is where you need to develop a plan to cope and to stay positive.

We always wanted to get on the ice right away to get the feel for the ice again. At that point we both knew what we had to do to get through this. We didn't talk, or very rarely, just little reminders: "Remember to bend, remember to breathe, just relax", just little words like that. You already knew that, but you said it anyway just out of habit, or as a way to deal with nervousness. I got to a point where during that time, I wasn't even aware of outside things or distracting thoughts. I was so focused on what I had to do to get the job done successfully.

As soon as they announced our name and we came out and got in our starting position, it was like, "Now I've got to concentrate on this." Just waiting for the music to start, was like time had stopped. As soon as the music started I shifted my focus to what I was going to do. At one point you get very light, like everything disappears, even the crowd. Outside thoughts are gone. They are always brushed away. There are definitely no negative thoughts, like those fearful anxieties we had in that minute before we started. They are gone. They came, they went. Then it was strictly concentrating on getting very much in touch: where I was, how everything felt, how my blades were running. Just getting very much in touch with my body so that I knew what to do with it, based on what I was feeling. "Let's bend, let's get down, let's loosen up."

In that little minute and 15 seconds, it is funny how much you think about. I was using that time, as well, to keep in touch, to know how I was feeling, how was the ice; is it fast, is it slow, and how are all the lights? It all takes place in that little time frame, the anxious terror to the complete concentration. By the time I stood there I knew where I was at, I knew where the body was at, and I knew what I had to do with it to get it through. When I was performing best during the event my focus was always on exactly what I was doing at that instant.

After Barb's fall in Sarajevo, my immediate reaction was, "You've got to finish the program." It is automatic. Instantly you put the fall aside. You've got to finish no matter what. We both went into that finishing. It was just a matter of executing everything that needed to be done. Everything after that went well, no problems. The best part was over, the double twists, they were great, we were fine. There was no break in concentration in terms of what was to come, no panic, no problems in getting back together. Because we've practised that so much, doing it is automatic, it just happens.

After that. . .it was awful! Everything we had hoped and dreamed for as skaters, was gone. There was nothing anybody was going to do to change it. That was a devastating thought, especially after coming in feeling pretty good, feeling like you were ready, like you had the

As I walked back and forth I would imagine a throw, a certain lift and I would feel my body doing it.

How do I feel when they call my name? Terror!

99

goods and were ready to deliver them. I look back now and I feel good about going out and doing the long program. It didn't go great, but it was all right. At that point I think I was playing for home. For us, there was no point in doing the long. It was over. All those things that you had little doubts about before, you now had serious doubts about whether you could do them.

I guess we just didn't want to speak to anyone. We thought about everyone at home and our coaches. They'd been through it all and getting the gold just wasn't going to happen. I remember going in the morning after the short program, and the only practice we did was at 6:00 a.m. - that is hard enough when you are feeling good. Lewis didn't come to the rink but Sandra was there. The three of us were standing around the rink. We couldn't even bring ourselves to skate. Our music was playing, like who needs it? How can this happen? Four years of hard work to have something like that happen. "It will never happen to me." Then there we were. It happens. You are out of it. It's over. You are right out of the scene. It's a one shot deal. Not many people truly appreciate how hard that is. That's it baby! In skating you don't get that feeling of working your way through the preliminaries, through the quarters, through the semis, to build up a sort of feel or momentum to carry you through. You build yourself up and all of a sudden it is over. We would have just as soon come home. It was awful!

We had the day off between the short and the long. There was that one practice that morning. That was it for the rest of the day. There was no other ice. We went through our off-ice program and even that we didn't feel like doing. It was also hard to go back to the village because everyone in the building knew as well. How do you face a person who has had the bottom pulled out from under them. Everyone was very good about it, but still, I'm sure it was as difficult for them as it was for us. It didn't help the whole feeling within the building and within the other athletes. I'm sure it brought back to them, the same fears everyone has, of not doing well. That didn't make us feel good, because we realized while being in the building, we made the rest of the building feel uncomfortable. It was real hard.

We stayed in our room. The rest of the skaters were there, and they were a little bit more in touch. They really knew where we were coming from. They didn't feel good about it but they took Barb out of the building, and I hardly saw her that day. It wasn't like we'd just missed and were a place or two out and still knew we had a shot. It was gone. Seventh place in skating, forget it.

The next day we skated the long. We went through it all. I went through all the same things but it was just like a chore. Like who needs it? We went through it but the over-riding thought was, "Let's just get this over with." And it was very hard to concentrate on anything. You didn't know what to do because we so badly just wanted to get out of Sarajevo. And it showed. I'm sure I missed the double loop, and a couple of throws. It just wasn't a good performance for us. It didn't make any difference in the standings. That overriding feeling - we just couldn't get rid of it.

You have to accept the fact that in the pairs dancing, the other person who is out there with you, is trying every bit as hard as you are, and wants to succeed every bit as much as you do. You do your best

We didn't talk, or very rarely, just little reminders: "Remember to bend, remember to breathe, just relax"; just little words like that.

100

to ultimately help them. That's part of the deal. That is the way it works so I wasn't mad at Barb. I was mad at the fact that there was no going back. We had done 5 World Championships. We knew all about it. I felt utterly powerless. No control at all. Just get it over with. Just get out of here. As soon as it happened that night, it was like we'd already written the whole event off. We were already thinking about, "Now what do we get ready for?" After the actual event was over we wanted to get out, but we sat there until the end of it all. In our minds we weren't on the ice. We weren't at Sarajevo anymore, we were now back in Western Ontario getting ready for the Worlds. We started to think seriously about getting out there and training again.

I got a little bit frustrated at the Olympics, because we wanted to get out the day after the long program and I think we could have. They said, it wouldn't look good. Having the position we had as a team, being a medal holder, being the second Olympics, being one of the seniors on the skating team, they said, "We want you to stay." I said, "What do you want me here for? I'm not movitating and the other skaters won't mind because we've had a very bad experience; they don't know what to say to us. Why don't you just let us go home, and they'll feel better when we've gone." The ladies were still to go. I think we were the first skating event finished. We were like a cloud hanging over everybody. We should have gone home.

Someone should be sitting down doing this type of scenario; what would you do here? Someone comes in who is a serious medal contender, it doesn't happen. What kind of an influence is that going to have, especially when everyone is staying in the same building? Everyone's eating together. Take all the situations that could happen, and say what should that person stage? Should they be given a choice? Should we send them home? No-one had done that. It is just like what an athlete has do to. You pre-plan your events. What influence does a disaster like that have on the rest of the athletes on the team? In Sarajevo you couldn't miss each other in an elevator, you couldn't miss each other in a staircase. When you are that close and have that many people on a very high emotional level in one building, and have something like that happen, what should you do?

For Worlds it was almost like the perfect preparation. The coach was there to oversee everything. Every time we went out and had practice sessions, they were flawless from beginning to end. The coach would start looking for things to tell us, like "Look ahead, stretch a little." He had to search for little things that come and go, just so he could feed back something to us. It was like the homework had been done. In the long program at the Olympics because of what happened, we didn't have the desire nor the will to go out and execute it. At the Worlds it was totally different. Everyone was going in with the original plan. (Paul and Barb won the 1984 World Championships with a flawless performance in Ottawa.)

Our training environment and our competition environment were always very similar. It was always a good atmosphere in which to work. Although Sandra was the one responsible for giving the program that flare and that uniqueness, we always wanted to skate for Lewis at a practice session. We had that feeling of wanting to go over and say, "Did you see that?" Even if Lewis was coaching someone

When I was performing best during the event my focus was always on exactly what I was doing at that instant.

101

else, and we put our program on, we wanted to skate well, because we knew he was looking at us out of the corner of his eye all the time, even if he was teaching someone else. I don't know whether he consciously did it, or if it was a natural thing he did to the skaters. He did it to all of them. You always wanted to hear from him if it looked good, or what needed to be changed. He always gave lots of positive feedback and he was very much in touch with where we were and what we were doing. I really enjoyed him. I can listen to him talk for hours. I enjoy his presence. I think we got along real well.

I first went to him when I was 16. I was still grasping with who I was, where I was going, what I wanted to do, what I thought I could do. I looked up to him. Then we grew closer. I can remember when we were having a real tough time between the Olympics and the Worlds. He didn't know what to do. Previously, no matter how we had felt, no matter how bad things were going, he always made us feel good, and knew how to get us going. Up until then, he always knew how to work us emotionally, socially, technically or whatever. He knew how to get us to where he wanted us to be. All of a sudden he couldn't do it. We knew it was frustrating for him, because he couldn't help us. I think the best things that came from that was looking for strength within ourselves. We tried to take on an attitude of, "Hey! Just enjoy it! Don't give up. Whether it be life in general, or in terms of skating." A difficult experience can make you realize how much easier it is to approach anything, a training day, a competition day or anything, if you are up. Make the best of it. Enjoy it.

For the winter athletes, there is no other event similar to the Olympics. For the summer athletes there are the Pan-Ams and the Commonwealth Games. They are both multi-sport, fairly high media profile events, that give a bit of that zoo-like feeling. You are just another act in the ring.

I remember when I went to the 1980 Olympics, I had never met Ken Read, or Steve Podborski. These were guys that you had read about in the sport pages. All the high-level athletes from all the other countries in the world, who you had read about, were right there. It was like being in 'celebrity city'. There is no other multi-sport event like that, so you never get exposed to it until you're at the Olympics. For me the first Olympics was terrible on the concentration. Wow! It was like everything that I'd always dreamed of. The fact that I was there to do a job was secondary. It was very bad. I often said, "Whose fault is that? Is it my fault? Or my coaches' fault? My association's fault?" I didn't have the answer. It seemed to me that people were more interested in telling me not to lose my ID card, instead of spending a little bit more time in trying to relate that experience of being part of that really big spectrum. Going into Sarajevo, I had a completely different focus. It was like this is just another competition; I'm here to do my job. My main purpose is to get that job done and do it well. The first time, I got caught up in all the distractions. Horrendously! After that, when we had new kids on the team, I always made a point of telling them, "Just remember your first job is to skate. You are going to be in a village of 1500 other athletes. You are going to see the bobsledders and skiers, and you are all going to finish at different times. You are going to see the Ken Reads and

What influence does a disaster like that have on the rest of the athletes on the team?

For me the first Olympics was terrible on the concentration. Wow! It was like everything that I'd always dreamed of. The fact that I was there to do a job was secondary.

102

Steve Podborskis. Just try and remember what you are really there for."

I think a lot more time has to be spent on getting kids ready mentally, finding out what they need to do mentally to be successful. I think a lot of kids have the physical skills to skate with the best of them. But whether or not they've got the mental skills is another question. They need to know what will work for them and what they need to do to make it work for them. I don't think any of us really sat down with anyone to seriously consider what we needed to do to be successful. How do the Russians come onto the scene and win or place in the first year of the competition? I've got a feeling we only give the kids the physical skills, and let them struggle with how they are going to cope with the scene.

I think a coach could do a lot. It is not something that is terribly complex. For some kids it might be more complex because they have a lot of outside problems as well. More time should be spent sitting down and talking and evaluating. "Now, let's go through the week, or let's go through the day, or let's go through the program, and evaluate. Did you miss this for some other reason? You're hitting 9, or 10 out of 10, now a 7. How come you missed it?" From what we've seen, when people miss, it is often not because they don't have the technical ability, because they hit ninety-five percent of them in training during the week. The mental control is probably the area for the most improvement.

I think coaching-wise, off ice program-wise, facility-wise, there is no shortage. There is no shortage of good coaches in this country either. I really think that where the fine line lies is in mental coaching.

The association has got this sort of mentality that you have to stay in skating for a long time to develop whatever it is they feel you need to get on the podium, to win. I think most of what actually happens is letting the kids learn themselves, taking three or four years at Worlds to find out what they need up here mentally. They certainly don't lack the technical skills. I look at what Barb and I won with this year, and we did virtually the same stuff technically that we did five years ago. We did no other major triples or anything, but we learned how to mentally get ourselves through the program. I look back at our first Worlds, and okay maybe a couple of elements were above our heads. It is fine to keep trying that sort of thing, your first or second year in, but you have got to sit down afterwards and say, "Now I missed this because. . .Maybe I still haven't got the technical skill for it, maybe it is something I should give another 6 months, and if I still haven't got the ability, it is time to shelve it."

After 1981, we had considered giving up because in the Worlds we had finished 11th, and again 11th, so we were going nowhere fast. We were thinking, "Let's get out." A really good move on the part of the association was sitting down with us and saying, "We really do believe you've got potential. Stick around a little bit longer." We finished 7th the next year, and 4th and then 1st.

Everyone keeps pushing, physically pushing. But are they mentally pushing as well? I don't think they are. That's why kids who look like they should be good, just aren't. I think post-competition evaluation is a real critical factor. Sitting down and learning about the kid

I don't think any of us really sat down with anyone to seriously consider what we needed to do to be successful.

103

Everyone keeps pushing, physically pushing. But are they mentally pushing as well? I don't think they are. That's why kids who look like they should be good, just aren't.

instead of just coming back in and saying, "Well you missed your double axel, let's do some more."

I think the mental set is probably the biggest area for improvement. If you start as a Junior, talking about it and trying some things, by the time you get into your first Senior Canadians, then maybe your first Worlds, you've got the mental skills to get you through. Maybe you come onto the scene and, boom!, third or fourth in the world, first time. People change, and grow over time but there has to be a faster way. There just has to be.

I don't think we use our best knowledge and experience. Let's use the experience, let's learn, let's find out what was good, what was bad, and take it from there.

12(b)
BARBARA UNDERHILL
1984 WORLD CHAMPION — FIGURE SKATING PAIRS

Before our short program at the 1984 Olympics, the adrenalin was flowing and I can remember looking around. There was so much excitement in the air. We had a lot of press going into it. We thought we could win or get a medal. I was so looking forward to getting the Olympics over with and moving on. There was such a build up. Finally that time had come, I was excited and I was up for it. Then I crashed!

I realize, when I compare the Olympics with the 1984 Worlds, that I have got to keep myself 'down' before I go out on the ice or it doesn't work. I have to stay calm, and completely focus on what I am doing.

At the Olympics a simple edge just slid out from me going into a sit spin. It wasn't one of the things we were worried about. It was just so stupid. Up to that point in the program it was great. Things were going so well. It was like we knew that we were going to do great. Then, all of a sudden, that one little slip.

Before the 1984 Worlds, I was much more careful, more focused, because I knew what had happened in the Olympics. I knew I had to really, really concentrate every step of the way. I could not break my concentration for a second. Before the Worlds I was much quieter,

I realize, when I compare the Olympics with the 1984 Worlds, that I have got to keep myself 'down' before I go out on the ice or it doesn't work. I have to stay calm, and completely focus on what I am doing.

105

much more to myself. Before the Olympics there were a lot of people around, the Canadian team and the other athletes from Canada were in the audience. Everybody was cheering. It was too busy. There was too much going on and I don't think I was focusing one hundred percent on what I was doing. I can remember warming-up. There wasn't really an area to warm-up in except behind the seats, so you could see the audience and everything that was going on. I can remember warming-up and getting really excited because I was listening to the crowd, whereas at the Worlds, I warmed-up alone in the dressing room, by myself, away from everything. I could just kind of get into myself. I didn't have that quiet time away from everything when we competed at the Olympics. It was much more out in the open. It was harder to get away. Actually, that could have been it. At the Worlds I knew I needed that time alone.

At the Olympics I was just raring to go, and I was jumping around. I should have been a bit more calm, and taken it just a little bit easier. I think I was just a little bit too hyper and excited before the Olympics. We may also have been a little more apprehensive, a little more nervous, because we hadn't competed all year. If we had competed we would have felt a little more confident, and a little more with it. When it comes right down to it, the reason for that slip was something else.

When it goes well, I concentrate every step of the way. When it doesn't go well you often don't realize you've lost the concentration until it already happens. You just drift. It is like you are sitting here and kind of staring, and you fall into a daze. You only realize it when you snap back. You think, "Oh my God, what happened?! That means I'm not concentrating on what I'm doing." Going into it I've got to be thinking about it. If it doesn't go right I wasn't concentrating enough. Once you've slipped or fallen, you're so worried about picking yourself back up that it is hard to know why your concentration is broken. You have to immediately focus again. Sometimes you don't snap back soon enough.

Before the event I normally get to the rink and immediately get changed into my training clothes. I go up to the top of the rink, above the audience where the ice looks clear. I just look at the ice and trace out our program on the ice in my mind. I'm looking at the ice and seeing us skating the routine and going through every move, tracing it out. People must think I'm crazy. What is she doing staring out at the ice? I usually jog around for a while to get warmed-up. I start doing my stretches and my normal routine. I do a lot of stationary jumping and jogging on the spot. It gets my heart rate up and just gets me warmed-up. Then I get quiet and go to my dressing room.

I've always done that mental tracing in the rink. It helps me to get the right feel and also the feel of the lighting. Inside the dressing room, the lights are much dimmer. If you go out onto the ice, without having gone out earlier, the lights are so bright that it is very shocking and it is scary. So I have to kind of get adjusted to that lighting. I also like to walk out when the crowd is in the audience and the judges are there, just to kind of get a feel for the audience, the air. Without that adaptation period, going from such a quiet dressing room onto the ice is difficult. It is a big contrast and sometimes it

When it goes well, I concentrate every step of the way. When it doesn't go well you often don't realize you've lost the concentration until it already happens. You just drift.

106

throws you off a little bit. So you have to know what to expect when you get out there.

When I am finished doing my hair and my make-up and everything, I do a little bit more warming up in the dressing room, usually stretching on the floor. After that, it is usually time to get my skates on. My skates go on about fifteen minutes before we go out onto the ice. Then I do a couple of things with my skates on, in the dressing room or in the hall closer to the ice, just basically to get my body loosened up. I like to do a lot of jumping on the spot, because I find it gets my adrenalin going and my heart rate up.

Then it is time to go out for the warm-up. We usually go out, do a couple of laps together, then break off and do our own single jumps, and warm-up on our own for a couple of minutes. We get together and talk about it. We discuss what we are going to warm-up before we go out onto the ice. If we have extra time left over, we decide whether we need to warm-up anything else. If we are first to skate, then when we have a minute left, we go over to our coach by the boards and rest. If we are not first, I get away from everybody. Usually I walk in the back hall. I go through the program in my mind. I go from the beginning, and I can hear the music. Sometimes I even go through the movements when I stand there.

Usually I go through the moves in my mind, really concentrating. If a certain thing is not going properly, then I think about everything going into that certain element. Say it is the double flip I was having problems with. Well, I look through everything in my mind that I should think about on that jump. Stay straight edge going in, keep my foot back, etc. etc., just little things that I have to think about when I go out there.

I'm visualizing as well as thinking that I've got to do this or that. Paul is usually pacing around, and every once in a while he says, "Remember to do this, remember to do that." Little comments here and there. But normally we don't talk that much before we skate.

Once we get out on the ice before starting I am still thinking about the program. Just mental reminders, especially if there is something I have to work on or if there is one thing bothering me, one thing that can go wrong. I think about what I have to do, to do it well. Usually when the last set of marks are being called for the previous skater, Paul and I hold hands and look at one another as if to say, "This is it." Just to kind of let each other know that you are there.

During the last couple of years I started trying to follow a consistent focusing pattern and to think more about the program. Before that I used to just go out and do everything by feel. Then I realized you have to be thinking or concentrating the whole time. You have to have exact thoughts going into everything.

I think we learned that after the Worlds in Copenhagen. Paul and I were skating a perfectly clean program and we could have won a medal there. We were coming around to the last 30 seconds, and it way home free. Paul was thinking, "This is it," and all of a sudden his edge slipped out from under him and he fell. As soon as you let your concentration go, you've had it. You have to keep it there the whole time, and I never used to do that. We realized through experience that you always have to be thinking or focusing on the right things. You can't look into the audience, you can't think about Mum, and

I like to do a lot of jumping on the spot, because I find it gets my adrenalin going and my heart rate up.

107

you can't let anything else get into your mind except exactly what you are doing.

We talked about what happened, and we both figured it out. That is exactly how you have to do it. That is why it shouldn't have happened in Sarajevo. I can't explain how it happened. It could have been a million things. It was one little edge that slipped out. I can't remember what I was thinking at that time. I just know that edge just slipped out on me. That was it!

Right after I slipped, it was like, "Put it behind you, you have to do the rest of it, you can worry about it when you get off the ice." We still had the rest of the program to do, and we didn't want to miss anything else. I just had to completely concentrate, even more, after that happened. We had to do the rest of it and if we had made any other errors, that would have been even worse.

As soon as something like that happens, it is almost like, "This can't be happening. This is a dream. It didn't happen." Then all of a sudden I got off the ice and it sunk in what had really happened. Once it sinks in it really hits you. When you are out on the ice you don't have time to let it sink in. You keep moving, the music keeps going and you have to continue.

That was a trauma. It was awful. Up until the Olympics I had a lot of problems with my skates. Because of the skates I was in, I wasn't skating up to what I normally could skate. I also had injuries. All through that, Paul was very, very strong. I looked towards him for strength because I needed somebody solid. As soon as the short program was over, Paul was crushed. It was weird because all of a sudden I felt it was up to me to be the strong one. I will always remember the next morning. We had a practice at 6:00 in the morning after the short program, and neither of us had slept all night. We were just absolutely devastated, and we had to come to this practice. Paul's face looked like a blank sheet. It was like nothing was there, nothing at all. I can remember the exact way I felt. I knew it was me that had fallen, and I had never ever seen him like that before, destroyed. I was the one having to say, "Come on Paul, you can't give up now." And he said to me, "There is really no point." When he said that to me I was crushed, because he never gives up. He's very strong, and when he said that, it was like a blow to the stomach. So we did the practice, which was like putting ourselves on automatic pilot. We just did what we had to do. I think we had a day off in there before the long program. I was trying to stay up, and I knew it was driving Paul mad, because he was in his room all the time, always by himself, very down, very devastated. My coach and I were feeling like, we've got to do something to get him up. I think I was okay, I knew that it was over for us but I knew we still had seventy percent to go. I knew we had to give it our best shot and I knew if we were moping around we weren't going to do it. I felt as though I had to be strong, but when we went out to do the long program, it was so hard to go out there knowing that there was no way we could get a medal. All we really wanted to do was go out there and skate well. All of a sudden we were out there and we were trying hard, but it just didn't have the sparkle it usually has.

I think if we had done well in the short program, the long program would have been good. We knew because of the fall that there was no

During the last couple of years I started trying to follow a consistent focusing pattern and to think more about the program. Before that I used to just go out and do everything by feel.

108

possible way we could move up. It was almost like we had given up. We knew ourselves that our goal was gone.

One of the hardest things, when we came home from the Olympics, was when we arrived at the airport. At the Olympics, we were with people who understood what we had been through. So we kind of put it aside, and so did they. As soon as we hit the airport and walked out, it was like it all came rushing back to us. The cameras were on Brian Orser and Gaetan Boucher and we were walking in at the same time. The way the people reacted to us was hard, because they didn't know what to say to us and we didn't know what to say to them. We just wanted to forget it and put it past us and just move on to the Worlds. They felt they had to say something, and they were really sorry. It seemed like a funeral situation. You never really know what to say to a person. No matter what you say it doesn't really help. It was really hard to deal with the people.

When we got home from the Olympics we tried to stay away from everyone and everything including the press. We didn't do any press once we arrived home from the Olympics. We held one press conference before we skated at Worlds, but that was all. Our coaches told our publicity person that we would give one press conference, and that was it. They do take a lot out of you.

Between the Olympics and the Worlds it was very, very difficult. It was hard because I would come into the rink and I couldn't skate like I knew I could. There were problems between Paul and I. Everything all of a sudden became very tense and we are not used to working or skating in a tense atmosphere. There was a lot of tension between us. When I got home from the Olympics I got into a new pair of skates right away. I had them waiting for me when I got home. I got into these skates and normally it takes me 4 or 5 days before I feel right in them. Well these skates were not working for me at all. I was having a lot of problems, and was getting very frustrated. I wasn't feeling good about myself nor were we feeling good about each other. I was in tears when I got off the ice and we would talk and cry and ask, "What is the problem?"

One night we went to the Cricket Club in Toronto to do an exhibition, because the coaches said they wanted us to get out in front of people and judges just to see if we could do it. It was a disaster. We were ready to hang up our skates. We were so frustrated. We just didn't do well at all. So we came in the next day, and both of us were to the point where we were so frustrated we were almost ready to give up. I walked in and saw Paul sitting in the lobby and it looked as though he wasn't going to come and skate. I put my skates on and went out anyway and tried to skate. I kept thinking, "It is going to be okay today, today it is going to be fine." Then I knew after I had tried a few things it wasn't going to work. I came off the ice and I was crying. Paul came over to me and we sat at the side of the boards and I cried. We just tried to come up with a reason for why things weren't working for me. What could possibly be the problem? Then our coaches called us into the office and we just kind of said, "What else can we do? There's nothing else we can do." The phone rang, I guess I sort of sensed that my coaches were going to say, "That's it. Pack up your skates." So I walked out of the office and went out onto the ice. I went over to Brian Orser, the Canadian men's champion, and I cried

Our coaches told our publicity person that we would give one press conference, and that was it. They do take a lot out of you.

That day I skated and skated and skated, until midnight. I just didn't want to get off the ice because all of a sudden I knew it was possible again.

109

on his shoulder a little bit. Then he said to me, "Why don't you go back into last year's boots? They worked for you then, it is worth a shot." They were downstairs in my car, for some strange reason. I ran down and brought the skates up. Paul put the new blades on my old boots. I went out and at first I felt a little wobbly because the other ones were so strong, but after a while I knew it was going to work. That day I skated and skated and skated, until midnight. I just didn't want to get off the ice because all of a sudden I knew it was possible again. I didn't feel clumsy out there. Everything was flowing naturally. Paul and I skated, it was unbelievable. We came in early the next day to skate. We were so high, so ready to go. It was like all of a sudden our problem had been solved and we knew that we could do it and we were ready. From then on we were doing clean run-throughs every day. We were the happiest people around and it was unbelievable that two people could change so quickly.

If you don't know what the problem is then that causes a problem because it causes other problems. Mental problems. I didn't know whether it was me or what it was. I started to get real frustrated, down on myself, depressed and so everyone else thought it was me. It was a vicious circle.

To compete well, I think it is really important for athletes to know what to expect when they go to an Olympic Games. If no-one has helped you know what to expect and you have not been in a major games situation, you really don't know. In 1980 we didn't really have a clue. There were so many different things going on. The opening ceremony, all these different athletes, all these different things are going on, and you are part of it. It is so exciting. You are not really concentrating on the one thing you came there to do.

I really think athletes need input so they know how to focus in on their own performance and how to keep everything else outside until the event is over.

In 1980, we found out that we were going to the Olympics two weeks beforehand. I really don't think that was fair. You should know at least six months before. Timing is such an important part of sport. You have to work your way up, set your goal and peak at the proper moment. If you don't know until two weeks ahead that you are going to be competing in the Olympics it is impossible to prepare properly. In our case we knew that we would likely win the senior pairs championship in 1980. But even though we were the top in Canada, they still didn't know whether they were going to send us because we weren't ranked in the top half in our sport. We should know in advance that if we are the top in Canada, we are going to go automatically. We didn't know that.

I think it is important for the Canadian Olympic Association to send the less experienced kids even though they may not be in the top half of their sport. They should be sent. Four years later, they're going to know what it is like and understand how to deal with it. I just felt so much more experienced the second time around.

I think a good way of teaching concentration is the mental imagery that I use a lot. A good concentration exercise for skaters is to take them off the ice, sit them down, play their music and have them close their eyes and go through their program in their head. They have to focus on every little thing. Initially you could sit them down and have

110

them talk it out: "'Okay I'm starting now, I'm skating backwards into my double flip jump, I've got to think of this, I've got to think of this, etc." They could talk out the program so they know what they are supposed to think about, so they don't just go through the motions without using their head. As an experienced skater, I look back at some performances I went through when I first started. I went through many without really thinking. I was just kind of going through by feel. It is a scary kind of feeling! You get off and go "Woo, is it over?" Because you weren't really there. You weren't actually concentrating each step of the way. You have to learn to be able to do that because with the pressure in that situation, you really have to know how to handle it. You get so hyped up, the adrenalin is flowing, you get so tense and say, "Oh my God, here I go". You have to try and stay calm and relaxed, so that you can think and focus properly.

I found we worked a lot better in a much more relaxed situation, and in Toronto it was very relaxed. Our coaches, Paul and myself got along really really well. It was a family type thing. We would come in, we'd joke around, we'd have fun. We'd get serious, but it wasn't ever, "Do this, do that!" It was never like that. We had as much input into it as the coaches did. We have never had anybody constantly on our tails. If our coach wasn't there that day we still worked just as hard. When he did come in that was great. He was a motivator. It wasn't like he pushed us, but he was able to motivate us. As soon as he walked in the door I felt like skating, but the days that he wasn't there I still knew I had to do it. It was easier if he was there. More than anything, it was the mood that he set. He would come in singing, telling jokes. It was so enjoyable to come into the rink, because we had fun.

At one point we went into the States, and we were taught by a coach who was much more strict. He was the type that told you what to do and if you didn't do it, he made you do it over and over again. I found that we didn't work as well in that stressful kind of atmosphere. I would actually be nervous for the lessons. I didn't like that at all. I would get to the point where it wasn't enjoyable. I think that you have to enjoy what you are doing to do it well.

It is very important for coaches to be positive. I really noticed a difference in how athletes feel about themselves, if their coaches are positive, as opposed to being negative. One skater's coach is always saying, "You did this wrong, you did this wrong". He never says, "You did well." That skater is very insecure, and she doesn't feel good about herself. Skaters who are always getting positive feedback are obviously going to be more positive about themselves. They are going to be more confident, and they are going to project that from the ice.

Our coach would always point out what we did wrong in a positive way. He would say, "Okay, try it again. One more time." It was never, "What did you do that for? Do it again! What do you think I just told you?" It was never with that tone of voice. It was always, "Okay, what are you doing? Come on, get out there again." It was more light in manner, he was never down on us. He was always up on us and that helped in getting his point across.

It is very important for coaches to be positive. I really noticed a difference in how athletes feel about themselves, if their coaches are positive, as opposed to being negative.

13(a)

GRANT MAIN & KEVIN NEUFELD

1984 OLYMPIC CHAMPIONS — ROWING, MEN'S 8 — PERSPECTIVE OF CREW

**GRANT MAIN
KEVIN NEUFELD
ROWING**

- 1985 World Championships — 5th (four without Coxswain)
- Gold Medalist (eight with Coxswain) at the 1984 Olympic Games
- 1984 Rotsee International Regatta — 1st (eight with Coxswain)
- 1983 World Championships — 8th (eight with Coxswain)
- 1983 Rotsee International Regatta — 2nd (eight with Coxswain)

Grant: Prior to the heats I felt ready. I think everyone else did too. A lot of that had to do with the fact that we had raced internationally and had tested our speed. We knew that we could go with anyone in the world. It was just a matter of putting it together. We had done two really good weeks of training that had sort of pulled everyone together, and everyone was feeling really positive.

I don't think there's any crew out there that could have trained harder than we did. I'm pretty sure everyone in the boat would agree with that. We put in a lot of hours, and a lot of quality work, which means intense in a short period of time, and not just going through the motions.

Kevin: For the first heat, I don't know if it was because I was at the Olympics, but I was thinking a lot about what I had done to get there, and all the work I had put in, and the sacrifices, and just thinking, "Okay, it's all coming down now. This is what you've been dreaming about. Let's go." I was just getting over-motivated. I was too anxious, putting the goal before the task at hand. Just thinking about winning instead of thinking about what I was doing in my seat so I could win. Fortunately it was just a heat and I had time to work that out.

We put in a lot of hours, and a lot of quality work, which means intense in a short period of time, and not just going through the motions.

113

One unforeseen thing that happened, and which helped, was the wind. We had anticipated, from what they were saying, that the prevailing winds were a cross-tail. You kind of hope that it's not going to be a direct cross-wind. And the longer we were there the more it seemed like we could be racing in that. And in the heat it was a cross-tail wind. That worried me a little bit. I think it throws uncertainty in the whole boat. That is something that I worked out between the heat and the final. I decided to get used to the fact that I could be rowing in those kind of conditions. Preparing myself to do that helped me win the final, especially given that the conditions weren't there. It was more of a head-wind if anything. So I was ready for a head-wind, and more, so to speak.

Grant: Prior to the Olympics, the one hassle that stands out concerned equipment. Some guys on the crew, and the coach, had to take it upon themselves to get us the best possible equipment to train in. I don't think that should be a worry of athletes, especially when the focus is on winning. You don't like a cloud hanging over your head, thinking, "What sort of equipment are we going to be using? Are we going to get the best shot or are we going to be behind the eight ball?"

Kevin: I mean athletes are out there busting their butts every day, 365 days a year, and without them you haven't got a Canadian Rowing Association. Without athletes it's pointless. The association has to just keep in mind that they're supposed to be working with these athletes and not against them. And I think that's been lost sometimes. Since the Olympics I think this has been worked out.

The Olympics was just another race, another stepping stone, and it was all in the plan, it's what our goal was, it was what we were gearing for, but we had been gearing for it for a long time. It was just another goal that we were trying to reach. Everyone was a bit wide eyed that it was the Olympics, but I don't think anyone was intimidated by it.

Our goal was to win. Every guy in this crew had that intensity and that desire that you knew every time, no matter what the odds were, they'd die on the end of their oar before they got beat. And that's a confidence that I know was there in that eight, before we started, and Neil Campbell, our coach, just brought that out even more.

Grant: I think a lot of that was brought out just by the work we did. You know it seemed each work-out we did built our confidence, and we'd come off the water just wasted, but knowing, "Wow, we had another good work-out." And I think those are real confidence builders, when you can go on the water each time and have a quality work-out. That makes a difference when it comes down to the crunch.

Kevin: The quality work is a confidence builder. The more you do the more you realize, yes, it can be done. And, at the Olympics, I just wanted to make sure that I put out and did everything correctly. Mentally, I had to account for more of the strokes in my race plan than you would in the team race plan. Just little things that I wanted to think about during the race. Before the race, I found myself going over the race in my head quite a few times during the day. I'd catch myself doing it and thinking, "Wow!" It wasn't necessarily like imagery, but just thinking, "Okay, after the start you will have to think about this. Here's where we're going to kick her down." Those reminders really helped with concentration, and made sure that

Our goal was to win. Every guy in this crew had that intensity and that desire that you knew every time, no matter what the odds were, they'd die on the end of their oar before they got beat.

114

when I started to get tired my mind didn't wander. I knew that I had something that I was supposed to be thinking about, and that kept my head in the boat on the task at hand. I had one of the best races I've ever had, and I think a lot of it had to do with just making sure I was mentally ready for it.

I've had success without doing that concentration, but it's because it was not as big as the Olympics or the competition was not as tough, so you can get away with a few lapses. Without that mental concentration I think I'm probably rowing almost as well, and pulling as hard, but it's just that little extra tuning that you don't want to leave to chance in a race like the Olympics.

Grant: I haven't been exposed to a lot of different coaches but in the case of Neil, our coach, as far as mental preparation goes, I don't think there's anyone in the world who can prepare a crew better than he can.

Kevin: I think Neil is incredibly smart and he's a people person, at least within rowing. I found he's very positive, but not positive in a phoney sense. A lot of times you can tell when coaches are pumping you full of nonsense, just saying, "You're doing great. Don't worry about that." You can tell it's phoney. Neil just takes a lot of the worries away. Everybody's important and you know that he's in control.

Grant: He asks for input from the crew. If he doesn't like what he hears, or if he thinks it's irrelevant, he won't use it, he's that smart. But he's a motivator and a confidence builder.

Kevin: The biggest part was the mutual respect that's there. It intensifies every time there's an exchange. I remember one piece, well before the Olympics, the boat was going, but it wasn't going great. A few of the guys were kind of frustrated and they looked to him for the answer. He just said, "It looks fine from out here. I can't tell you anything unless I get in that boat. You guys have rowed long enough, you tell me what's going on. What do you think?" That kind of respect for us just pumps you up, because you think, well, here's someone that's definitely working with us, not just sitting up on the chair and saying, "Okay, do this, and do this, and do this." He's saying, "Let's work together." And I know for a fact that if anything happened at the Olympic final, if the Americans would have caught us say, he would have blamed himself. He would have said, "I didn't train them properly." And we would have been doing the same thing, saying, "No, it's our fault." Whereas I think a lot of coaches would rather stand back and say, "You guys blew it. You choked." He cares a great deal about the people that row under him and he worries a whole lot. He carries a lot of pressure; it takes years off his life.

Grant: I think everyone in the crew identifies with him and he identifies with us, if that makes any sense. That makes a big difference because I think it tightens up the whole crew. There definitely was a feeling of comraderie. It stemmed from Neil and what he instilled.

Kevin: Part of the reason for his ability to identify with us is he's done it before, and he's a worker and a fighter. He rowed for Canada in two Olympics: the last one when he was 38 years old. He knows what it's like to go through the pain that we go through, and he's even said during workouts that he doesn't like putting us through it because he knows what it's like. That has a special quality to it,

Without that mental concentration I think I'm probably rowing almost as well, and pulling as hard, but it's just that little extra tuning that you don't want to leave to chance in a race like the Olympics.

115

because a lot of times you find coaches that just sit back and read the paper and say, "This is what you're doing today."

Grant: Yeah, with no feeling in it. And he's got an incredible eye for telling when you've hit the limit. He reads the crew really well, which is pretty hard with eight guys.

Kevin: And he'll say, "Well, I don't care what the training paper says, if it says you're supposed to do one more piece, you guys are dead. Why do it?" When we go out and do a workout, say we're scheduled for four eight minute pieces, and we've finished the third one, and people are falling out of the boat, he'll say, "Take it in." Whereas if you knew the coach wasn't like that, maybe you'd pace yourself for four pieces. You'd pace yourself to make sure you could get through the fourth piece, and maybe you'd be just as tired at the end of the fourth, but you'd have developed a bad habit of not being totally intense. So you go out for every piece. The first one, you go out to kill yourself knowing that if you can't do it, he won't make you.

Kevin: At Los Angeles we tried to make training seem not special, we geared it down. The group of guys we had in our eight are incredibly competitive and intense, so when it comes time to race, you know everyone's going to be fired up. You don't have to run around pumping somebody up the night before, making sure they're ready, because they wouldn't have gotten that far if they didn't have that attitude.

We went out on the water about 35 minutes before the race, and just went through the warm-up. We do a specific amount of strokes, and race starts, to get ourselves going. Then you have to be in the gates three minutes ahead of time. The boats are 17 metres long, so it takes a while to line them up. We had a bit of a head crosswind, so the boats were blowing everywhere. I'd say we actually sat there for ten minutes. I don't remember anyone saying much.

Traditionally, everyone is quiet in the boat, and the cox is the only one who speaks. When it comes right down before a race, you don't want to do anything that is going to disrupt what is happening, so you let one person take care of things. Our cox, Brian, wouldn't say too much to try and motivate us before the race, because he knows everyone's thinking about their own thing anyway. So you listen for a command, whether to stop rowing or start rowing, or whatever.

For the qualifying heat, I remember I was too nervous to row efficiently. I was looking at the competition, just taking it all in; these are the Olympics, you know.

But for the final I didn't look out of the boat. I stared at the bottom of the boat. I just said, "Okay, we're just doing a 2,000 metre piece. You're going to go as hard as you can and you're going to row as well as you can." I thought about what I wanted to think about during the race, and the first thing at hand was the first few strokes, making sure that I was just clean and pulling hard. I was surprisingly relaxed at the start of that race. I think a lot of it had to do with just not looking out, and not letting anything bother me, just worrying about my seat.

Grant: Everyone was a bit focused in on themselves to make it go as well as possible, and get a positive feeling in the boat. I go through a bit of a ritual right at the starting gate. I make sure about three or four times that all my equipment's tight. I tighten up the rigour bolts; doing that sort of takes my mind away from any other distractions. I

I was surprisingly relaxed at the start of that race. I think a lot of it had to do with just not looking out, and not letting anything bother me, just worrying about my seat.

116

think about relaxing, trying to keep my shoulders untensed. That's pretty well my focus, just keeping everything warm but not getting tight, because it's very easy to get tight, especially when you are sitting there for about ten minutes. You're at your catch position, which is not comfortable, and you've got to try and maintain a certain degree of flexibility so that you don't seize up. We were doing a lot of going up to the catch position, waiting, and they would almost start us, and then someone would have blown off, so they'd say, "Lane seven, sorry," and everyone would relax for a while, and then we'd go back up to our catch position for the start again. Didn't France false start?

Kevin: Yeah, they let go, and stuff like that. But we didn't have to watch what was happening. Brian, our cox would say, "Okay, the hands are down." He would give us enough time to get ready. He could see the starter raise his flag and say the command.

The first half of the race I was just thinking about what I was doing; about working efficiently, and making sure I wasn't putting out too much, but putting out enough.

Grant: That was basically the same for me; I just focused. We did a start in 20 which is high, you're basically going for broke for the first 20 strokes and that's just a flurry. You've got seven boats with a lot of meat in each boat pounding through the water. But after that I just concentrated on getting in and out, and making sure that I'm working efficiently, that I'm not tense, I'm just trying to relax on the way up the slide. There's not much time on the slide anyway, but just getting in and out together. The position that we were in was nice too because we were out in front a bit, so out of our peripheral vision we could see pretty well. You don't need to look, you can see all the boats in your peripheral, so that's almost a bit relaxing. You're not thinking, "Oh no, we've got to catch up!" You're thinking, "Okay, we're where we should be and let's just keep it there." We've raced from behind and we've done well from behind too, but it's a different sort of inner strategy; you've got to start thinking, "Oh man, I've got to dig deep. Things are bad now, but they are only going to get worse." Whereas when you're out in front, especially in that final, it makes a difference with the way you motivate yourself.

Kevin: You can relax so much more. In 1983 we raced from behind all the time, and it was a feeling like you rowed to a certain point, and then you just shut your eyes and went for it, and hoped you caught up. Whereas in the Olympic final we seemed more controlled. The emphasis was for them to catch us.

13 (b)
BRIAN McMAHON

1984 OLYMPIC CHAMPIONS — ROWING, MEN'S 8
— PERSPECTIVE OF COXSWAIN

A s a cox you need super-psych. You have to be so confident because you're just there holding onto the boat. All you've got is the microphone. All they can hear is your voice, and your voice has to be confident, enunciated, and clear. I'm in the stern and I'm facing all of them, but they can't see the finish line. I can see it, and I'm driving and talking to them with confidence. "This is what we're going to do, this is how, I'm looking out, we've got half a length on these guys, we're gonna need five strokes, I want you to put 5 strokes together, with the legs because we're gonna need another seat from the Aussie on the right side, we're gonna need 5; 1, 2 . . . then you've got to go to work on them now . . ." The voice always has to be as if you know exactly what you're talking about all the time. Whether you always do doesn't matter, your voice still has to have confidence. The crew can tell just by your tone of voice what you were doing the night before, what you're going to be doing today, how nervous you are, because you have talked to them for two to three hours at a time during each training session for several months.

To get myself confident I listen to a lot of music and I walk for miles and miles by myself with my Walkman on, talking to myself. I have this neat little ability, or mental capacity. I probably row or cox

I probably row or cox about a million and a half, or two million races before I get to the actual race, so that when I get into the starting gates and back my boat in, there isn't anything that can happen to me that I haven't already taken care of in my mind.

119

about a million and a half, or two million races before I get to the actual race, so that when I get into the starting gates and back my boat in, there isn't anything that can happen to me that I haven't already taken care of in my mind. All I have to do is open my mouth and I've already thought about what I'm going to have to say for any situation that's going to happen. I visualize every single stroke, millions and millions of times over. For example, who's ahead here, and what you've got to say at each point of the race.

I've had that mental capacity since I was in Grade 12. I started off coxing, I've never rowed myself, and that's the way it's always been. It just seemed the right thing to do because I'm quick, but I'm quick because I like to take my time to figure out the race plan, so that I have that background before I go out on the water.

I have to do that thinking when I'm walking. I can't do it sitting still because I have to start bouncing, I get pumped, I get excited, and I have to get all that out of me before I hit the water. In the water you have to be nothing but confident.

When visualizing the race it's as if I am sitting in the boat and I simply visualize everything, every possible scenario I might have to deal with. For example, I have to figure out what I'm going to do at the end of the first 20 strokes. I'm going to have to tell the guys where they are, so I have to figure out how, and in what order, I'm going to do that. Once that's done, so many strokes have elapsed, we're already half way down again, and something more has to be injected. Let's say another crew has decided it's going to start to come up, but that's not likely because I've watched all the tapes; I know who is going to go, and when they are going to go. I am lucky we had all that at our advantage, we could watch exactly where the other crews make their move, and how they go up. You simply take all that information and just read it, and read it, and read it. By the time you hit the water, you're ready with a race plan.

The coach didn't want to hear about the race plan, that's the last thing he wanted to hear about. You don't talk to him about the race plan, because you, "Go full power from start to finish," that's his race plan. If you lose, it's because "you rowed too long in one spot." But that isn't really what happens.

Neil Campbell, the coach, is there to make sure you can go full power from start to finish. And if you can't do that, if you fall out of the boat before you hit the finish line, then it's his fault because he didn't train you properly. Neil's biggest job with our crew was to keep them from working too hard. He had to keep them from overtraining. He stopped them before they killed themselves. They showed up with huge cold sores, massive body viruses and body infections, because they'd just literally rowed themselves into the ground. I mean, their heart rates were at 200 for 2 hours in the morning and 2 hours in the afternoon.

It takes everything at this level to win a gold medal, not just the athletes, but everybody working together. Unfortunately, this doesn't always happen. Let me give an example. In the spring of 1984 our new racing shell, purchased in Germany, was going to be flown directly from Lucerne, to Los Angeles in a refrigerated container. We were supposed to pick it up in Los Angeles the week before the Olympics. That's the most absurd thing you can ever imagine

120

because you don't just simply jump in a boat, and race in it. I mean you have to train in it, and get used to it.

The day before the race in Lucerne we got our brand new boat. We said, what the heck, let's rig it up and use it anyway. We were all excited and every little bit helps, it really does. So we raced it and we won. Then on Sunday afternoon we were loading the boats on the trailer. We said we want ours on the trailer to New York; we're going to go down, pick it up, train in it all summer, and then take it down to Los Angeles ourselves. But the administrators said no. I guess it wasn't in the budget.

It was the first time that Canada had ever won a race in Lucerne. We'd never won a gold medal at that regatta, and all we were simply saying was, "We won the gold in this boat, we want this boat." The people who told us that we couldn't do that, I'd never met before in my life. They were on the executive. Jim Joy, our technical director, is an excellent dude, but he's just got so much garbage to deal with. The only way he can really win is to not pay attention to some of those other people. My crew was starting to get jumpy because they could see what was happening. So Neil just said, "Fine, here's the money, I'll buy the boat." It was a lucky thing to have a coach like that, but those are the type of people you sometimes have to deal with.

You just go out and you work with your crew, you work with your boat. You have one goal in mind, that you want to win. You're there to win, you're not there to fool around and "t & t", — "trips and tracksuit," — that's what some of those other people are in it for. Most often problems between the athletes and these other people connected with the sport arise from a lack of communication, but everybody ends up trying to blame each other.

Before the Olympic final, I was ready. I had to be. I got out with that confidence in my voice. As a cox, if you don't have that, you really shouldn't be there. If you don't have it then, you aren't going to find it on the way down the course. I asked Neil before we went on, "How are we going to do? Are we going to win?" I have to ask him that because it's easier to cox a race if the coach gives you the confidence and says, "Yes, you can win". If he said that we can win, then all you've got to do is go out there and do it. It's not like you have to go out there and hope you can win. You go out there and you win. You think positively like that.

All the way up the course during the half-hour warm-up, the crew is preparing mentally and physically. Everything is completely together. All 8 are doing the same thing at the same time, and yet each one is scared. They're scared as a whole and scared individually. Yet I'm the only one allowed to talk. The stroke man looks up at me every now and then. Just before the race we were sitting in those gates, just sitting there forever. I felt it was just no good, because I had them on the water for half an hour getting them warmed up, getting them into their second wind, getting them ready to go, and now here we were just sitting, coming down. I was trying to keep them relaxed, because I knew, the longer they sat there, the more nervous they would get. I talked to them, and gave them little things to do: "Check this, check that . . . check foot stops, tuck in your shirts,

After the final start I was thinking about just keeping the boat straight, because I've got nothing but raw speed, that's all that I have at that time for the next twenty strokes.

It's a neat race plan, a real tough-guy race plan. "Hang with them, and then we're going to spend it all."

keep breathing." I just tried to keep things going, to avoid letting them sit there worrying in silence.

You've got these other crews beside you, and you're all doing the same thing. When you're talking, you have to be that much more confident than they are, because they're all looking over here weighing up the competition. But you never look right over at them. Everybody understands that. It's part of the tradition of rowing.

Then the starter called every lane. He said, "Sit up," then "Êtes vous prêts?" And then someone jumped the gun; I think it was France. We just floated out, so everybody took a few strokes and then we put all the boats back into the gate again, and lined them all up. We did it very quickly.

After the final start I was thinking about just keeping the boat straight, because I've got nothing but raw speed, that's all that I have at that time for the next 20 strokes. I had to make sure that my strokes are exactly right on, so I'm counting the same strokes that the crew are counting. I'm going perfectly straight. I count a couple of them loud, but not the rest, just so that they always know, because they might lose one, or I might lose one, and we have to be right on. They just have to go as hard, and at as high a rate as they can. But they have trained for that, and 20 strokes they can do, just as hard and as high as they can do.

Then I called it down after that, I called, "Lengthen" and I started to bring them down, slow their slides, and started to work the technique again, because they were going so crazy at that time: physically crazy, because you've only got that first minute, and the lactic acid level gets to the point where your body is just hanging on for 5 minutes. But you do have that first minute to just go bananas, so it's important that everybody goes bananas together to get what you need right off the start, and to carry that momentum into the race.

Further down the course, once I had them lengthen after the twenty, we were starting to bring the raw speed under control. We were going to work our way to the 500-metre mark, but before we got there, I had to tell them where they were in proximity to the other crews because they're not allowed to look out of the boat. They've just exhausted so much physical and mental energy that I have to be right on the money to tell them where we are, and what we're doing.

Everything has to be exact, the way it should be set. Whether we're behind or ahead doesn't matter, but the time I choose to tell them, after using that much energy, has got to be right with the flow, so that it carries right on. Then we go again, and we hit the 500 metre mark, and we easily do a little "10" just to bring things together, snap it up, and I worked them 5 at the catch, and 5 at the finish. First 5 at the catch, so I get everybody going in together, thinking about rowing in together; for the second 5 everybody is finishing it off, right on. We're in the middle of this race and I just simply say, "I need 10 strokes," because they're just so ragged, because they're beating their heads against a wall. That's my job, to keep them together, so for the 20 strokes they just focus on technique or pulling.

Five strokes with the legs is the way we move through people in the opposing crew. You can't really go to work on a crew that's right beside you, you have to pick another crew and go to work on them

122

because they've brought the rate down. You just simply work your way through that crew, and as you work your way through that crew, you hope you can lose the other crew. I have that speed on tap, and I just have to be careful where I use it, and how I use it. For example, I could go all the way through one boat, just power right through that boat, and then when the crew gets to the end of that boat, they could be right out of gas. So you only have to use enough power to get through, and then a little later you can use a little more.

When we hit the 900 metre mark, that's where we do the big piece, the 30-stroke piece, because all the other crews row just to stay in contact with the leader in the first 1000. It's a neat race plan, a real tough-guy race plan. "Hang with them, and then we're going to spend it all." We just simply say, "We're going to spend it, all the way down."

We got to the 900 metre mark, 100 metres before the half way mark and I said "We'll go, everything we have!" Then we threw in a huge, huge piece. We decided on this because if they're all going to push at the half way mark, we're going to go that much before the half way mark, and that's what we did. Everybody in the crew knows when we're going, how we're going, why we're going, everything's there. We go, and in just 10 strokes before the other crews are going to go, we got them. We started to move. Their cox is telling them that they're going to start the hardest piece they've got in 10 strokes, but we're already moving away, and they have to get the momentum up and try to catch us, and we're still moving away! The rest is history.

14
BOB MOLLE

1984 OLYMPIC SILVER MEDALIST — WRESTLING

BOB MOLLE WRESTLING

- Silver Medalist (+ 100 kg Freestyle) at the 1984 Olympic Games
- 1985 World Cup — 4th — + 100 kg Freestyle
- 1983 World Championships — 5th — + 100 kg Freestyle
- 1983 Pan American Games — 3rd — + 100 kg Freestyle
- 1983 World Cup — 3rd — + 100 kg

My situation was totally different from other people's at the Olympics because I had had a back operation three weeks to the day before I wrestled my first match. The week prior to the operation, I was bent over, and had lost the feeling in my left leg because my sciatic nerve was pinched when the disc ruptured. The national team doctor called up our coach, Mike Jones, and told us that there was no possible way I could recover from back surgery and be able to step on the mats. So I thought it was up to me to get down there and prove him wrong. It was my once-in-a-lifetime shot to do it.

I had the confidence to come back and do it because a lot of people had supported me throughout my couple of weeks stay at the hospital. The doctor who did the surgery was very supportive. He said, "I haven't seen anybody walk out of here in a week, but it's up to you; you can do anything, it's all in your mind."

Also, a former pro wrestler, Gene Kiniski visited me in the hospital just after I came up from surgery. I was in tears at the time because a couple of people had said that I was done for, and that I couldn't make the Olympic team. Gene came walking into my room early in the morning and said, "Hell, we'll prove them wrong. What do they think we are, average people or what?" That was it, it just kind of clicked right there. We had trained together before and I had

I had the confidence to come back and do it because a lot of people had supported me throughout my couple of weeks stay at the hospital.

125

trained with his son. We always felt that we were superior to other people. I don't know whether we are or not, but we always took that attitude. He's played pro football and wrestled, so he has a keen idea of what competition is all about, and the price you have to pay to keep above the rest.

Gene made me get up every morning and walk with him through the hospital hallways. He's quite a motivator. After a week, I went right from the hospital to his place. I'd lost twenty-seven pounds and he fed me. We would go bike riding and swim in his pool every day. But I couldn't wrestle at all in those last few weeks.

My goal for the Olympics was to win a medal. After the operation, in those last three weeks my goal was the same. I looked at the operation differently than most people. For me it released a lot of pressure. Prior to my operation, there was a build-up for me to be a possible medalist. Afterwards people didn't expect me to do anything. I liked that, it relaxed the pressure.

I believed that I could win a medal because of my past experience. The international circuit gives you more confidence than anything else. When you go around the Soviet Union, you know that you are wrestling the world's best. At age twenty I was already fifth in the world and I had won a bronze at the Pam Am Games. You just keep on gaining confidence to the point where you can 'be' with these people.

My mind changed in the last couple of years about preparing for competition. I don't think there are any big surprises. It comes down to who is training the hardest, and the combination of athletic ability and mental preparation. I don't expect anybody to beat me because I train harder than anybody else.

I do mental rehearsal. I watch other wrestlers on video. I know what other moves I have to stop to beat that opponent. I go over those moves in my mind. I do that anytime or anywhere.

I always try to release the pressure before competition by sticking around people. I'm very loud and always joking around, like nothing's wrong. I take a different attitude than a lot of people. I'm kind of the comic strip of the team, always cracking little one-liners.

The day of the competition I try to run my routine identical to what I usually do. Before my final match at the Olympics, sitting outside the hotel room having a bull session with the boys for a while, then going for a swim, the same as usual. I don't want to change anything in my life that would upset me. I don't care if it's a beer at midnight or out talking with the boys. It relaxes me and makes me feel good. Sit down, fall asleep, wake up in the morning, kid around with the boys, go for a swim; that's exactly what I do. If there is a big event coming up, I might think too much about it, and apply too much pressure to myself. If I just go around casual, like everything else is all right, then I'm ready when it comes time, a half hour before the match. Right before the match I just do my usual routine of warming up, making sure everything is loose and warm. If I feel warm I feel a lot better. I go through the moves that I have to defend against. I go through those moves in my head, and physically with a training partner. At important international events in the past, I've blocked out the crowd from my mind by telling myself that I'm an underdog.

126

During the match, I'm going over in my mind, what's working, what's his stance, defence, offence, and what are his reactions. It all comes naturally. If you have to think about it in the match, you're hesitating too long. It's got to be a reaction. You've got to react normally to whatever he does. You've got to have the counter to it. You have to have done that move so many times, that when he does this, you know how to counter it. It's just a natural reaction in your body.

Between matches at a competition I do the same thing that I always do: be normal, joke around, go eat, go for a snooze. When the match is over, it's over. I've seen too many people die because of the pressure between matches.

That's pretty well how I prepared for my very best international performance. It was a meet in Italy and I was in a final against Poland. The day before the match I felt weird. The temperature was eighty-five degrees and I wasn't used to it but I sat outside in the sun for a couple of hours and felt good. Then I had a good dinner. My match was the next morning. That night I ran over six miles with my coach. He couldn't keep up with me, and yet he usually just kills me on runs. I felt great about it. I stretched out and the next morning I felt so confident going into the match, it was unreal. I dominated him 12-0, which means "end of match."

Prior to that match, the Olympic trials had just finished for Canada. I'd made the Olympic team and the pressure was off. Many of the Canadian Olympic team wrestled well because they knew that they had made the team. There had been a pressure release.

My worst international performance was in the Soviet Union. There were so many little variables that conflicted: their day is our night; we sat in Customs for five hours; they searched us over like a toothbrush; we were shoved into a cab and driven for a long while; it was minus 40 and your Walkman froze when you stepped outside; you couldn't go for a run because we didn't have the toques and heavy clothing. It was a lot of turn-offs, just getting in there, being shoved into a room, and getting telephone calls in the middle of the night. I was so naive to that situation. I would get telephoned; they'd talk in Russian; I'd put the phone back on the hook; and a couple of hours later some operator would call again. The whole set-up was a hassle. People want to trade everything you've got. There were just so many changes.

The person I lost to was a joke. The match should never even have been close, physically. What happened on the mat was a big turn-off. They call "cautions" right away for passivity, if you're avoiding wrestling. I tried some offensive moves and got cautioned and then cautioned again. I let it get to me. It seems like you're fighting three referees, plus the opponent, and the crowds hiss. The referees dominate the match so much it's just ridiculous. You have to experience it to believe it.

Over the years my coach Mike Jones has been a major factor in keeping me active in wrestling. He's kept me mentally prepared. For someone who doesn't know us, it might seem different than it really is. Mike treats each athlete in the way that works for him. For example, he didn't compliment me at all. He looked at my bad points, but always in a joking atmosphere that I like. He's comical. Just before my match he'll say something like, "There's a guy up in the stands

The day of the competition I try to run my routine identical to what I usually do.

127

that has bet a steak that you're going to lose this match". He'll shoot little subtle hints into you all the time. He never gives away any emotions. He'll never say, "Great match". He'll never grab you or hug you. This is his classic line: "If you want compliments go to your mother." But you've got to understand him to appreciate him.

I've dealt with him for four years now and I'm accustomed to his coaching, and I enjoy it that way. He'll make sure that you are warm before the match and he'll say, "I've no worries at all, you're going to dominate this guy. You've just got to do this and this." And we'll communicate. It's just like when you're in a hockey game in Saskatchewan, you can't hear all the other people yelling, but you always hear your mum. It's the same way with Mike at the side of a match. There are four or five thousand people screaming, and yet I can hear Mike's voice on the side saying, "Single leg, drop down, high crotch," or whatever. He's following it, and in the middle of a match I can look over and he'll just talk to me all the time. I can understand totally what he wants me to do. I'm tuned into him totally. That communication is vital for my success. I see him every weekend and we're wrestling together all the time. He trains with me sometimes, but he's a little small for that. He's only one hundred and eighty pounds and I'm over two hundred and fifty pounds. That's a lot of strain on his body.

I've heard nothing but negative comments from him for four years. To tell you the truth I don't know how it comes through so positive. If there is any way he can put me down, he will. For example, I lost one match to a kid from the States. He was about three hundred and sixty pounds. I was beating him 6-0 and got lackadaisical and he just rolled me for a pin. It came out in the wrestling news with the title, "Molle pinned." Mike photocopied it and put it up in the wrestling room, the football room, all over, just to remind me, "Look what happened here, this 'lard' guy just beat your butt." All the way back from the tournament I heard that constant ribbing, "Yeah you lost to a 'lard'." But somehow it doesn't come through as negative. On the surface he doesn't seem to care, but at the same time he really does care. He'll say anything, just as an incentive, "Yeah, you owe me a steak, come on, let's go!" Gene, and Mike above him, had the greatest influence on my mental readiness for the Olympics.

We once had a sport psychologist come in to the team. One day between practices our manager said, "Have lunch, then you have to go to this meeting with a psychologist." All you could hear were groans. It was a bad start because this was the atmosphere: we'd been to 8 o'clock practice; we'd been running and weight lifting. We had been in there for about three hours. What do you want to do after three hours practice? Do you want to stand there and listen to someone, and do little papers and stuff like that? All you want is to go home. If I'm training twice a day, really hard and intensely as we were, I want to get away, listen to music, and sleep.

We sat down for fifteen or twenty minutes and tried to get in this totally relaxed state. I think I can do it myself, but because somebody in the administration put this person in here, we have to do it his way. I remember the one thing that we used to do every day, that I didn't like at all. You'd have to get into your "state of mind", and think about that place where you feel really relaxed. We used to sit

It's just like when you're in a hockey game in Saskatchewan, you can't hear all the other people yelling, but you always hear your mum. It's the same way with Mike at the side of the match.

there for about twenty-five minutes. It was clear that some people didn't want to be there, and they were just hurting whatever he was trying to do. If you don't want to go, don't show up. That is the attitude we should have had, because you're not respecting someone else who it could have helped.

Going into the Olympics I knew technically I could beat a lot of people. It was just a matter of putting everything together. My leg was improving with time. There was a lack of balance but my strength was starting to come back. I grew in confidence every day. But realistically, to tell you the truth, I didn't think I had a chance at the gold medal. I didn't think I could push the top wrestler to where he would be extremely tired.

Mentally I was a 'ten' out of ten, going into every match except the final. I was probably around 'six' going into the final. The major difference was when I stepped out onto the mat. Right at that moment I think there was a change. You've got fifteen thousand people sitting in the Coliseum; you've got the trumpets going; and you can't hear the trumpets for the crowd who were giving a standing ovation because you've got to wrestle with an American in the final. I was trying to block that out of my mind, but I didn't do it very well. I've had big tournaments in the States before, but this time I let it get to me a little bit.

This time I couldn't block it out because I doubted my ability. I don't think I had confidence in my conditioning, and my technique wasn't there. I couldn't lean forward on a single leg because I didn't have the balance yet. I knew how powerful Bruce was because I'd trained with him. I knew exactly what moves worked on him, and what didn't, and what I had to do to beat him. I would have had to wrestle with my head, because physically he is stronger than I am. I don't say quicker, but he was technically stronger. At the same time, if I had wrestled over my head I could have beaten him. But I never once "shot it out".

But somehow it doesn't come through as negative. On the surface he doesn't seem to care, but at the same time he really does care.

15
ALWYN MORRIS

1984 OLYMPIC CHAMPION — PAIRS, KAYAK

ALWYN MORRIS CANOEING

- Gold Medalist (K-2, 1000m) & Bronze Medalist (K-2, 500m, with Hugh Fisher) at the 1984 Olympic Games
- 1977 & 1985 Recipient of the Tom Longboat Award for Outstanding Native Athlete of the Year
- 1983 World Championships — 3rd — K-2, 500m, 6th — K-2, 1000m
- 1982 World Championships — 2nd — K-2, 1000m, 9th — K-2, 500m
- 1981 World Championships — 5th — K-2, 1000m, 6th — K-2, 500m

I n 1982 Hugh Fisher and I were second in the Worlds. We were on the inside of that course, the Russians were on the outside. We had a bit of a headwind, they had no wind. That was the closest anyone had ever come to the Russians in the 1000 metres. Hugh was devastated by coming second.

I thought, well, I gave it everything and I was second, I was happy we had done well. Hugh was devastated and we had a hard time talking. The next day something really stupid happened. We picked up a weed on our rudder and were right out of the race. I was devastated and Hugh just laughed about it. It was really confusing, but you learn from those experiences.

It was after that experience in 1982 that we plotted our Olympic course. We wanted to win. Once we were second in the Worlds we knew we could win. We did everything in our power to put ourselves in the environment to win, including going any place, getting the right people around us, making time available, making it the priority. At that time I wrote down that my goal was to win a gold medal in 1984.

Before our first final at the Olympics which was the 500 metres, we did our on-water warm-up the way we normally do. We came off the water and watched some races on TV, Larry Cain's race and others' as well. I remember standing around watching. We normally don't do that. Before a race we usually do our own thing, the most com-

We did everything in our power to put ourselves in the environment to win, including going any place, getting the right people around us, making time available, making it the priority. At that time I wrote down that my goal was to win a gold medal in 1984.

131

Hugh said afterwards that maybe we just weren't as focused on getting down the course following our own goals. He felt we were more worried about, "Can we beat these guys today?" And as a result we had a hopeless start.

fortable thing we are used to. When we got back on the water, there was something missing. We were talking, but it felt like a little bit of intensity or direction was missing. We talked all the way to the line. We said what we were going to do, and what was going to help, but it was like we were talking at a superficial level, rather than really deep. That's what it felt like. The words that we were saying to each other didn't feel like they were inside. As much as we knew the race plan, and what we should do, the minute we pulled the first stroke there may have been somewhat of a lack of communication about the race plan as a whole. Hugh said afterwards that maybe we just weren't as focussed on getting down the course following our own goals. He felt we were more worried about, "Can we beat these guys today?" And as a result we had a hopeless start.

Later we watched the tapes over and over again. We know where we made our mistake, right in the transition, which is a critical place to make a mistake. When we should have come down with the stroke rate and up with the power, we came down with rate and just played. Instead of getting intensified in our power at that point we just kept the power the same. Once the boat starts to accelerate it gets easier to pull, but as you start to drop the stroke it gets harder to pull. You have to remind yourself, "Now the transition," so you have to add the power to keep it going. But what happened was the power didn't come on and the stroke rate dropped. Then we were just paddling. You try to remember your race plan and not worry about outside influences. We followed our race plan but we made a mistake in the first part of the transition. We dropped back one boat and we never had enough time to get it back.

If the race had been a little longer we might have gotten it back. At about 150 metres into the race, Hugh called a "hutt" a little bit early, and everything came together and we were able to fall back on plan B. Terry (sport psychologist) was always suggesting "Plan B". We probably should have called for plan B after 50 metres, because we had a tremendous finish and paddled right through the whole pack to come up to get the bronze. If we hadn't dropped that boat length, maybe it would have been a different story. I think we were as good as, or better than, anyone in that water.

What probably would have helped would have been not watching the other races on TV. That just made the point that we have to do well now. We have seen Larry race a hundred times but we have never watched him on TV. When we watched him, we realized, "Here we are, this is the Olympic Games." At that point we both thought about that, instead of thinking, "We've been here before, we know what we're doing." When we started to talk on the water before the race, it felt really strange; it didn't feel the same. On the way to the line the boat was running as fast as it always did, but there was just that lack of depth in communication. Maybe it's because we watched Larry on TV. We watched everything prior to ours on TV and we'd never done that before. It was a change in pattern. All of a sudden there was a recognition of where we were and what we were going to do, what we were planning to do. As much as we thought we had that under control, we were missing that depth which we always had. That was a difference.

After the 500 metre final, we were so mad and frustrated and disappointed in ourselves for making a mistake, at one of the most important events that we'll ever participate in during our lives. I remember going to the podium, and a lot of people were cheering. I didn't listen to it. I was mad, I almost cried. We came third. As we were walking toward the podium I was really down on myself and I guess Hugh was down on himself too. I was not even going to look up. I remember the music played; that whole ceremony was just a bad blur. The organizing committee had given us some flowers. I just had to get some relief somewhere. I remember I just went "bang" and stuffed the flowers into the hands of a buddy of mine from Kahnawake. I said, "You've got the flowers, keep them and leave me alone." I remember paddling back and we didn't talk about the race at all. When we got off the water, the reporters wanted to find out what was going on. Nobody around knew what to say to us. We tried to make somewhat of a joke of how we were feeling, then we just shook our heads and moved on. We tried to be serious enough to get our point across, that we had made a mistake and that's part of the game as well. We had another day we had to get ready for.

The whole period from the moment we crossed the line to the time we left the site was really a down period. We were trying to realize what had happened and trying to get ourselves ready for the next day.

Going to lunch, everybody was still down. They were happy for Larry, but at the same time they didn't know what to say to us. Hugh and I talked. I thought that would help, but it didn't. I talked to Hugh and I asked, "Well, what do you think happened in the race?" Something went wrong right after the start. I didn't know what at the time, but we dropped pretty quickly.

We saw the replay and I said, "Why did we drop?" Hugh got really mad, just fuming and I said to myself, "Get out of the room!" I walked around the hotel grounds, then I jumped in the pool. As I sank to the bottom, I thought, "Okay, that's it!" It felt like it took me fifteen seconds to drop to the bottom. I had time to think . . . "Okay, that's it, no more, this is it!" I remember pushing off the bottom and jumping out of the pool. I went to Hugh and I said, "Okay, I'm not going to be mad anymore. We've got lots of work to do tomorrow." I could see that he was still really frustrated. A lot of people were coming up to us saying, "That's okay, you have another day tomorrow." That was hard to take at first, when you're down on yourself. We know we have another day, don't bother us. Then you realize we do have another day, and we have to approach it by following our plan and racing our race.

The next morning we got up and Hugh called me in. He asked me, "What are we doing this morning?" I said, "Hugh, we're going to do our race plan." We talked about the race plan and it felt a lot more genuine, without even being at the course yet. I don't know how long it took Hugh to come around, but at this point he took control, and I took control but without taking control from each other. We sort of just blended together as a team. That was missing the day before.

As much as we both had to be together, we both had to have control of ourselves and control of one another, in a sense. The communication between the two of us had to be strong, yet compromising,

We tried to be serious enough to get our point across, that we had made a mistake and that's part of the game as well. We had another day we had to get ready for.

I don't know how long it took Hugh to come around, but at this point he took control, and I took control but without taking control from each other. We sort of just blended together as a team.

133

without compromising everything. As much as it's a team event, you still have to be a very strong individually because you are not going to let that person behind you feel like you're letting him down. The trust was there. In order to have that trust, we had to be individuals. We had to show our individualism and our strength without hurting one another. The day before, we were weak people. We showed our personalities, but we didn't show our strength. By not showing our strength, there was an idea of, "Well, maybe he's not pulling so hard today!"

When I said, it's over for me, at the bottom of the pool, in a way I was showing that it was over. I'm going to do this tomorrow, and you're going to be with me whether you like it or not, without ever saying it in those words. Taking charge. These are after-thoughts. It's not what I was thinking when I was doing it. I knew we had to have another focus for the next day. You've got to be really strong yourself. You can't rely on that other person to be strong for you. You have to be one, and still be two.

You've got to be really strong yourself. You can't rely on that other person to be strong for you. You have to be one, and still be two.

Before the 1000 metre race we went out and did our warm-up. We talked a lot and we even did a few extra hard pieces before the race to really feel good about it. Both of us had always felt that the 1000 metre is the race that we really excel at. We've always treated the 500 as a bit of icing. At the Worlds it always comes after the 1000. At the Olympics it came before.

Out on the water it wasn't a superficial type of thing, there was laughter, we were talking. Then we got the lane draw and we saw the Swedes were on one side, the French were on the other side. We sat down and went over what we wanted to do. We'll go at 1:40 and then we're coming home. We know we're good in the first half at 1:40.

Before the 1000 metre race, our focus was there. The plan for the race was there. Physically I felt fine and mentally I felt strong. I knew what we were there to do. Waiting for the gun at the start was a period of quiet. We just sat there trying to keep the boat in line. Just a matter of waiting and keying in to the sound of the gun. At that point, we just blasted off, just reaction. From the start on, nothing was in my mind other than the focus of what I was doing in the boat, and controlling the pace rate, and the plan, and pulling. I could feel myself pull the stroke all the way through, and not just going through the motions of the stroke, as had happened the day before in the 500. I could feel my body in space, and feel pressure pulling the paddle. I could feel myself lift myself. I felt the boat move.

Before the 1000 metre race, our focus was there. The plan for the race was there. Physically I felt fine and mentally I felt strong. I knew what we were there to do.

We watched the races in the morning but not on TV and that was fine. We got ready, got on the water, went out. We went through the 500 metre mark at 1:40.01. From there Hugh called the signals. The last peek I took, we were about half a boat down from the West Germans, so that must have been about 200 metres out. From that point on, I didn't even bother looking. The plan from that point was that we were going to dig in. I had to look to see if we won, I didn't know. Hugh said he had to do the same thing, whereas in the 500 final Hugh said he felt like his peripheral vision was really strong, and he could see everything that was happening around him. For the 1000 final he "put his visor on," which kept the focus on the back of my head.

Right after the race the French came right over to us and we started to laugh. It was a flood of emotions. You just don't know what to think. All those emotions that are running through you. Then when we got out of the boat Hugh collapsed on us. I let some other people attend to him.

There is no one word in my vocabulary to describe what happened that day: the whole thing about what I did on the podium; the pressure of what I had decided to do and why I was going to do it; questions of justifying why I wanted to do it. A voice said, "Am I being political; am I being over and above what I really want to do? Who am I?" It didn't come to my mind the whole morning until we crossed the finish line. Then I said, the pressure is on me now. Now I have the chance to do this.

On the way to the podium you don't see anybody. You hear a lot of roar. I felt like I had a ton of bricks behind me pushing me through. I couldn't keep my mind on what I wanted to do, to raise the eagle feather on top of the victory podium. There were so many other influences. As much as we'd been on the podium before, this was a new experience. It wasn't the same as the Worlds. I remember people yelling "smile". The whole ceremony is just so interesting. You're just so choked up, what does it all mean? You're trying to justify something that you've worked 10 years for and it just took 3 minutes of your time. You just can't . . . There are just too many outside influences . . . too many things running through your head.

In a media interview after our race I finally expressed what it meant for me to raise the eagle feather. It felt like it took years to say it, even though it actually only took about 30 seconds: I'm proud to be an athlete, a native and a Canadian. What I had done was important to me because I hoped my grandfather was very, very proud. That's what I felt. I got emotional about it. (Note: Alwyn's grandfather was a Mohawk Indian from Kahnawake, (Alwyn's home) who had died before Alwyn was able to reach this dream goal.) I wanted to do something that signified being native.

First I thought about wearing the kostowa (a Mohawk headress) on the victory stand, but it just wasn't me. About a week before the Olympics I finally decided, "This is what I'm going to do. I am going to raise the eagle feather." This is something that is universal and still carries the message that I want. In traditional values, an eagle feather was presented to someone who had accomplished something special. It meant a number of things: life, honour, courage. Those are the 3 basic values. I said to Hugh, "this is what I'm doing. It's settled". When my friends got there with the kostowa I said I didn't feel comfortable with that. They said, "You do what you feel comfortable with." That was like a voice of confidence. I just didn't feel comfortable with the kostowa. As much as that is part of my heritage, that is not me. I was given the chance to be who I was and be native. I guess I was stressing the idea of remaining an individual.

We worked on our mental training for a number of years prior to the 1984 Olympics, with Terry Orlick. Before that I really didn't do that much in the way of mental preparation. I used to key off my opponents, without putting my own plan together. When I had problems technically, I would visualize movements without a paddle in my hand to help me feel where my body was in relation to space. That

You're just so choked up, what does it all mean? You're trying to justify something that you've worked ten years for and it just took three minutes of your time.

I'm proud to be an athlete, a native and a Canadian. What I had done was important to me because I hoped my grandfather was very, very proud.

135

When I had problems technically, I would visualize movements without a paddle in my hand to help me feel where my body was in relation to space. That would help me put my technical game back together.

One of us would visualize and the other would hold the stop watch.

would help me put my technical game back together. Terry made us think of why we were doing things and why we should do things. He had input in different areas, including using a stopwatch, where we would visualize our race as a whole and get closer and closer to the real time on the watch. That was a new experience, something we had never done before.

Initially he made us think about our training, about our goals and about what we were doing to reach them. That sort of prepared us for the next phase. His input had a direction to it. The practical side of his involvement was somewhat along the lines of, "Where is the benefit and why are we doing this? Is this focus really going to help us? Do you know your best focus?"

Since we worked with Terry the practical things we did changed, like having and sticking to a race plan, visualization, and learning to relax. It wasn't necessarily structured time, it was free time because it became a game. It wasn't like training, it was a game. Sometimes it's really hard to close your eyes and visualize, but if you visualize for a game, it becomes easy. Hugh and I would visualize our race. We would have a competition to see who could come closer to the real time. One of us would visualize and the other would hold the stop watch. All of a sudden it became more and more complete as we came together.

I've been keeping a diary since 1975. I recorded all the training I did, how I felt that day, whether I felt tired or fresh and whether I got the most out of my work. If I was tired, I recorded whether I still felt I was able to push. Sometimes I would include whether outside influences, girlfriend or school had been bothering me.

The race evaluation forms that Terry introduced were another tool that we started to use. They made us think. It's easy to forget about something, and it's really easy to fly off the handle. They bring you back to the basics as far as learning from the experience, rather than letting the experience fly away. By going through that whole race again, like with the Olympic 500 metre, we can come back saying, "This is not going to happen to us again." With the race evaluation forms the learning part stays in your mind.

I guess there was a lot of skepticism when he first got involved with the team. When a new stimulus comes in, you start to wonder, is this really going to help the end result? The whole idea of sports psychology was something new. We didn't know it, we didn't feel it. Was this really going to help us? We didn't know. I think we became really good friends before I started to realize that what he was doing was right. There's got to be a basic trust and basic understanding right off the bat. We hung out together while we were in Europe, and we talked a lot. The basic questions that came from him that helped were: "What are you doing?" and "Where's your focus?" — They made me think, "Did I have a focus? Did I have a plan? If I don't have a plan, am I shooting in the dark?" I guess Hugh did the same thing. They seemed like appropriate questions. It wasn't something new but it was an innovative approach for us.

I think when Rob Sleeth, our coach, first started working with us, he was intimidated. We were loners, and we did our own thing. Nobody wanted any part of us, but we worked together, and formed a bond. As he started to work with us, we became more focused and

136

planned. He knew what we were doing in workouts and in mental training. The whole idea of key phrases became important. The phrases meant more after we worked on focusing than before. It was fun, but it was also serious. Before the 1000 final his last key phrase was, "It's time!" That's all he had to say.

When we haven't performed well it was usually because we weren't thinking about what we should be doing. We let outside influences hamper what we were doing in the boat. That means from a seat breaking, to poor weather, to watching what was happening around us while we were racing, instead of following our focus plan. When I've thought about why I was doing things and prepared myself mentally, I've performed well. By focusing more, being mentally tough, not letting the outside influences come in, and keeping my train of thought, I was able to do better. There are things that you aren't going to be able to control. We had to do the best we could, regardless of the outside influences, and we had to adapt to whatever happened. You have to accept the fact that you cannot control certain things. The idea is to prepare yourself in a way that you will be able to perform no matter what the environment.

By focusing more, being mentally tough, not letting the outside influences come in, and keeping my train of thought, I was able to do better.

We're not there to play around anymore. This is not a game. We're out there as professionals in our train of thought. We may not be professionals in our pay scale, but we are certainly professionals in what we do because of the attitudes we have to take with us into those forums. That's important. We are not just a bunch of kids playing. We are adults who are representing ourselves and our countries.

When I'm training, I'm focused. I train to the best of my ability. By focusing all the time on what you're doing when you're training, focusing in a race becomes a by-product. They complement each other.

We put in the same amount of training hours as other top athletes in our sport. We do basically the same kind of off-season work. But we recognized a lot of problems we had in the past and we corrected those problems as we matured. That's why I think we could have beaten anyone on the water.

Training with intensity is just a matter of digging in. You say, "I'm here to train, and I'm not going to waste my time! If I don't train that way, I'm going to be the ultimate loser, no-one else." It comes down to a personal vendetta against yourself, but it also comes down to personal satisfaction. When I say I've done my best and worked my hardest, I feel good about that. If I am going to be second or third, it's going to be because someone else has superior ability. I have to accept that too, but I'm not going to question my training. That's the last thing I want to question. Knowing how to focus gives you that little extra push when you have to push in the everyday sessions. On training days when I feel a little flat, to get myself "up", I try to key off another person. If I see someone is working hard, then I know I can too. As much as I may feel flat getting into the workout, and I may be flat for part of it, I'll recognize the fact that I can do it. I ask myself in a positive sense, why am I here? At that point it becomes a mind game. I'm here because I want to be the best I can be. Then I'm ready to focus.

Training with intensity is just a matter of digging in. You say, "I'm here to train, and I'm not going to waste my time! If I don't train that way, I'm going to be the ultimate loser, no one else."

137

16
BRIAN ORSER

1984 OLYMPIC SILVER MEDALIST — FIGURE SKATING

BRIAN ORSER
FIGURE SKATING

- Silver Medalist — 1986 World Championships
- 1985 St. Ivel Ice International — 1st
- Silver Medalist — 1985 World Championship
- Silver Medalist (Men's Singles) at 1984 Olympic Games
- Silver Medalist — 1984 World Championships
- 1984 Skate Canada — 1st

My first event at the 1984 Olympics was the compulsory figures. I don't place as well in the compulsory figures as I do in the freestyle. The previous year, I was 8th in the compulsory figures, and pulled up to 3rd after freestyle. When I went to the Olympics, I wanted to at least keep that spot, or try to move up one or two places, which I did, because I was 7th in the compulsory figures there. That was the best I could do at that time, just because there is so much work to do in one year. It is hard in compulsory figures to make a big jump even though you do improve a lot. I had improved a lot. I had made a lot of changes during the training year. We had a coach come over from Czechoslovakia. He is known as a figure expert. He is also politically very strong with judges and the international skating union, and very well respected. We worked the summer with him.

I also went to Toronto and worked two days a week with judges. Rather than work against them or be afraid of them, I worked with them. They came out and analyzed what I did and that was a big help and made a big difference. I knew I was mentally ready to go out and do the best I could do. I finished 7th in figures so I was pleased with that. "Figures" is more of a mental game and you have to have your

I also went to Toronto and worked two days a week with judges. Rather than work against them or be afraid of them, I worked with them.

The feeling is what you are after, rather than just picturing it. It was through actually feeling it in my mind that I started to make all my jumps consistent.

heart rate very low; you have to be totally in control and not let anything from the outside bother you. In free skating, however, you need a lot of energy. When the audience is rowdy you can feel the vibration from them. For me that helps the free skating, which makes it exactly the opposite of the figures. I know where I have to focus for each event.

I went from Orillia to train in Toronto a couple of days a week. The change in environment and skating with the others was a big help; watching them work, in a way almost competing with them, because they were going to the World Championships and the Olympics too. If they would push extra hard that day, I would push extra hard that day or vice versa. We sort of helped each other and I couldn't do that here in Orillia. The rink we have here is very small, there is no seating, and this is the first year that we have had heating in the rink.

I do have down days when I don't feel like pushing it. My coach never really pushes me or screams at me. When I feel like working he really works me. Then there are days when I go out there, when my mind is really not on it, and I don't really feel like being there. He will say, go home or take an hour off, or come back later. If he is understanding, all of a sudden I feel better. That is just the way it works. He has known me for so long, he knows exactly how much I can tolerate. If it is something small, he will say, "You're okay. Just go back out on the ice." He knows what to say. He can read me very well. He is always there so that if I want to let some frustration out, he is there to take it. I put him through a lot, but he understands what I am going through and a lot of things I say just go in one ear and out the other for him. We are very close in terms of our working relationship. It is almost like a big brother or father type thing. There is a lot of mutual respect, and that is what you have to keep.

I think a lot of success is a mental thing. How well you prepare and whether you really work hard. If you don't work your skills along with what is going on inside your head, it just won't work out. There are times when I really push myself. It is a good thing because I want to do it and I enjoy it. Of course there are times when I hate it but put myself through it anyway. But most times I enjoy it and my coach makes me feel good by doing it. I think there are other skaters that do it because they have to. They are "driven" to, and the coach gets really upset and makes too many rules. That is one good thing about Doug Leigh, my coach; once I'm away from the rink, I have my own lifestyle and I have my own life. If I'm doing something that is hindering my performance at the rink then of course he would say something about it. But he has never put a curfew on me. He has never ever said, "I don't think you should go out this weekend because you have a performance on Monday." He leaves it up to the skater. A lot of times he would say to me, "Did you have a great weekend?" And I would say I didn't really do much this weekend because I wanted to skate well this week. It is mostly what I do for myself. I have been trained that way, whereas some skaters really haven't been. Doug used to put his foot down when I was young. He was very demanding, very strict, very loud and I see him like that with the younger kids and I feel sorry for them. But as they get older, all of a sudden they start working themselves and become very disciplined.

140

They don't need to be told and that makes it a lot easier and a lot nicer to train.

I see some kids my own age in some of the other schools where they are really forced. It is too much like a real training camp and too work-oriented. Their visors are on and they don't see what else is happening in the world. From my perspective that seems to affect the enjoyment. With figure skating, I find to be able to go out and work and really benefit from it, you have to enjoy it and you have to want to be there. I depend on adrenalin when I skate. We train hard. I get my endurance and strength up but when it comes to going through a 4½ minute program, I count on having the extra adrenalin, which comes from the enjoyment and excitement. If skaters don't have that during the year, it won't be there all of a sudden.

The figure skating association always sends the team over to Europe early if we are competing in Europe, so we can get adjusted to the time change. The Olympic year we went to Mannheim, West Germany. I've trained there before, so I knew the facility and the accommodation was ideal. The Canadian team was then told they had to go to the actual Olympic site early because the women had to have their outfitting and femininity test so that meant we all had to go. Our ice time and practice time was to be limited at the Olympics so I wanted to stay in Mannheim an extra 4 days, which would still get me to the Olympics a week before my event. We went through a lot of hassles trying to arrange it. Not so much arrange it, because Usha, my choreographer, had booked flights and confirmed them, no problems. Our association at home didn't want me to stay. They wanted me to go with the team and be part of the team. At this point I was thinking of myself and I wanted to do whatever I would benefit from. That is where Doug stepped in and really put his foot down. He said, "I will take all the responsibility, we are going to stay and that is all there is to it."

That training really made a huge difference, because in Sarajevo we only had an hour and a half practice a day, which was split up between figures, the short and long. We went to practice times which were at 6 a.m. and at eleven at night. And you are back at the rink at 6 the next morning. It was just a crazy schedule. I just didn't want to be there. They were afraid that my uniform wouldn't fit and all these things. And I said I don't care if my uniform doesn't fit because all I want to do is go out there and skate and do well. So I stayed in Munheim and got away from the team. I was on my own, and that took a lot of pressure off me. The last few days out of the whole year were the ones I benefitted from the most. They were saying, "No you can't." Four days later I took a 2 hour flight right to Sarajevo and I felt great when I got there. I knew what I was doing and we just put our foot down and did it and that was the best thing I could do.

My realistic goal for the Olympics was to be on the podium. I was not sure of which position because I knew it would be difficult to finish on top, to be first. Scott Hamilton was 3 times world champion and was the favourite to win and that was pretty secure. I didn't take my sights off winning, I still was going after that. As it turned out I won seventy percent of the competition. To place second overall, I had to beat a fellow who had been 2nd for the 2 years before that. I was 4th and 3rd in 1982 and 1983, and he was 2nd and 2nd, so I

We made a video of a perfect program and of all the elements in my program individually, perfect elements, and we had them repeated a number of times, sometimes up to ten times with the more difficult ones, so I would get a picture of a perfect element and a perfect program in my mind.

My imagery is not so much visual. It is more just feel. I don't think it is visual at all. When I'm watching it on video I look visually at it and then I get this internal feeling. When I'm actually doing it I get the same feeling inside.

I normally do a high quality training, and that is influenced even by what I wear. I can't train in sweat pants and a sweat shirt and an old T-shirt.

knew it was going to be difficult to beat him. So I was hoping to be on the podium. That was my main goal. Going in I fully believed I would be on the podium.

In the 1980 Olympics, I didn't even make the team. In the 1984 Olympics, I went from not even making it to being 2nd. 1981 was my first year being on the world scene, and between 1980 and 1981 I made a big step by really working hard and really pushing it. We set our goals for the 1984 Olympics back then. My goals back then were to be on the podium, and actually to be the Olympic Champion. That was what we were going after. We knew it was realistic because in 1981 I won my first senior title in Canada and that's when I got my birth on the world scene and when I finished 6th. So that was quite a feat for somebody in figure skating, a judgmental sport, to go in the first year and be in the top ten. Once I was there I skated very well. At that point I knew I had to keep skating well each year, because if you don't skate well they just put you down and just forget about you real fast. After that year, I knew that being on the podium at the Olympics was very, very realistic. Then we just made steps each year and set realistic goals each year. In 1982, I was aiming for the podium and I finished 4th, and that was a bit of a disappointment. In 1983, I was aiming for the podium, and I was 3rd then. Each year we made a step.

Ever since I've been young I have always done imagery. That is how I learned how to do a lot of my own jumps. I would be working on a triple toe loop for instance; I would be thinking about it so much and I would be at home in bed thinking about it and all of a sudden I would get the feeling of it in my head. The feeling is what you are after, rather than just picturing it. It was through actually feeling it in my mind that I started to make all my jumps consistent. It was just self-discovery. I guess I just wanted to land these jumps so badly. It was like when you have a dream about something and you think you have actually done it. Initially it was just specific elements that I was working on. It was never ever something that was impossible to do, it was always something that I was very close to doing but not quite there. I can remember one specific jump, the triple toe loop. I was thinking about it in bed and when I went to the rink the next day, I was thinking about the feeling and all of a sudden I landed my first one. The night before I had the feel of it. I couldn't wait to get to the rink the next day so I could try it, to see if that would work. There was a certain feel I was thinking of and I said, I will try that tomorrow, and it worked.

We did a lot of imagery in training. We also work with video a lot, looking at perfect jumps. We made a video of a perfect program and of all the elements in my program individually, perfect elements, and we had them repeated a number of times, sometimes up to 10 times with the more difficult ones, so I would get a picture of a perfect element and a perfect program in my mind. If I am having problems with a jump, we'll go back to a video, for example of the Olympics or World Championships where that jump was successful. We will watch it a few times to see exactly what we are doing there. Even watching I get the feeling of it.

The videos we used at the 1984 Olympics were definitely very useful. Going to the Olympics with the very limited ice time and practice

142

time, I watched the tape probably 4 or 5 times. It was almost like having an extra practice session. I would sit in my room and watch it with my coach. There were a couple of jumps I was having problems with, and watching the perfect one on tape 10 times over, just one after another, bang, bang, bang, I got the feeling back. So for me I benefit from it, but the program on tape has to be really clean, so what you have to tape is exactly what you want to do at the event. It has to be a perfectly clean program. If there is a flaw in that program and you see it over ten or twenty or thirty times, the chances are that you will do that flaw again just by watching it. Subconsciously, all of a sudden, you have that same mistake before you can realize it has happened.

When I was younger, I didn't realize what imagery was, I just knew it helped me with my jumps. I never talked to anybody about it. If I was working on a new jump, I'd be lying in bed or sitting in the car almost ready to go into the rink. I would be sitting there and thinking about that jump, because I wanted to land it so badly. So I'd go through it in my mind and get the entire feel of it from the beginning to the end.

In skating, doing the elements is more of a feeling. People do jumps technically different. For instance, I do an axle jump, on a very tight circle, whereas some people do it on a very large circle. It can be successful both ways, but with me it is more the feeling that I get, and it is combined with adrenalin.

My imagery is not so much visual. It is more just feel. I don't think it is visual at all. When I'm watching it on video I look visually at it and then I get this internal feeling. When I'm actually doing it I get the same feeling inside. It is a very internal feeling that is hard to explain. You have to experience it, and once you do, then you know what you are going after. I can even get a feeling for an entire program. Sometimes in a practice I get myself psyched into a program that will win the Olympics, like I won the long program last year. I step on the ice and go to my starting position and I get this feeling, "I'm at the Olympic Games," and I sort of get the whole program flashed before my eyes and I get this internal feeling of how this program will be and usually I'm fresh and usually it will be a perfect program. I don't just step out there in training and just say, here we go, another program.

Before I go to a competition I do a lot in imagery. Once I'm there on-site, at the event I try to keep myself very low key. I skate well in practice to show them what we can do, although we don't want to show them everything. I'm in a position now I don't have to show them everything. I learned from my own mistakes in the 1982 World Championships. I went there wanting to skate well. I was the only person doing the triple axles, so I was doing ten or twenty of them in practice just to show them I could really do it. People used to get excited about seeing triple axles then, and I was just showing off and doing them all the time. By the time it came to compete I was just exhausted. So the next year I learned from that and kept myself pretty low key. I didn't over do it. That is one thing that happens to a lot of the skaters. They get there and they think they have to show others everything they have ever done in the first two practices, and it doesn't count then.

At the Olympics and at Worlds this year and last year, when I was in my room by myself, I put my costume on and went through my program with my costume on, just to get the feeling of that.

I normally do a high quality training, and that is influenced even by what I wear. I can't train in sweat pants and a sweat shirt and an old T-shirt. I like to go out in skating pants, nice body suit, something colourful. When I wear sweat pants I know that won't be the day to do a clean run-through which runs with pizazz. So I very rarely train in that. That is all part of getting into the right feeling for training.

To prepare for my competition performance, before the short and long program I always go out for a walk, an hour or two hours before, regardless what the weather is like, even if it is raining or snowing. We had the Canadian Championships in Brandon, Manitoba one year and it was forty below. I went out for a walk and took a few deep breaths and went through my program in my mind again, while I was walking. Sometimes I get to a fast part in my program and start skipping and picking the pace up and doing a lot of mental things. I know a lot of people try not to think about the event, try to keep their mind away from it, but I'm more into it when I'm down there. My mind is on it the whole way. When I was at the Worlds last year in Ottawa, I had a lot of friends there and they came to see me the day of the long program. I was sitting in my room and it was two or three hours before I had to go to the rink. We were sitting there watching a television program and they were talking to me and I didn't even hear them. They were laughing, because they couldn't believe I was so much into the event, "Nobody was home!"

At Olympics and at Worlds this year and last year, when I was in my room by myself, I put my costume on and went through my program with my costume on, just to get the feeling of that. I'm moving and doing landings and even trying to do some cuts on the floor. If somebody could see me doing that, they would think I was out of my mind. At that time I'm by myself in my room and just go through it. After that is usually the point where I take off my costume, pack it in my garment bag and start getting ready.

This year in Toyko before the short program I went to the ice rink early and didn't even go to the actual ice surface. I went to the dressing room, dropped off my stuff and went out for a walk. After my walk I put on my warm-up suit. What I do most times is go into the rink and go directly out to the ice surface, with all the TV lights on. There will be somebody skating, or they will be flooding the ice. I just go in and stare at the lights and the audience and get the feel of that and get myself into that scene. Last year at the Olympics, the change rooms were down this little stairway. It was like going down to a basement or dungeon, and what was happening upstairs was like a totally different world. So I put my skates on and went upstairs early enough for warm-up so I could get the feel of everything. After warm-up I had probably 10 to 15 minutes before I did my program. I stayed upstairs in that whole scene. There were some curtains. I even walked behind the bleachers, but I stayed up there. Once I'm there and I'm into it, and I see the lights and the audience, don't do anything to take me away from that.

For my on-ice warm-up I usually do just one of everything. The adrenalin is flying and there is no stopping me. I constantly go over to the coach more than anybody else in the whole competition, and it is only a 6 minute warm-up. I just coast by him and he just gives me a nod. I very rarely have problems with any elements at a warm-up so I

144

never have to go over and say, "What is wrong with this jump?" I just go over, and actually he never says anything. I just go over and he just gives me a nod. I guess I go over there for that nod.

I keep a very blank mind. I just go through the motions and don't think of anything. In a warm-up there are 6 or 8 skaters on the ice. You are aware of where they are so that you don't get in their way or they don't get in your way. That sort of thing keeps your focus so I don't start thinking negative things. It just kind of keeps me busy.

In 1982 I skated first after warm-up. That was the year I never slowed down and kept going to the last minute. Then, "The first skater is Brian Orser," and I went out and never really had time to bring myself down and talk to Doug and get my thoughts together and get myself psyched. The next year I skated first again, so Doug told me to get off the ice a minute and a half early and I came right off the ice. Most people stay on the ice. I got right off the ice and pretended I was skater #2 or #3 and I went around and paced around a little bit, and got myself psyched up and that worked. I skated much better. I learned from that experience.

Sometimes there are up to 6 skaters in a group. With a 4½ minute program and with the time it takes for marks, you can skate up to half an hour later. So you have to keep yourself warmed-up, but you can't keep yourself moving too much or you will burn up too much energy. Sometimes I will go off on my own and my coach just stands there so that I know where he is, if I need him. He never follows me around or discusses things. I see that with other coaches and skaters. The skater would just love to say, "Get off my back right now!" but don't want to say it at that point. I just go off on my own. I know exactly where he is and I will come back to him and give him a little nod and he'll come walking with me. Then all of a sudden I will just hang a left and go off on my own again, and he'll know exactly what to do. Stay there. Sometimes I will spend the whole time with him, sometimes I will spend very little time with him, sometimes if I have half an hour to wait I will take my skates off and put my shoes on and jump around a little bit and stretch. When the skater before me is on, I always sit down in a chair, and not move around too much. I feel good doing that, so I do it. If I had to stand on my head before I skated, I would do it.

I'm not thinking too much of my program with actual steps and that sort of thing. I'm just getting myself psyched into getting the adrenalin going. I know that it has to happen. The whole scene makes it happen. I don't like it to happen too soon. Sometimes I get all hyper and I don't need it yet. When the skater before me is on, that is when I get hyped. The hardest part, the most vital part, is when the last skater has skated and I go out on the ice and his marks are coming up. We have to stay in our own little area for 20 seconds or so. I have the same little routine that I do, and that's when it comes to a head as far as adrenalin needs. When I watch it on TV I don't even realize I'm doing this, but I can see myself so ready to go. Like a horse that is ready to go before the gun goes off. I do that each time. I do the same stretches each time and I can see the determination, putting my hands together, punching my fists together, and I always look at Doug and give him a signal, like I'm okay kind of thing. Then they say, "next skater representing Canada . . ." then I go. I come out

There is a certain mood I have to get into for my program. There is a feeling in my program. I have to get myself into the mood of the progam theme.

145

to a stop point and they just start my music. I've been standing there and I get ready. There is a certain mood I have to get into for my program. There is a feeling in my program. I have to get myself into the mood of the program theme. I have different moods that I have to get into for that program. For instance, this year, my short program was "Cats", so I had to get into that. My long program was a James Bond film, so I had to get into that mood.

I get into the mood before the music even starts. I'm totally into myself at that point. I go out and they say, "Brian Orser of Canada." I make my presentation to the crowd, a smile or something. When we are performing at home, in Ottawa at Worlds for instance, there would be some stamping or they will start whistling or calling your name but I shut it all out. I become the character of the theme. I probably have the same expression a diver would before they make the dive. I think that is concentration, but it is also trying to get in that right mood.

During the program, I'm not thinking about anything, I'm just going through the program, like I do at home. I remember at the Olympics the first 1½ to 2 minutes is the crucial point, that is really hard. Once I got past that, I remember at one point I looked around and saw all the Olympic symbols on the boards and thought, "Wooow! I'm at the Olympics!" I had finished the hard part and it was at a non-crucial point. That is when I took a breath and looked around and thought, wow! This is while I'm doing the performance. I've never done that before. All of a sudden the next piece started and then I went right back into it.

Three weeks before the Olympics, we had the Canadian Championships in Regina. That was my all time worst performance. My all-time best that year was my performance at the Olympics. I think because it was an Olympic year and they had hyped the Olympics so much that when I got to the Canadians, I couldn't get into it. I remember sitting in the bus from the airport saying, "What am I doing here? I don't want to be here." I had a hell of a time getting myself psyched up for that whole week. Even though I still won I really bombed the long program because I had my focus on three weeks later at the Olympics. I wasn't activated, I wasn't on the ice at all. You could really see it from my expression, the way I skated. I remember the press asking, "What are you going to do, are you going to do so badly at the Olympics?" And so on. . .I said, "Don't worry, I am so glad this happened at the Canadian Championships because now this is behind me and I can focus on the Olympics."

At the Olympics things were different from any event I've been in. That helped me a lot as well. I went to watch the Olympics in Lake Placid, but being a spectator and being a competitor are two different things. Wearing my Olympic uniform all over the place, seeing all the other athletes in the cafeteria, that whole scene. The environment was uplifting. Not having the focus on just figure skating was good, because there were the skiers and they were having their problems with conditions, and there was the focus on Gaetan Boucher winning a gold medal. There were all kinds of things that took the limelight off us which was great.

This year I skated great at the Canadian Championships, it was my all-time best. There is no comparison as to how I felt. Last year I

All you have to do is do something once to know that it is in there and try and find that feeling. Sometimes it just takes lying on the bed for an hour and thinking back to how that felt.

146

missed the first element. For the rest of the program I was thinking negative things and saying, "God, don't fall." Normally I never think that way. I go for the feeling, I never think about technical terms, I never think about my arm, I never think about that sort of thing. I try to get the feeling before I do it.

A lot of times during a practice session when I help a skater with a jump, it is not so much that the left arm has to be here, the right arm has to be here. It is all in the type of feeling that you have to develop. When you land that jump once, you can think back to how that felt. All you have to do is do something once to know that it is in there and try and find that feeling. Sometimes it just takes lying on the bed for an hour and thinking back to how that felt. Sometimes it just comes to you. Other times I've lost it. I had problems with my triple axle and I lost it for over two months. I'm expected to do that now at a World Championship. I went back and watched the tapes and the feeling came back again.

I am the one who has to go out and skate. No one else can do it for me, so I like to be the one to get myself in the right frame of mind. I have to do my imagery when I feel like doing it, when the time is right for me. Even when I'm driving sometimes, it is terrible but I'll be driving and thinking about my long program. All of a sudden, I'm driving from Orillia to Toronto and I'm in Toronto and I think, "Wooow, what am I doing here?"

I have to motivate myself. If I go out and screw up it is my fault. I know at the Nationals I didn't skate well and I knew it was my fault, because I wasn't psyched for it. There was nobody else to blame.

I know I have benefitted from being here in Orillia. Our entire club has always worked together even though there are 6 or 7 different coaches. If I have a problem and my coach is busy, I can go to another coach and ask him to have a look at something, and not worry about competition between coaches and competition between skaters. In some of the clubs so and so's skaters will fight against so-and-so's skaters. We are away from all of that. Everybody works together.

I have friends away from skating here. That also helps me get away a little bit. You can't have your mind totally focused all the time. Ten years from now I don't want to look back to this time of my life and regret doing it. These are supposed to be the best years of your life. This past few years I have been going out to the rink and working, and of course last year, I was thinking about the Olympics most of the time, but thank God I had my family and friends to take my focus off a little bit and take away the tension.

This year, I had a problem with a pair of boots, and I had only had them for a month or so. It was the beginning of summer. I was thinking I have been off for a while, I haven't got my feet used to them yet, although the boots didn't feel right. In fact the boots didn't feel right when I first put them on, but I gave them a chance because I hate blaming equipment. Finally I got to the point where I said it is definitely the boots. If it is not, I think it is anyway, so let's ditch them and get a new pair. So I got rid of the boots and got a new pair and started skating better. So whether it is the boots or not, or whether it is in my head, it worked. Change it, get rid of it, get a new one. Don't talk about it. Just do it!

I have friends away from skating here. That also helps me get away a little bit. You can't have your mind totally focused all the time.

147

I have been influenced by my father a lot. He is goal-oriented and I sort of watched him grow from the beginning in business. He started off as a helper on a coke truck and now he owns the largest bottling company in Canada. Coca Cola, Schweppes and the whole thing. So he has worked his way up, and I watched him do it and the way he has done it. He never really sat down and talked to me and told me to set goals and that sort of thing. I have watched him.

Doug my coach is also very goal-oriented and very positive and that has also helped. I remember when I was younger we used to sit down and fill out a form because we were going to summer skating school. We would get a form and fill out what we wanted to accomplish at summer school. It is a very small thing but that helped me a lot. You say, by the end of summer school I want to be doing triple toe loops, or triple axles. So you go into the rink on the first day and say, "Yeah, I better get my butt in gear for that one!" I wrote this down so I should be doing it. A lot of the time the kids just go through the motions. They go to summer school, they go to the rink each day, they put in their time, they go home. No specific goals. If you write something down, sit down and think about it for five or ten minutes, at least you've thought about it. Okay, I want to win Canadians, win something. It is such a small thing but it can turn out to be a big bonus.

I was disappointed after this year's Worlds, very disappointed. I didn't skate up to par. Three days before I left to go to the World Championships, they diagnosed that I had pneumonia. I was going through all that therapy and couldn't take proper medication for it because of the doping control. So I had a heck of a time and it put a damper on a lot of things. I wasn't feeling one hundred percent. Also there was a lot of pressure because I was expected to win. I never thought of coming down with pneumonia and not being able to count on an extra little boost of energy. You don't prepare for that sort of thing. Under the circumstances I did pretty well. I never told the press, I never told anybody I had pneumonia. My family knew and my coaches knew and that was about it. Of course a lot of our team members knew, like our team officials, but no-one else knew. I didn't want to make any excuses. They would say that it is an easy out. I was pleased with the outcome just because of that. I was also very pleased with the figures because I moved up to 4th this year, which was a big step for me. At that point, everybody thought I had it in the bag. I was feeling a lot of pressure. The day after I finished my long program I could hardly move. My back and neck were so sore just from tension. I didn't really know I was carrying so much there. I could hardly get out of bed the next day it was so sore. I have never experienced that before.

I think this year it will be a little easier going into Worlds because I will be going in as the underdog. Last year I went in as the favourite, Scott Hamilton retired and I was favoured to win. I did a very good short, very good figures, the long wasn't my best and it wasn't my worst. It was enough for 2nd place. The skater who won deserved to win. He skated very well. He skated cleanly. He keeps me on my toes.

I think back to the Olympics and I see tapes and pictures of the Olympics, and I get that feeling of how I was there when I was part of it, which was a really neat feeling. It's very unique and very special.

148

Even some of the kids that I talked to that didn't do well, still had the same feeling about the Olympics. I want to experience that again and I want to win. That is what I want the most, because that is the ultimate. Having it in Canada in 1988 is also good.

A month and a half ago at the press conference after the World Championships the Russian skater was there with me. He speaks pretty good English but he didn't answer any of the questions himself. His translator answered all of them for him. They asked him about the Olympics and the translator said, "Yes, he'll be at the Olympics and he is going to win the Olympics." I looked over and got this sort of fire inside me and thought, "No way is he going to win the Olympics in Canada, there is no way!" If I have to stick it out three more years, I'll do it, because I don't want him to do it, especially not in Canada. It gave me a little shot.

I looked over and got this sort of fire inside me and thought, "No way is he going to win the Olympics in Canada, there is no way!"

17
ANNE OTTENBRITE

1984 OLYMPIC CHAMPION — SWIMMING

> **ANNE OTTENBRITE SWIMMING**
>
> - Gold Medalist (200m Breaststroke), Silver Medalist (100m Breaststroke), Bronze Medalist (4x100m Medley Relay) at the 1984 Olympic Games
> - Gold Medalist (100m Breaststroke), Silver Medalist (4x100m Medley Relay) at the 1983 Pan American Games
> - 1982 Commonwealth Games — Double Gold Medalist (200m Breaststroke, 4x100m Medley Relay), Silver Medalist (100m Breaststroke)
> - 1982 World Championships — Silver Medalist (tie) (100m Breaststroke), Bronze Medalist (200m Breaststroke).

I had a knee injury right before the Olympics. I didn't start doing whip kicks again until two weeks before the Olympics. On a ten point scale, my physical, technical, and mental readiness for the Olympics was a "nine". Without the knee injury it would be "tens" for all of them. I was just not mentally ready. I didn't have enough time to recover, for the strength to be there. But I liked the attitude that I went with. I just went to the race saying, "It's anybody's race; I could do it, but I might not." I went in with a real loose attitude, and that's the best way for me. I always have to joke around. I can't get tense about a race. I was just glad to be there. I had thought that I wasn't even going to be able to go to the Olympics because of my knee injury. I wasn't going in with high, high expectations, but I was very psyched up after Alex Baumann's swim because I was in the next event.

When I was younger, before I started swimming, I remember watching the Olympics on TV and saying, "I want to go to the Olympics and win." I started swimming when I was thirteen. My goal, which I've always had, was to win a gold medal at the Olympics. That's the only goal I've ever had.

Three months before the Olympics, I firmly believed that I could win a gold based on my training. I had been doing really amazing workouts. A lot of athletes get really scared and think that Canadians can't do it. I don't get psyched out by the other athletes. The Russians

I just swam because I had fun and I loved it.

151

When I was younger, before I started swimming, I remember watching the Olympics on TV and saying, "I want to go to the Olympics and win." I started swimming when I was thirteen. My goal, which I've always had, was to win a gold medal at the Olympics. That's the only goal I've ever had.

When I'm daydreaming I feel the excitement, and then when I finish and I see that I have won, I always see myself coming up out of the water, holding up one fist and saying, "Yeah!"

or Germans don't scare me. As long as I'm doing really well in workouts, that means that I'm doing really well all over. I never really have any problems in my head. I don't let anything bother me very much. A lot of things happen which I should get uptight about, but I just say, "Oh well!" I've always been like that. Maybe Paul, my coach, does the worrying for me. He takes care of little details.

In preparing for the Olympics I usually had no problems at all in keeping motivated to train. There were times when I'd say to myself, "I don't feel like going swimming today," but I'd go and get in and have fun. I just swam because I had fun and I loved it.

I think I trained differently from other swimmers. I usually did 4000 metres each workout, and a lot of it was high quality. There was just one main set. Also, I needed to do a lot of stroke work because I have a weird stroke. My training is altogether different because other swimmers do low pace times, and we do high pace times.

I used to daydream a lot about swimming, especially before going to the Olympics. It started before the first meet I'd ever won and I've done it ever since. I would just go off into some little space where I'd "see" myself swimming. I'm in my body but I can also see myself. It's just me swimming, and I can feel the excitement. I see myself swimming, and then I see myself winning. When I'm daydreaming I feel the excitement, and then when I finish and I see that I have won, I always see myself coming up out of the water, holding up one fist and saying, "Yeah!" This is what I always wanted to do at the Olympics, win the gold and be able to go, "Yeah!" I never actually held up my fist at any other meets. I saved it until I achieved the one goal that I'd always wanted.

I've always been the type of person that goes off in a daydream. People will be talking to me, and I'll be "out of it". People will see it in my eyes, that I'm not comprehending. I can just blank things out. I do it with everything, but I did it most with swimming, before the Olympics.

The night before a competition I listen to a tape on my Walkman. I did that at the Olympics too. There are a couple of songs that really psych me up. The beat goes with my stroke. I can see myself swimming with it, I can feel my stroke and I sort of get excited. I don't go through the whole race. I just see parts of the race, maybe my start and my finish; just the best parts.

I don't have the typical pattern of preparation. Some athletes really get screwed up when things aren't just the way they want them to be. But I'm not like that. The coaches tell us little things about what to expect, but I never notice the kind of stuff that worries most other people. I'm weird! People say, "Oh God, aren't you nervous?" and I say, "No, I only get nervous two months before I'm up on the blocks — no need to get nervous now." I know that I'm different. A lot of people have to be really quiet and not bothered with people, but I have to joke around with people, go, "Yeah!", and punch them around a little. I'm a very physical person.

The ready room was a tent at Los Angeles. In that room I don't look at the other swimmers because they sit there just staring at you, trying to scare you. They make noises and that kind of stuff. I hate when people try to scare me before a race but I use it to my advantage because it makes me feel even tougher. It just makes me want to beat them even more.

Usually before I swim, the coaches say, "Why don't you go out in this split, and come back in this?" It doesn't take me long to adjust. I'm really good at pacing. I can usually feel what pace I'm in. The coaches know me. They know that with my stroke I have to take it out fairly easy, and then build the whole race. If the coach gives me pre-race splits that I don't agree with I say, "That doesn't feel good doing it that way." My coach and I respect each other's opinion. We've tried to experiment and we've ended up going with what feels best.

Two or three minutes before the race I feel sort of numb. At that point I don't close things out. If a lot of people are standing at the end of my lane yelling for me before the race, I see them and I smile or laugh at them. At the Olympics I knew all those people were there, and I was looking up and saying, "Oh, look at all those people watching me swim." It's only just before the race starts that I focus in on the job.

Between heats and finals, if I swim a bad heat I just say, "Well, it's a morning swim, I'll do better tonight." Then I work on the mistakes I made, or on whatever the coaches say I should do about my splits.

Since the Olympics I'm finding myself very unmotivated. I don't daydream about swimming any more. I used to do it naturally, but now I don't do it at all. Now I'm daydreaming about new goals that I've set for myself, like what I'll be doing in communications after I've finished school. So I'm wondering if it's just time to quit swimming. It's hard for me, because I've always just had that one swimming goal. It has always been there, and I would always daydream about it, or not daydream at all.

I don't have any regrets. I'm really glad that I went to the Olympics and did what I did. I've always done other things while I was training: I rode horses, and went out with my friends on weekends. I didn't miss out on anything because of swimming. It wasn't like I hibernated. Otherwise I wouldn't have been able to take it. I would have quit if I hadn't been able to lead a full life. There were times when I had to give up things, but that's nothing major. Everybody has to give up something, at some point in their life.

There are a couple of songs that really psych me up. The beat goes with my stroke. I can see myself swimming with it, I can feel my stroke and I sort of get excited.

My coach and I respect each other's opinion. We've tried to experiment and we've ended up going with what feels best.

18
STEVE PODBORSKI

1982 WORLD CUP DOWNHILL CHAMPION — ALPINE SKIING

STEVE PODBORSKI ALPINE SKIING

- Member of 1980 and 1984 Canadian Olympic Teams
- First North American Male Skier to Win a World Cup Downhill Title — 1982
- Top Ranked Downhiller in the World for 1980-81 by the Federation Internationale de Ski
- Winner of 8 World Cup Races
- Bronze Medal — 1980 Olympics — Downhill

Without knowing what to expect, the Olympics can be a horrible time in your life. Look at Lake Placid. It was the worst two weeks in my life. First, I got searched at customs. I have been travelling across the States for many years, and had never been searched. But because it was the Olympics they opened all our bags. Then we got to the race site and they said that we couldn't take the bus across this bridge to take our ski bags into the waxing rooms. We were supposed to unload our skis, put them in a pick-up truck, drive the pick-up truck across and unload them. Totally ridiculous. An hour and many arguments later, we drove the bus across and unloaded our skis. Then the bus got stuck. We finally unstuck the bus by pushing it with a snow cat, drove to the village, and went through a lengthy check-in procedure, which is no big deal unless you haven't experienced it. But there was a photographer who decided he had to get all these wild shots, and he had to have them right now. I finally said, "Look man, I've got to go, it's 3 in the afternoon, I haven't had lunch, I've got lots of things to do." He started giving me this story about how he has to feed his wife and children. I don't need that, I'm here to do something, not stand taking pictures on ice sculptures all afternoon. What irritated me most, was that an official from the alpine team who was supposed to be on my side, was saying, "Steve, take it easy, you've got to help the poor guy." "Who's side are you on man?" I was going crazy, I didn't need it. Then it got worse.

We were the darlings of the Games that year. The press said, "They have a good chance for a medal." Then a couple of days later,

Without knowing what to expect, the Olympics can be a horrible time in your life.

"They are probably going to win a gold." Then, "They could win more than one medal, they could win a gold and a bronze, or maybe a gold and a silver, they could win three medals." Finally, "They are probably going to win three medals." They kept going on like that. The racers were all saying, "Wait, anything could happen. Take it easy." We were all blown up out of proportion.

Unforeseen things were happening all the time, like surprise press conferences. I was walking through the village and some official says, "Good to see you are heading to the press conference." Press conference! The Olympic committee, or whoever was in charge, was setting up things to help promote the sport; very well meaning, but it wasn't designed to help our situation, which is performance, not promotion. Things like that were constantly happening.

This press conference came out of nowhere. I still don't know who organized it. I went but I was getting pretty irritated by this point. We were getting up at 5 in the morning to get to the hill on time for a 10 a.m. run. It was really a hassle. I looked around and didn't recognize anybody. All the regular reporters who we talk to all the time had been sent out elsewhere. They are the ones who know the racers, how old they are, and what is going on. The ones here were all the editors and were there because it was a heavy story. They were smoking cigars and the place stank. The first guy says, "You look pretty small to be a downhiller, don't you?" Another says, "What happens if you knock down a gate, does that disqualify you?" I'm thinking, "Give me a break, I'm not here for that. If you want to know information like that ask a coach, ask the program director, ask somebody who is not performing." By that time I was just irritated. I didn't realize this was part of the whole scene.

We also had to go to cocktail parties. It seemed we were there to perform for the people who were running the show and keep them happy. That was disturbing to me. It seemed we were not there for us. I somehow had the mistaken idea we were there to race, that we were supposed to be there to perform for ourselves and for Canada.

It was interesting, but it wasn't enjoyable because there was so much pulling on me. After I finished my event, I had a good time. Up to that time it was really crazy.

As I pushed out of the starting gate, I thought, "It is all over. Thank God it is all over, the crap is over. Now all I have to do is ski." I normally never think things like that but it just kind of popped into my head. I threw all the hassles into the back of my mind and pushed out. That was a great feeling because I was already into the race. I was finally finished with all that crap, and into what I was there to do. It was a relief to be skiing. I had a good run too.

Prior to expecting to be a medalist at the Olympics, it is important to know what to expect. Everything was unforeseen in 1980. We had a very good team, and that was my first Games. We were on the doorstep of Canada and there were a lot of Canadians and extra officials there. Our ski team had built up this whole system that worked for World Cup racing. We raced World Cup races 10 times a year. Then we went to the Olympics and outside people started telling us how to run our show. Our masseur was living at the other side of Lake Placid in a house. It is very hard to get a massage over the telephone. We

156

also had two coaches, our ski man, and our team manager living far away from us at that house.

In preparation for the 1984 Olympics, we had a big meeting in Calgary one summer and dealt with all those problems. It is extremely important to recognize the fact that many teams have built up a system that works, and that's why they're successful. It is not the team that should have to fit into the Olympic system. The system should fit around the team, so that they can continue to be successful. A racer has reached the ultimate in performance by working in a way that works. You can't expect him to change everything in one week and still beat everyone else in the world.

The system you are used to or are comfortable with, should be the one you follow for the Olympics. It seems so simple. Yet when you get to the Olympics you have these people who think, "We've got a lot going on here fella and we can't cater to each sport." But I think that's what they are supposed to do. In my opinion, if you want people to win, then allow them to win. That means let them do what they know works, because they have been doing it more than some official has. As an athlete you get one chance every four years.

When we're in Europe racing in the World Cup, the head coach is the team leader, the manager, and the boss. He's the one who sets up all the interviews and knows what the routine is. It is not some official from Ottawa. When we have had problems before, it was when an Ottawa team manager or official came in and started running things. When people go to these officials who are supposed to represent us, and ask, "What should we do, the officials don't go to the coach and say, "Well what should we do?" They say, "The racers will do that." It doesn't make sense from the racers' point of view. They should go to the one who is actually, literally running the team on-site. The coach is the guy who knows what to do for performance.

I was on the National Team for eleven years. I finally retired after the 1984 Olympics. The first year I won a World Cup was in 1979. It was a mental step that allowed me to do it. I'd been on the team for some time. I knew that I was a good skier. I was racing in the first seed and I was in the top three once or twice. As I was sliding down the course one day in St. Moritz, I looked around at the other guys and they were all nervous. It was a new course and they were all pretty scared. I realized that I was not scared. I wasn't intimidated by the course. I thought, "Gee, I can win here. If I do everything right, I should be able to win here. I can win." It hit me like a lightning bolt. I said, "Well, why not?" And I just went out and did it. It wasn't as if it was a shot in the dark. I had ability to win, all I had to do is do everything right. That thought sort of hit me and I won the next two races after that. Everything really clicked from then on. Expecting to win wasn't a large leap in credibility. It was a recognition of the fact that I could win if I did things right.

I think the training I did over the years was quite a bit different, particularly from the Europeans, and also somewhat different from our own team. I found early on that there was very little feedback from the alpine team in a real day-to-day manner regarding my dry-land training. That's just a natural problem in a country like Canada, simply because of its geography.

As I pushed out of the starting gate, I thought, "It is all over. Thank God it is all over, the crap is over. Now all I have to do is ski."

The first year I won a World Cup was in 1979. It was a mental step that allowed me to do it.

157

I started working with a dryland coach after my brother hurt his knee and started to cycle; subsequently I hurt my knee and started to cycle as well. The trainer and I had daily conversations about how my training was going, how fit I was, how I was feeling, and we worked together to develop a weight training program. Our summer training program, which in my opinion is the foundation of the skiing, was superior to what everyone else was doing. I was not great in cardio-vascular type events. With the cycling I became adequate.

In preparing for a race, part of our whole thing is ritual. The ritual of arriving at the race on a certain day. Then the first inspection and the training runs, usually on Thursday and Friday. Then the race on Saturday, day off Sunday, travel Monday. There's a whole build up to a race that's really consistent in World Cup. In the Olympics, it is a different story. The race could be any day of the week, plus you have things like opening ceremonies which you don't have at World Cup races. The downhill event is the first day of the Olympics, which is the day after the opening ceremonies. The opening ceremonies aren't set up around the downhill training schedule, so it makes it different from the World Cup.

Before I arrived in Sarajevo I thought there was a good possibility I could win a medal. I was quite realistic. My goal going in was to get a medal. After looking at the course, in my deeper subconscious, I thought, "When is the next World Cup race?" The hill had been changed quite dramatically from the year before when we had a pre-Olympic race, in which I placed second. So I was a little disappointed that they had made the course somewhat less terrifying. It wasn't as favourable to my style of skiing. Deep down I felt I didn't have a chance. Of course I was trying desperately to deny this little thing, and I tried very hard in the race and ended up getting an eighth place, which is obviously nowhere. It ended up being a disappointment for me. That's the nature of downhill in the Olympic Games. The Olympic Games by its very nature is a compromise, particularly related to the outdoor events that aren't on a standard track. That's just one thing everyone has to deal with.

I had some good results prior to Sarajevo and I knew I was getting pretty peaked. I expected the course to be the same as the year before where I had a second place. I knew that if I had a good day on that course, I had a good chance to win a medal. The change in the course at the Olympics was my monkey wrench. When they changed the course, my goals changed. If I had won a medal, I would have been really happy. After they changed the course, if I had've won a medal, it would've been a miracle. That's how I looked at it.

Physically, I was one hundred percent. I was fit. Technically, on a scale of 1 to 10, again, as good as I could be, maybe a 9; technical equipment, I had the best. It is as simple as that. I could not fault my equipment at all. Mentally, I was probably a 6 or a 7, because with a week weather delay we didn't get the good skiing, and also I knew the course wasn't going to be as good as it could be for me.

There are many factors that go into a performance. The equipment is important, the skis, and boots, and suits. By the time you get on the hill you have a lot of things behind you, good summer training and good ski training. Everybody basically has the same tools, within

158

a certain leeway. But there's only one guy that wins, the guy with a desire, who wants to win the most.

Another thing that is very important, that gets you to the point where you are one of the elite, is the ability to actually visualize not only the way it looks when you are going down, but how it feels. The ability to feel the muscle tension that you actually go through when you make the turns, and to experience what attitude your body is in is really important. I feel what things will feel like and see everything run through in my head. I have a moving picture with feelings and sensations. When I'm doing these mental runs, I'll do the run and if I make a mistake, I'll stop the picture and back it up. Then I run it through and usually get it right the second time. I run through the entire course like that. This ability is sort of an ingrained thing. It takes years and years of practice of visualization.

When we have fall training camps, we'll set a course, and we'll run it for a week. Over the first four runs the guys who were winning the timed runs were the top racers, Ken, or Todd, or me. By the end of the week the young guys were winning the runs and we were getting farther back. We had explored the full potential of the course in about 4 or 5 runs. Then we started to go over the edge and lose ground. The young guys don't learn as quickly. They can't do the great things as well in this mental picture. That is my assumption, and I'm pretty sure it is correct.

When they used to ask Jean Claude Killy to describe a course, he would describe it and come in within a second of the actual race time. One time someone said to me, "Steve, quickly describe the course for me." I said, "Well, you go out of the start, you go left, you go right, you go over a jump, you go along a flat . . ." He timed it without me knowing and I came within a second of the time of the race. That is the kind of tune your mind and body gets into.

The way to memorize the course is to make visual clues and then start to link them together so they are continuous. You find out just how hard you have to turn at each gate and then it starts to become easier to integrate. It takes a lot of effort and concentration to be able to do this. But after you have been on the tour for a long time, you know the basic hill orientation. There's about 2 miles and you know it all. I start at the beginning and link it all together. The first thing you do at a race is get on the hill and inspect. You go to the start and just slide down at whatever pace you want. They give you an hour or an hour and a half to get down the 2 or 2½ miles of hill. I start down, come to the first corner, look around the corner and see how tight it is, what condition the snow is in and how much room you have there. Then I decide on a line, or the best approach to enter and exit the corner. One of the important factors is the exit from the turn and where you are going for the next one. If I hit this turn better, I will be going that much faster for the next one, so I will have to integrate that with the rest of the course, in a flash. You memorize the direction you are coming from, entering, and the direction you want to be going, exiting, and where you are in relation to the next gate.

Then you get to the second gate. You think okay, relate it to the first one. Gee, this is a little tighter than last year, so you're going to have to move the first line. You don't actually move back uphill, you think okay, just tighten that up here. It is all done up in your head.

You have to take your body and image, and picture the other guy's line, and somehow find your style within his line. It is a very creative process.

159

I was aware that I had to enjoy it, or I would never have been able to go on for that long.

On our team we follow the same routine throughout the week so there are no surprises on race day, like sudden traffic jams.

Then you start drawing your line, section by section all the way down. But it is a whole. The line from the first gate, weirdly enough, affects the line at the last gate. The farther away it is the less bearing it has, but they are all together. I look at the section until I have it ingrained. Then I close my eyes and see exactly the same thing. I see the course. I see mostly the surface snow and where I am going around the corner. I also feel what it will be like to do that. I see out of my eyes, I feel the tension in my muscles, the pressure on my feet and on my knees, and my balance. One of my biggest technical problems was standing too upright. So I would feel myself being low in the upper body when I was racing in my mind.

The mental part is amazing. Let's say there's a corner I'm having real trouble with. If, as I am going down, I think, "What are you doing here?", I just mess up. If I'm in the same place on the hill but approach it with a sort of mental clarity with a specific focus, that makes it possible. The mental clarity, and the ability to integrate it quickly, is a learned thing. The young guys have not learned to do it as well as the old guys. The old guys get into the course faster. That is a learned process, no question.

I worked on my imagery a lot in training. It is critical. We study the course, we work on our line and on our mental approach. In the evenings we look at videos of certain sections of the course before races. We have section times of most parts of the hill on the video. We see who is the best in those sections and basically copy the line. You have to take your body and image, and picture the other guy's line, and somehow find your style within his line. It is a very creative process. That goes on constantly in training. The young guys watch the old guys, the old guys watch each other. We are all trying to adapt.

My problem was that I was racing against natural athletes who work their arses off. To beat them, assuming I have all these gifts as well, I have to work my arse off a little bit harder. When you have all the same tools as everybody else and you want to get ahead more, it is the work aspect that gets you through. I certainly worked harder than other athletes in a lot of areas. I did a lot of things besides just cycling and weight training and doing it on the hill. I even worked on ski boot design. Putting a little bit extra in allows you to get a little extra out.

I always felt I had the talent, I had everything, and I worked really hard, maybe harder than others, and I was quite successful. And I enjoyed the whole thing. I made sure I enjoyed it. The stuff I did, I did it right. I did quality work and enjoyed it. It was fun to ski, and all that stuff was enjoyable. I was aware that I had to enjoy it, or I would never have been able to go on for that long.

In fall training you get an hour of downhill training, total. That is 60 runs. It takes at least 40 days or more to get 60 runs, so if we get a minute of training in our specific event per day, that's a lot. When you think of it in those terms, you realize it is very important to get the quality. It is not just taking a lot of runs. You can't ski yourself into shape.

To prepare myself to do quality runs in training I make sure I am in good physical shape, and I make sure when I do my free skiing that I try to make good turns. When I get to the starting gate, it is

160

almost a race run. I have thought about the course, I have prepared mentally for the run, my boots are done up the way they should be, I'm concentrating, and I make a good run. I don't screw around because I only get a few runs a day. That's it. Plus, if you are not concentrating when you are going downhill, you don't just bump your head on the end of the pool, right? It is "tits up" if you make a serious mistake. You have to be continually aware.

The mental preparation for my event kind of built up through the week. But the night before a race I never got uptight about the whole thing. At that point I just thought, I've spent the whole week training, I've spent years training before that, I can't do anything more now, so forget it! I'd run through the course in my head. If it was bothering me, I'd run it through until I knew I had done everything right. Then I was okay. I'd just say, "Go to sleep and do it tomorrow."

On our team we follow the same routine throughout the week so there are no surprises on race day, like sudden traffic jams. We get up at 7:30 a.m. even though the race is at noon. We get up at the same time and just follow the normal routine. I have a regular old breakfast, jump into the van, and drive up to the hill. We get up on the hill at least 1½ or 2 hours before the start. When I arrive at the hill I know exactly what I'm going to do. I know which hill I'm going to ski for warm-up, approximately how many runs I'll get in and how long the line ups are going to be. It's all there in my head. We ski for an hour, then get to an inside area where we change into our suits. I like to get to the start areas at least half an hour before the first racer.

It is very frustrating when there are eighty million buses in front of you, or if you are not allowed lift privileges, or somebody changes the parameters of what you are doing, as in the Olympics. It can blow you away. I can handle this now. After a while you know that it is going to happen. In the little league you just freak out. Now, having gone through the experience and still having skied well, with zippo warm-up training, I just say, "Hey, listen, I can handle this." Because I can. It is not ideal, but you still have to do well.

Half an hour before I race I start getting nervous, just like I am now. Everytime I think about it, it sends me off the deep end. At that time I'm starting to get pretty well "into" the whole thing. My heart rate is up, my breathing is erratic, I'm sweating and I don't talk to anybody. I go into the starting area and find my ski man, get my skis, and check out where the binding guy is, because he is going to adjust them for me. I say, "Hi!" to everybody and let them know I'm there. I give my goggles to the guy so he can put a new lens in, same fellow every time. I wander around and chat with people and do my stretching. The ski man brings my skis over at least 15 minutes before I start, gets them all adjusted and done up tight and then says, "Good luck." Near the end, I do my final stretching. At that time I'm really not thinking too much about the course. I take off my clothes, get into the starting gate, and I sort out what is going to happen. By that point I'm down in this primal thought pattern. I'm thinking, "Go for it! I've got to watch this corner, I've got to watch that corner. I've got to go for it." "Go for it" is sort of the theme that's running through my head all the time. There are a few points in the course where I may have been having trouble, or I want to do something in particular, so I think about that, but I always think, "I want to go for it, I

By that point I'm down in this primal thought pattern. I'm thinking, "Go for it! I've got to watch this corner, I've got to watch that corner. I've got to go for it!"

161

want to go for it, I want to go for it!" Then when I push out of the starting gate I don't think about anything. If you have come very close to being in a car crash, that's what I feel like. My body just slips right into overdrive, it just reacts. The only reason why I still manage to ski through all this is because the skills are so deeply ingrained in me. My body knows what to do, and I just let it go. Usually it makes the right decision, obviously, because I have had some success. That's because it has had tested moments before and I can apply them to the race.

The race happens so damn fast. I'm looking, I'm feeling and I'm hearing. A tremendous amount of data is going in, and I can't describe to you how much I see. I can see the changes in the snow. I know how much it is going to grip and let go. I can feel the tip of my skis, as a discreet part of my sensory input. I know what is happening out there. The whole ski is an extension of my body. I can feel out there. Very strange, but I can feel the change as I go over a small patch of ice. It goes under my ski at a fairly slow speed, relative to the speed I'm actually going. So there is a lot of input and a lot of data being analyzed. It's very important to be able to "read" all this stuff and have it come through. I don't have time to think, "Oh well, it looks like I'm going to have to change my weight here." You're going very fast, eighty miles an hour. I would be past it by the time I finished the thought.

If I ever got distracted by the thought of outcome during a race, it was really a bad thing. The only outcome thought I had consistently, was when I was about to fall. "This is not going to be good for my run." When I went over the edge, I'd think, "That can hurt." But just before falling, I'd think, "This is not going to be good for my run. You can't mess up the run!" Then once you are past the point of no return, I'd think, "Oh shit!"

I have had things happen in races that I totally forget. Someone would say, "Oh you nearly ended it on that turn." I would think back and I really had caught an edge. But I was so busy trying to do the next thing, which is the right thing to do, that I'd forget about that one before. That happened all the time. It is a very primal kind of thing. It is not thinking. It is not conscious. It is not like I have to get higher or try harder. I was getting to the point where I could integrate it pretty quickly and it was just a question of going for it.

I discovered that after a certain point of nervousness, I would start to deteriorate pretty rapidly. There was a real drop-off point in my ability to perform if I got too nervous. For a three year period I was seldom out of the top fifteen, maybe twice in three years, which is unheard of. Being in the top ten or top fifteen is quite respectable in downhill and I was in the top three, twenty times, and there were eight times when I won a World Cup race. Once I reached a real good steady state and I knew how to do it, I was very consistently in the top three.

There were a number of factors that influenced this, like the ability to control your tension. You need a certain amount of tension to be able to go. Primitive thought pattern. On the other hand if you are too far gone, you just go off the deep end, you lose control. So it was just being able to find that little narrow comfort zone, to get into the right area. I had to learn what was important and what wasn't.

162

In discovering the proper tension level I was on a continuing evolution the whole time I skied, but I think I really hit the key after 4 or 5 years on the Canadian team. I found out there was a difference between winning and losing and took a while to zero in on it. It wasn't conscious until one time I went too far. Then I really noticed I'd gone overboard. I was way too nervous and I just blew the race. I thought, "Gee, I have to find that balance in there." Then I honed in pretty quickly. The way I did it, once I had an idea it was there, was to get really hyper for a race, and find out what reaction I got. Then be really laid back and see what the reaction was. Once you find out the outside limits you can get to, you can get quickly to the middle. Find out where it is.

Towards the end of my career I felt the difference between winning and losing was not great. If it wasn't my equipment, then it was probably just my desire wasn't up, I wasn't quite hyped enough. It is not unusual in our season to kind of "lose it" in some races. Ten World Cups, the Canadian Championships and World Championships. That's a lot of first class competition over three continents.

Learning from your mistakes is probably one of the biggest things influencing real excellence. And the sense of the ridiculous is another thing. You have to know when this is just ridiculous. Everyone is so intense about ski racing, but let's be realistic. These are just grown men, flopping down the hill at 80 miles an hour, on plastic and wood sticks, and this is ridiculous. If you can have a little balance in your perspective, take a step back occasionally, you'll be okay. If you learn from your mistakes and eliminate distractions, it really will help. The challenge ultimately, is establishing consistency and consistent behaviour.

All through the week prior to a race we tried to draw out the lessons. There are always places to improve. After a training run I tried to adjust to the course in my mind to fit in what I wanted to do next time. By the time you race you should have a good idea of what's going on.

After the last race on the hill I usually just forget about it. It's history. There's nothing I can do to change my performance. Each race is unique, even year to year on the same hill. So once it is over it is dead, it is gone.

After a really good race I made it a point to remember what I did right. I didn't worry too much about the actual on-hill stuff. It was just the mental approach I was interested in and how it worked, what level of activation I was at. What factors had changed it. One year I was standing at the start and I heard Klammer was winning the race. I thought, "Shit! I can't let him win, it is just not right. I've just got to do it today." Those little things you have to remember. You have got to remember what turns you on. It is amazing what these little kinds of things can do for you. Of course he didn't win.

By the time you get to the level I'm at, you have pretty well developed a pattern and it certainly works. You are "there", and unless there is some major fault, no need to screw around with it. By talking to the top guys you find out the sort of things they do, and they do what I do. Some of the guys on the team would ask, "What are you doing here?" I'd say, "Well, you have got to come in here and think about doing this, and this is what it will feel like." They'd go, "Oh,

Learning from your mistakes is probably one of the biggest things influencing real excellence. And the sense of the ridiculous is another thing.

The coaches who I felt best about simply said, "Yes, you can do it." They just provided basic support and helped me believe I could do it.

163

yeah." Then they would start thinking about what it is going to feel like.

The coaches who I felt best about simply said, "Yes, you can do it." They just provided basic support and helped me believe I could do it. John took part of the load off us by saying, "all you have to worry about is the race. I'll worry about the other stuff." He did it that way and it was very good. You just had to race, so that was what you thought about all the time, and you didn't have to worry about other things. It worked very well.

With respect to improving the readiness of elite Canadian athletes at the Olympics, I make the assumption that the athlete is already doing everything he can and that the changes that have to be made are in the organizational set up. First, the organization should fit into the athlete's pattern, not the athlete into their pattern. The second thing is to help the athlete gain some kind of Games experience, where they come in, have a sort of ceremony, and have events throughout the week. It is important to get the career guy in there to see what the Olympics are, to give him the Olympic experience.

The Olympics are the biggest media event in the history of mankind, every time it happens. The Calgary winter Olympics will cost twice as much as the summer Olympic Games in L.A. It is huge. With all the hoopla there, the top ministers and officials are going to want Canadians to win, but the racers have to learn how to deal with it.

You can either learn by having negative things happen to you, which is the worst thing, or learn by drawing upon other experiences, which is better. Then you can go in saying, "I know what happened before, I saw that Heiden didn't do any interviews before his Olympic race. Maybe that is a good idea for my situation." Maybe it isn't. You just have to find what works for you. Hopefully the top sport administrators will work with you to achieve that.

When I first started to do very, very well in Canada, Ken Read was also doing very well. Needless to say the press discovered us, and they thought nothing of phoning us at 4:30 in the afternoon their time, to find out what was going on. In Europe that is 10:30 at night, the night before the race. It was like a Stanley Cup final there and some guy would phone me up and start yakking. I'd said, "Do you have any idea what you are doing? It is 10:30 p.m., I'm in bed and I've got a big race tomorrow and you are asking me how old I am." It used to drive me nuts. Of course I learned to deal with that in two ways. One, don't let any calls come through. The second thing is not to worry about it. I had to learn how to deal with the press. One of our biggest problems was educating the Canadian press, because we had been used to the Europeans, who have this long-standing tradition, so everybody knows what the score is. When the Canadian press comes in they just say, "Well, I'll go over and see Steve in his hotel." It's easy, since they know where it is. In Europe there is a real etiquette, you just don't do things like that. The athlete has to have some private time! But the Canadian guys don't know that, so it is not their fault. But is it our job to educate the press? How far does it go? It would be great to only have to ski.

Advice to press. Don't phone the racer to get basic information, because that is not his function. Talk to his coach, he knows everything. Don't talk to the competitor about anything but his perfor-

164

mance and do it at an appropriate time. I had so many phone calls, "What are you guys doing tomorrow?" People would phone in Europe and if they couldn't reach other people they would ask for me because they know my name.

The media should have a fully-packed press kit. They do in most cases. At any kind of major interview if they ask a question that's already in the press kit, like "How old are you? Where were you born? How long have you been skiing?". You should assume they will ask questions not answered in the press kit. If the guy hasn't felt that it was important enough to do his homework, everybody else will suffer because of him. If you end the interview at that point, believe me, it really changes their attitude. Everybody begins to think of good questions that are part of the Games, or part of the race.

The racer shouldn't have to pay for the reporter's laziness. Not because I think the racer should be coddled, but in a situation like the Olympics, it is really difficult, and if you want to perform, the fewer distractions the better. Why should I have to sit there for hours answering questions that I know are in the press kit? I'm good at doing interviews because I've done literally thousands of them but for the younger guys it is a real distraction. They keep answering questions until the barn burns down around their ears. That is where our sport administrators could help the racer.

I wasn't exactly pleased about my 1984 Olympic performance. It is really hard to come back and have everybody ask why you failed. However, over my career I had lost a lot more races than I won, so I knew how to handle it. I had been thinking about quitting as well. If I had done really well, I would have had an easy decision, I just would have quit. But since I didn't do well, it was harder. I had to ask myself, "Should I go back and keep hammering again? Do I have enough energy?"

Having been around so long, I had developed a good ability to hold myself at the right level as long as demanded, and accept coming down as part of being up. I sure came down after the Olympics, but I knew it was going to happen. I did a number of other World Cup races after I came back to Canada, the Canadian Championships, as well as a race in Aspen and Whistler. I came back pretty strongly. I was skiing well. Good results. March was my last race.

In order to do as well as I wanted to do, and keep winning, I knew I would have to do more work than what I was prepared for. I would have had to train more than I wanted to, and do more of everything. And I felt that when I finally got on the hill, even though I'm a better skier than some of those guys, they would have beaten me because they have hunger and they've got fire. After eleven years on the team and the World Cup circuit, I was simply burned out. Not like a burned out cinder of ash lying on the ground. But as far as racing goes, not the bright flame. I knew I wasn't going to pull it off the way I wanted to.

The media should have a fully packed press kit.

The racer shouldn't have to pay for the reporter's laziness. Not because I think the racer should be coddled, but in a situation like the Olympics, it is really difficult, and if you want to perform, the fewer distractions the better.

19
LINDA THOM

1984 OLYMPIC GOLD MEDALIST — SHOOTING

I know why I have been successful. First is the support and total commitment of my husband, Don. He was very quiet in the background, but he encouraged me at every step. Even when I was away a month at a time he never complained. I know he missed me very much and he often felt like a single parent, but he never made me feel guilty. Quite the opposite, in fact he made a point of making sure I was guilt-free. He would even hide difficult things that were happening to him at work, so that they wouldn't affect me.

Our children were quite young but were encouraging, as well as being proud and tremendously positive. They were both convinced I would succeed. All during May and June of 1984, eight-year-old Samantha would tell anyone who would listen that her mother was going to win an Olympic Gold Medal.

There are three other factors which, combined with family support, formed the fabric of my success: first class coaching, funding from Sport Canada, and positive psychology.

In the days before government funding a shooter saved money to attend one major international match a year, or maybe one every two years. Shooting clinics and training camps were either very few and far between, or out of the country. Now that we have some funding from Sport Canada, training camps, although sparse, are held and

For me those developments made the difference between standing in the crowd and standing on the podium.

the team can get to them; the team can also occasionally afford help from experts in the sport sciences.

For me those developments made the difference between standing in the crowd and standing on the podium. Now I can structure my annual training and competition plan using international matches at carefully spaced intervals. Shooting at these matches helps me to test and fine-tune my preparation and shooting routines, coping strategies and ability to adapt to different circumstances, to gain invaluable experience and insights from world-class competition, and to get to know other coaches and athletes and compare notes with them.

It really helps to be there and to see other shooters get nervous too and blow their shots. You realize they aren't invincible. A big green light goes on, you realize you can win. Then when you do win, you are confirming what you felt, and gain even more confidence.

Coaches are so important. You can win at the provincial or in some sports perhaps at the national level without a coach, but these days you don't break world records or win Olympic Gold without one. And not just any coach. It takes world-class talent to produce world winners. It's hard to believe that a decade and a half ago we didn't have shooting coaches in Canada. Joe Liota, who is head coach of the pistol team, did a great deal to change that. He learned all he could from other coaches and still reads every book he can get his hands on. I think he's the best on-line pistol coach in the world.

Joe deserves the greatest credit for my victories. He taught other coaches I worked with and got sport science experts, including Jack Leon to share their knowledge with us. He pushed hard for training camps and trials and funding for international matches to season us. His dreams and goals were just as big or bigger than mine. Joe was like the hub of a wheel, all the spokes led to him.

The big thing that really helped me when I came back to shooting after raising my family, was that I had a national coach, Ed Kelly, at my home range, the R.A. Gun Club in Ottawa. I knew Ed from years before, and we quickly re-established our friendship. In fact we found we could rag each other really hard, which is a wonderful stress release valve in situations where concentration and effort become so intense.

When I started to work with him I made a conscious effort to listen to him instead of fighting him; to unlock a door somewhere in my brain and allow everything that I had previously learned about shooting to pour out, and let pour in everything he might tell me. Each thing he asked me to do I gave an honest try. I knew that if it didn't work, he would be the first to agree to drop it and try something else. I was very aware that we had so little time, less than two and a half years, to the Olympics.

We worked together for over a year, and made tremendous strides. All his help, the hours he devoted to training me, was strictly voluntary. I wanted to give back something for what he'd given me. However, Ed Kelly, unlike most other human beings, didn't operate on praise. I kept on, mostly unsuccessfully, trying to find what might work. I kept on training and competing, and slowly making progress, although it seemed to me that for every step forward there were several dunkings that went with it.

168

One day, at last, I won an international medal a year after I had come back to shooting. The medal was small and thin compared to some, but I cried. It meant so much to me.

"That's bloody fine," Ed managed to whisper as his jaw clenched and unclenched with emotion when I showed it to him on my return. That was it, the only way I could thank him was to bring home heavy metal. I don't think I could have had a more powerful motivator.

I broke through to gold in Zurich that year, and then added a bronze and a silver at the Pam Am Games in August in Caracas. On December 7 1983, seven months before the Olympics, Ed died of cancer. The only regret I have is that I didn't get to share the Olympic medal with him.

Positive psychology is so powerful in enhancing performance. Since I'm a convert to positive thinking, I get evangelical about it. People who have always operated that way wonder what the fuss is all about, to them it's 'part of', not an 'add-on'.

Before the Olympics I put in as many hours doing the various aspects of mental training, including reading books and thinking about how I was going to perform as I did in everything else combined, range training, aerobic training, stretching, and weight training.

I have wanted to be on the Olympic team since I was eight. I promised myself that I would train so very hard if I could ever be good enough at anything to have a possibility of making the team. My possibility came along thirty years later, almost too late, as one television commentator mentioned after I had won. I told Don about my childhood dream, and was about to ask what he thought. Without waiting for me to finish, he said, "Do it, you've got to do it!"

My goal was to win the gold medal. I said to myself, "If I'm going to win a gold medal, what kind of score am I going to have to shoot, and what can I realistically feel I can do?" I had set myself a score of 594 out of 600. I had my intermediate goals and short-term goals all planned out as to what progress I would have to make to achieve that in the end. I was getting there, my average was coming up. But it still wasn't high enough.

The second last competiton before the Olympics I shot a 590, which is my highest score in an international match, and it's a Canadian record. At last I felt I belonged to what you might call the "590 Club", or in my terms, that's a lifetime world ranking score. It was reassuring to know the world record was only two points above that, 592. It is now 594. I really wanted the world record but the primary goal was to win the gold medal. But I felt that I could equal the world record or break it.

I felt that I could be more determined than the other competitors might be, and therefore that I would win. Somewhere deep down in the core of Linda Thom existed a belief that I could do it, or I would never have come back to shooting after seven years off. My coach, Joe Liota, who had been Ed Kelly's mentor and who became mine, reminded me, "You were talking about the gold medal right from the beginning."

My determination grew and I became confident, but doing it was not so easy nor so quick! I had to overcome things that I learned in my youth, when I was taught to be self-effacing and humble. It's fine

Before the Olympics I put in as many hours doing the various aspects of mental training, including reading books and thinking about how I was going to perform as I did in everything else combined, range training, aerobic training, stretching, and weight training.

My determination grew and I became confident, but doing it was not so easy nor so quick! I had to overcome things that I learned in my youth, when I was taught to be self-effacing and humble.

169

to have humility, and I don't like arrogance. I don't feel I'm arrogant and I hope I don't appear to be. But you have to be determined to win! If you're not determined, you're not going to win. Somebody else is going to win because they've got that much more gumption. It's just as simple as that. You have to believe in yourself.

You train and strain and compete for a whole gamut of reasons. The first that always springs to my mind is to see the Maple Leaf go up the centre pole and hear them play 'O Canada!' Of course I did it for my country, but I also did it because I thought that I could, and I wanted to. You have to start out with yourself.

My mother was the positive force in the family. She's the one who sustained us and said, "You can do it! It can be done. Yes, you can!" There were very few things in my childhood that ever were said like, "You can't do that because you're a girl, or because society says you can't."

My Dad was an excellent rifle and pistol shooter, and he taught us to shoot safely and well in a sand quarry, miles from anywhere, but he never wanted to join a club in this country. Only once did he ever shoot with me at a club.

Joe Liota was always saying to look at things from a positive view; look at the things you want to do, and ignore the other things. It took a good six months to understand what he was saying to me. In shooting we had always talked about the "sevens and eights" and the "fliers" and we compared tragic stories; it was sort of a race to see who had the worst thing happen to them. Joe and Tom wouldn't listen to me unless I talked about the tens, and the things that went right. Tom Guinn, a very successful and experienced teammate, loaned me his 'bible' "Inner Tennis". He, Joe, and Bob Todd, Technical Director of the Shooting Federation of Canada recommended other books such as "In Pursuit of Excellence", "The Winner's Edge", "The Inner Athlete", "Psycho-Cybernetics," and Don got me to read "Zen and the Art of Archery". All these books are talking about the same thing - how to use your inner strength, and how to stop blocking yourself and let it come out.

Joe just turned the world upside down for me. I was determined to understand what he was trying to say, such as concentrating on the "tens" and virtually denying the fact that you had ever in your life shot a "seven". Now I see it so clearly. I'm practically fanatical about it because of how much it can help you.

A turning point was a clinic which I attended in February 1983. The clinic was given in Toronto by Lanny Bassham, who is a World Champion rifle shooter from the U.S. Out of his own competitive difficulties, experienced at the 1972 Olympics, he had dug around and developed what he calls, "The tools of mental management." That man really spoke to me.

One thing he said was so important, "You've got to write it out. In this country and the United States too, we don't write our goals out." We're a very literate society otherwise, but we don't seem to write our goals out.

One of the most important things he found useful for himself was to write out the goal in the first person, present tense. "I am the 1984 Olympic Gold medalist in Ladies Match Pistol," in my particular case. And he said, "Write it out in your diary every night, every single

170

night, and one of two things will happen, either you won't believe it and you'll stop writing it, or you'll keep on writing it and you'll succeed." But he said, "It really works."

Although I have a journalism degree, I don't like sitting down and writing and I have to make an effort, but I did make an effort to write my goals in my diary. For 18 months I wrote that I was the Olympic Champion, every single night in my diary, and it came true. It helped me grapple with myself and my image of myself as a champion.

"Imagine yourself on the podium," he said. "You have won. You know it's behind you now. The flag is going up and the anthem is being played. There are the reporters and they're interviewing you. Visualize all of these things, and savour them."

"Act as if you are going back over your life, the gods have given you the chance to relive this. You've won it. It's yours. You've got the gold medal. But the gods are giving you the chance to relive and savour your experiences." You can say, "Hey, I can enjoy this. I'm not just in a headlong rush." I can also notice the other things in life and enjoy the little steps along the way.

My coach, Joe said, "You know it's just like little stepping-stones across a creek. You're hopping across and every now and then you slip down and get your feet wet, but you get back up on the next stone and you keep hopping across." And then he said, "The last jump is over onto the bank." And then when I won he said that evening, when I saw him, "Now you're safe on the other bank."

You must take things in steps. You couldn't possibly jump the river in one leap. These mental images really helped. Lanny Bassham also told us about the television cameras, and about the crowds at shooting events in Europe. He went through all the things that might shake you up, like having your gun stolen. That happened to him at the 1972 Olympics. Now I take pieces of the gun so that the gun can be replaced, and I also take an extra pair of glasses.

While I was sitting in the chair watching Lanny Bassham talk to us, I realized that I was going to have to make a commitment or I wasn't going to follow through and put to work the tools he had given us in that seminar. So at the end, feeling very shy, very doubtful, I forced myself to walk up to him. I looked him straight in the eye and I said, "You really spoke to me." And I added, "I'm going to be there." And this slow smile came over his face, and I could tell that he knew what I meant, that I was going to be there on the podium, that's what I meant. I didn't have to say anything else. The Shooting Federation paid quite a lot of money to bring him up to Toronto, but it sure was worth it.

I train differently than most shooters, but more and more are now beginning to train like I do. Tom Guinn, who came second in the World Championships, helped me a great deal. He did a lot of aerobic training as well as wall work, which is holding the empty gun against a blank wall and watching the sights while coming through on the trigger, stuff other people only get to dream about. He and Joe, my head coach, got me into what the rifle shooters do, stretching, aerobics, holding the gun, and other work besides just the range work. It used to be quite rare for shooters to do anything else but go to the range and shoot.

One thing he said was so important, "You've got to write it out. In this country and the United States too, we don't write our goals out." We're a very literate society otherwise, but we don't seem to write our goals out.

171

I also did mental training of one sort or another every single day of the week. By that I mean reading positive books, thinking of myself as a champion, or thinking about some aspect of shooting. In connection with this, I wrote out my shot plan in detail - how I wanted the trigger to come through, positive and smoother, and break in good time before my eyes and arm got tired, and before I lost confidence.

This is important because eventually your eyes start lying to you. You think that you are seeing the sight sharp and clear. It's not that your eyes are wrong, but that you are waiting for the shot to break, and your brain starts lying and saying, "Yes, it's still good, let it go." But what you are looking at is an image, micro seconds old. While you are fresh, and you've got all that oxygen in your muscles, the best thing is to settle in, "Bang". That's when you want the shot to break, before you start to say, "God, when is it going to go?" Eventually if you raise too often without having a shot break, you are tempted to break the shot yourself, and you don't get away with that too often.

I wrote all of these things that I wanted to happen, the optimum, in my diary.

I would also write down and remind myself of interim score goals. In addition, I wrote about my family and things I wanted to accomplish in my daily life, because you mustn't forget that side of yourself. In spite of the fact that you're really living very much in your sport, that is not the real world. The real world is out there earning your bread and butter, raising your kids and doing all that kind of thing.

I'm sorry to say this, but it's true. You occasionally have to remind yourself that those things are important too, otherwise you can fall off the edge in sport. Whether you win or whether you don't win, there's a big cliff for the unsuspecting at the end of it all. So I would write things like, "Whether I win or whether I don't win, my family loves me, my husband is going to be there to kiss and hug me." You do have to keep sport in perspective. Maybe it helps knowing that although you are striving for this, and it counts a hell of a lot to you, if by chance it doesn't occur, despite your best efforts, it is not the end of the world.

You have to have control, and you need it all day if you are going to shoot at 9 a.m., 1 p.m. and possibly at 3.30 p.m. in a shoot-off. I predicted that the person who was going to win would be the one with the best control. I resolved to have the best control and proceeded to describe what for me constituted control, but not over-control.

Becoming passive on the line, that's when I really run into trouble, and it takes time to turn it around and get back on track.

I've found out how to detect the distant early warning signs of becoming passive, or losing control. I went through all kinds of mental repetition routines to find out what was the best thing.

Control for precision shooting is not the same as for duelling, these are the two halves of the Sport Pistol course. In precision shooting I have to be determined and I have to really concentrate on my "tens", and accept the fact that the blasted gun, no matter how still I can hold it, is moving. The temptation is to "point shoot", but you can't. You have to "area shoot". The ten ring at 25 metres is so big. Your gun can wander around in that area and you'll still get a ten, whether it's at the top, the bottom, or whatever. Your gun has to float in an

172

even, smooth movement. As soon as you detect corners, then you'll know that you're controlling the gun, so you put the gun down, take a breath, and start over.

Control also means putting distractions out of your mind. I have very good peripheral vision so I wear blinkers. I also wear a hat with flaps which extends the blinkers, and I wear hearing protection. In training I wear a pair of ear-muffs, but when I go into competition I wear ear plugs as well as ear-muffs so that I have double protection against distractions. In competition everything is heightened including your sense of hearing. You are in a vigilant, alert mode.

You also aid yourself by recognizing that there are competitors. You recognize that the crowd is there, the sun is shining, and there are butterflies around the target. Then you say, "Fine, what a wonderful day for shooting, this is where we are going to produce tens, and this is how we are going to do it."

The control is never relaxing totally. I mean, you can relax to a degree. Relaxation is important, but it's important for a shooter not to totally relax or you'll really become passive and that's not a good idea. You want to relax your muscles so they are not tense, but you've got to keep that something inside you, that "This is what I'm here to do" determination. You've got to keep your thoughts in that direction and not let anything interfere.

Imagery is another part of my mental training. I have a good imagination and I can visualize things. I'm told that unlike a lot of women, I am spacially oriented. I can imagine an object like a car or a rock, and in my mind walk all the way around it, or turn it as if it was on a turntable, and see all the facets of it.

Even so, when Tommy Guinn introduced me to mental training, which involved visualizing sharp sight alignment against fuzzy targets, I could see the rear sight, but I couldn't see the front sight, or the target was clear and the sights were fuzzy.

"Visualize this, and train," he said. "At first it may not come, but persist with it and it will slowly come, and the sights will clear up." At first it was as if I was mentally throwing barriers in my own way, but eventually it did come true. I was able to visualize after two to three months.

He told me to do this at different times of the day, and not necessarily for 15 minutes at a time either. I would do it anywhere. Usually it was only an image, but occasionally I did find myself raising my arm. Once I was in a bank queue, raising my arm. "Whoops, what am I doing?" I didn't have my gun with me of course!

When I do mental imagery I see the rear sight not as a notch, but as two light bars, and the front sight is really sharp. I usually look at the centre, or a little bit to the left of the centre, of the top of the front sight. Then I can see the target as a fuzzy grey blob. I'm not conscious of my hand, I'm just concentrating on that small part of the sight. Right now with my eyes open, I can 'see' the sights hovering around the middle of the 25 metre target.

It used to bother me that I would get up on the firing line and what I actually saw wasn't as perfect as what I could visualize. Previously it used to be the reverse, my mental image wasn't anywhere near as good as the real thing.

I've found out how to detect the distant early warning signs of becoming passive, or losing control. I went through all kinds of mental repetition routines to find out what was the best thing.

You want to relax your muscles so they are not tense, but you've got to keep that something inside you, that, "This is what I'm here to do" determination.

173

I actually shoot in imagery because it is important not just to hold up the gun, but also to imagine the shot going off. That is important to me because one of my bugaboos is not having the shot go, and I wind up 'pumping iron', doing several raises just to get the shot off.

You want to make up your mind before you raise the gun that this shot is going to go extremely well, so I imagine firing. I see myself inside myself, shooting in regular motion. I can feel the initial pressure of the trigger, and then I'm looking at the sight, and then the shot goes off itself.

The shot has to break by itself because if you think about it going, you are going to disturb the gun. The shot breaks without thinking about it. You have trained your reflexes to come back through the trigger positively.

Then I'm outside myself, an observer. I see the bullet going in slow motion through the middle of the target, cutting the paper through the "X" ring, and the paper starts to fly, all in ultra-slow motion.

For months I did this, virtually every time before I fired on the line. I would sit down and do several raises and shots in my mind. I would do it for five minutes, ten minutes, fifteen, or anything up to about 30 minutes.

I wouldn't spend more than 30 minutes in preparation, and that would include diary time. I would be doing imagery as I was doing the diary work and I would write what I wanted to do and say to myself, "What am I going to do in this training session?" I wouldn't just get on the line and pump rounds down range, but would actually go to the line with an intent, a goal, even if it was just to make sure everything was smooth.

When I go to the line, and set everything up, and take the gun in my hand, I also mentally go through my shot-plan checklist before I shoot. This strategy started out very mechanically with a physical list of words which I have on the shooting table, and which I read exactly. These words represented every single step involved in shooting a shot. Then I reduced these to key words so that I could go through the list faster. Finally I didn't need a list anymore. I would usually write one word to emphasize what I wanted, such as "trigger" or "smooth". Then this shot plan rehearsal became a mix of simple verbal reminders and images which I "ran" before each shot.

As for success imagery, I didn't do as much imagery of being on the podium as I have heard some athletes do. But I would imagine to myself, "How would a champion act? How would a champion feel? How would she perform on the line?" This helped me find out about myself, what worked and didn't work for me. Then as the actual roles I had imagined came along, and as I achieved them, that in turn helped me believe that I could be the Olympic Champion.

As the springtime came along I would say to myself, "I don't know exactly how I'm going to win, but I know I'm going to win. I've got the technical expertise, the ability, and the determination."

My mental preparation for competition starts the night before. I sit down and write everything in detail in my diary about what I will do the next day. Each little step is written out, such as getting up at 6.15 a.m., stretching, having a shower, brushing my teeth, packing, getting dressed, checking the room, putting my gear in the car, having breakfast, going to the actual location of where I'm going to shoot.

174

Everything is pre-planned right up to the time I shoot, during the match, and afterwards.

I also get to know the range officer ahead of time so that I'm familiar with whom I have to deal. Before the shoot I put my equipment near the line. As soon as I am allowed I start setting up. When the 10 minute formal preparation time is announced, I push my stopwatch to time myself while I smoke my sights, put up my 'scope, set out my magazines, ammunition, rosin, and screwdriver. I set it up so that I'm not scrambling around in my bag. I reassure myself that I have everything ready.

Once I've set up I usually sit and look through my diary so that I don't miss a step, like visualizing shots. I may write down one word like "determination" to remind myself what I want to do that day. Then I do a few raises.

Once again I get up on the line, I fit the gun in my hand, take up my stance, line up dead-centre with the target, make sure that my grip is absolutely correct, then I just wait for the command to load.

I'll be thinking about the shots and what the sights will look like. I try to occupy my mind with constructive thoughts to avoid invading negative thoughts. If these start to creep in I'll immediately focus on what I have to do. I'll go through the shot sequence. Or, I'll pick a mental image. Sometimes I imagine a Russian whom I shot with. She was so steady. When the shot broke the gun never moved. She followed through beautifully. She calms me down because I know I can do it too.

If I'm already shooting, but feeling uncomfortable, I'll say to myself, "You candy-ass!"

I'll start thinking about Les Desci, who's got one leg off above the knee. He's constantly in pain, and if it's hot and humid, like it would be in Los Angeles, he'd be in even more pain because the stump would be sweaty and bothering him. He's always got that to contend with, so what am I doing looking to find things to be wrong?

Disabled athletes inspire me because they have to be so determined just to get to the point where they start to train, just to get up in the morning and start to dress, they have to go through so much effort to do things which you and I don't even think about.

If I start to get distracted I refocus right back to the task. Sometimes I even say to myself, in Joe's voice, "Show me how to shoot a ten." You'd be surprised. Most people shoot tens when he stands behind them and says that. Or, I'll think of my old coach Ed Kelly, how much faith he had in me, and how proud he would be of me, and I get right back to my routine.

After shooting five shots, you sit down while everything is scored. When the scores are announced to everyone up and down the line, you have to ignore this. I don't count my score and I don't count anybody else's score because that is a distraction I don't need.

Over the years I've discovered that every time I was aware of my own score, then my performance would deteriorate. Early on I would actually hum to myself to block out the announcing of the shots. Now I'll sit with my screwdriver in hand so that I'll remember to adjust the sights when I go back to the line. I think of what I want to do in the next series.

When I look through my 'scope, I'm not counting the value of the shots, what I'm doing is concentrating on the group to see whether I've got to click the sights up or down or sideways. When the target crew have stopped announcing, and they tack up a new target, I'll check to make sure the target has been properly stapled and then start focusing on the shot. I make sure that my magazine is in. That whole routine fills my focus and the time until there is a fresh target. Then I'm starting afresh.

All of that is how I prepare mentally for competition. Unfortunately, I can remember one competition in Mexico, when I felt great and had everything planned but things didn't go well. Both my coaches were behind me. They are both very good observers. I was getting some tens, but there were several nines just outside the ten ring.

During the match I would go back to Joe and say, "Here's a super opportunity because this is happening while you are watching. What did you see, what should I be doing?" He would give me a focus point. I would focus on that but I came up with a lousy score. Afterwards he said, "I don't know what the hell was going on, I called almost all of those shots tens." I think that there must have been something disturbing me, I was anticipating the shot so slightly that not even my coaches could see.

There was also a three quarter hour delay before the shoot. I said, "Fine, this is bothering other people but it isn't bothering me." I know for sure that it wasn't bothering me.

My very best international performance was somewhat different. My personal coach, Al, was behind me. I didn't talk a lot to him. Before a shoot I always say, "I'll come back from the line, but don't say anything to me unless I ask." He was good about it, he really buttoned his lip.

The match was really great, it just went like a dream. I can remember thinking positive things. Thinking about the individual shot, and saying, "This is going to be a ten." Kristina Freis of Sweden tied with me. We were in a shoot-off, and I said to myself, "Sister, this is the shoot-off. There are a lot of people standing here and I'm going to show them how it should be done." I shot 150 out of 150.

I've already told you about the positive thinking which I learned from my coaches, the books I read, and Lanny Bassham's clinic. In addition, Joe invited a psychologist to work with us. Joe had met Jack Leon at a party. Jack works as a counsellor at Mohawk College. He's not a 'jock', but Joe thought that he might be suitable, and Jack thought that he might like to work with the pistol team.

Joe got Jack to run a clinic with him. Jack didn't know beans about shooting, but that didn't matter, he was talking about the principles of team building and the principles of not allowing things to distract us, the principles of looking at what we wanted to do and not what we didn't want to do. He had run seminars before for nurses and other groups. The shooters reacted positively to it. They weren't threatened by Jack. He wasn't trying to say, "I'm better than you," in some way or another. He was really giving of himself. This reassured everybody.

At the end of the first clinic he asked us to fill out an evaluation form. I had felt that he was unsure of himself and tended to dump on himself a bit. I felt that we didn't need someone insecure coming

Over the years I've discovered that every time I was aware of my own score, then my performance would deteriorate. Early on I would actually hum to myself to block out the announcing of the shots.

176

to an international match, and we might have to carry his socks for him. Jack really took all the criticism as constructive. He used it to change his behaviour. After that he walked around as cool as a cucumber, just like the rest of us. We all attended several clinics by Jack and benefitted greatly. We did team building and became more aware of each other's likes and dislikes, and how we could inadvertently distracting each other.

He was good because he was there for the shooters and not for himself. He said that beforehand, and he really meant it. Some people will say that, then go off partying somewhere. He was there one hundred percent doing his job night and day right along with the coaches, when we needed him, or Joe thought we did.

The coaches and the consultants worked tremendously hard. Jack and Joe worked together to develop pre- and post-competition evaluation forms. At first, the coaches got very little sleep because they were constantly going over things with the athletes. Afterwards they realized that they had to shorten the forms for their own sake, as well as for the athletes.

Several days before the event we filled out our feelings, our goals, our expectations and we made out a detailed competition plan. This was discussed, and if the coaches felt the athlete's goal was unrealistic they would say so. They didn't want the athletes falling on their faces.

Right after the match we filled out a form to tell how we felt during the match, how we had felt so many minutes before the match, at the match beginning, during the match, and at the end of the match, whether our score goals were achieved or whether they weren't, what distractions there were, how we felt, how did the coaches perform, how did the psychologist perform in relation to that athlete.

Most of us filled these out either right on the site or that evening following the match. Then we discussed the form usually with the coach and psychologist together, or whomever we felt comfortable with. This would usually take a half hour. The coaches kept the form and the athletes were encouraged to write out the things in their diary. In fact there was a question on the form, "Have you written this in your diary?" Because of the pressure of time, we often found ourselves discussing our forms together with everybody who shot that day. We felt trustful enough of each other that we didn't mind talking about what was going on.

The general feeling was that these forms were helpful, but that there was too much on the form. They went from a very condensed version that we felt didn't cover enough areas to an expanded one, which was expanded further, then finally cut down. They were very open to athletes' suggestions about what should be on the forms and how things should be stated.

The athletes also felt that the forms should go to the coach and sport psychologist and no further. So the forms are kept confidential.

The coaches realize the value of working with these forms and they don't want to stop doing it. Its very valuable to make sure the athlete is focused on the task and that he is not being unrealistic and the athlete has the opportunity to go "one on one" with the coach to talk about his feelings before the match and after the match. From this, athletes come to realize that losing is not the end of the world. The coach's task is to reassure them and let them talk it out. Athletes tend

We did team building and became more aware of each other's likes and dislikes, and how we could avoid inadvertently distracting each other.

177

to be very hard on themselves and get closed up. It's a delicate balance because as a coach you've got to let the athlete know that we expect you to improve and we expect an effort out of you.

I knew I was going to win at the Olympics. All week I had a quiet feeling, not a big feeling, but a quiet feeling that I would win. Every now and then I'd sort of check on that, "How does it feel? Great! I'm still going to win. The gold medal? Yes, the gold medal." And it just went on quietly all week, and then that day I thought, "Well, gee, everything feels so positive and yet I didn't shoot a great score this morning," and then I managed to put that out of my mind and just carry on, and then I just felt better and better and better.

I had my whole preparation done ahead of time. I do a complete dress rehearsal the day before so there weren't any surprises. I even paid for an extra night at the motel. Also, beforehand I imagined what sorts of questions the media might ask, and we told the coaches that we didn't want reporters interviewing us before the match.

I got to the line at 8:30 a.m to shoot at 9 a.m. Then I just set up what they would allow me to set up and I thought about my match. I did some raises. I had read that a lot of successful swimmers prepare by actually doing the motions that they will be doing in the water. We had a huge gallery. But I had mentally prepared myself for the fact that they are going to be for me, and they are a good crowd. I just said those positive things to myself.

Immediately before the start I was looking at the range with the sunlight on the target, and I was thinking, "This is nice, and still there's no wind." I just thought about how I wanted the shots to go. I don't dwell on individuals or anything like that, I dwell on what I want to do. I sort of observe the other things, but I dwell on the task at hand.

But I also had this feeling beforehand that the control wasn't perfect. I was a little edgy. During the event I wasn't trying to powerhouse myself into control, but I was using things like focusing on the task at hand to gain the control and reassure myself. The odd time I'd think about, "Well, I know the sighting target's going to go well, but then what about the first target?" This shows that you're thinking too far ahead. Just think about the one-shot. Think about the shot, and it's just an extension, and you'll just carry on, and the ice will be broken, and it'll be smooth and you won't think about this and you'll go on ahead. Don't anticipate trouble. Just simply come back to what you are doing. You tell yourself, "I know I can do it, I know I'm really capable, I just have the ability and that's that."

When the competition started you could have heard a pin drop, but when the scores were announced the people started cheering for the people who had got 50 out of 50. So I thought, "Oh, that's interesting, they're cheering, and the range officer asked them not to." So I thought, "Ah, I know how it's working. They're being absolutely quiet while we're shooting and they're rewarding those who are shooting well." So I thought, "When I shoot my 50 they're going to cheer me." I shot a 50. They cheered. I thought, "That's wonderful! This is the way it's working." So it was a potential distraction but it wasn't. I turned it around.

When the scores were announced I just recognized my score, sat down and thought about my relaxation. I have a bad lower back so I

178

do sidebends, walk up and down, and sometime I push on the chair just to stretch a bit and maintain my determination.

Then there was a break. I had planned out exactly after the first half what I was going to do in those four hours. I ate part of my lunch, and thought about what I wanted to think about. A couple of competitors came into the trailer too and we just sort of said, "Hello," to each other, but we kept to our own thought processes. I had a book there to read and I had my diary if I wanted to refer to it. The book I had was totally irrelevant to shooting. I just said to somebody, "Lend me your book", and I opened it in the middle and started reading. I wasn't involved in the story. It was just occupying my mind and it was keeping me from thinking about negative thoughts. I had practised so much about maintaining the positive attitude that I really did maintain a very positive attitude.

Joe was concerned, though, because when we walked out of the range after the first half he could see that I wasn't terribly pleased with my score and he said, "Well, I'm sorry, but you worked really hard, you made things work for you, and brought them together, and I'm proud of you. What are you going to do this afternoon?" Of course, he wanted me not dwelling on the past but going forward. And I said, "I'm going to put every shot in the centre of the target!" So he said, "Fine." That's all he had to say to me. We communicated very well.

During the morning shooting I had felt better and better and I finished quite strongly. Then in the afternoon it started again - with my first target I was a little edgy. But then I pulled it together and I just cleaned up.

I was feeling very, very good indeed after I finished although I still didn't know the results because the second relay had to shoot their second half. I didn't want to go back into the range even though I had finished shooting. So I walked around just outside and every now and then soembody would come out and I'd say, "Oh, how is Ruby Fox doing?" "What did she have this morning?" "How's she doing now?" The person would reply, "Oh, she's losing some points, not a lot but she's losing some." And I thought, "Oh, that's interesting." So I just waited.

Then Joe came out of the range at the end of the second relay and he just looked at me with a big bright smile, his whole face was lit up and he said to me, "Well, lady, it looks like you're in a shoot-off." We gripped hands but we didn't say another word, we just had big, big grins. He knew I was feeling very, very happy. I knew then that I was going to win, and he knew it too.

I knew I would win if I went into a shoot-off situation. I thought, "She's lost it now." I knew I was stronger in duelling, the shoot-off. But I also knew Ruby was an excellent competitor. It went right down to the last shot. Ruby's a friend of mine but you have to put that friendship into neutral when you're on the line. You have to put your feelings aside and treat them as you would any possible distraction and do your best.

I knew I would win if I went into a shoot-off situation. I thought, "She's lost it now." I knew I was stronger in duelling, the shoot-off.

179

20
JAY TRIANO

CAPTAIN OF MEN'S BASKETBALL TEAM — GOLD MEDALISTS — 1983 WORLD STUDENT GAMES

Coming into the Olympics we had just finished a tournament with Italy, Yugoslavia and Australia. We had played a one point game with Italy and beaten Yugoslavia twice and they were supposed to be the second and third favourite teams in the Olympic tournament. At that time we were playing well and I really believed we could beat both of those teams and get into the gold medal game at the Olympics. I wanted to win a medal, preferably gold. All the talk and hype was about the Americans and how tough they were going to be, especially in the United States. When I thought of all the countries there, we had the best chance to beat them, and I believed that on a given night we could have done it. In Edmonton at the World Student Games the year before, we had played well and showed we were at the top of the world in our game.

At the Olympics I felt physically ready but mentally, I expected more. The Olympics didn't hold as much power as I had thought. I had expected to get goosebumps and be really awed by everything, but it didn't really come out that way. That first game, I saw the rings on the floor, but I expected it to be more of a lift. I was looking for

At the Olympics I felt physically ready but mentally, I expected more. The Olympics didn't hold as much power as I had thought. I had expected to get goosebumps and be really awed by everything, but it didn't really come out that way.

Before I can do anything else, I have to train. If I have something to do that night, like going to a show or going out with the guys, I have to finish my training before I go out. It's like a religion.

the "lift" of the crowd but they were so far away from the court that you couldn't feel them. I didn't really feel I got enough psych from the crowd. We'd just finished playing a tournament in Canada where we played in the University gyms. There, when you stepped out on the court the fans would get you 'pumped' straight away. They were 'right there' and they were excited. I look to that adrenalin flow to give me a boost. I expected it to be there going into the Olympics.

As a whole the Olympics were very powerful emotionally and psychologically. At the Opening Ceremony, you get all those chills and everything, and I think that brings you up to a different level. I don't know how much further you can go from there. Maybe we were already at that level when we went into the gym but we expected more, I don't know. It is not as though we weren't psyched up, it was just not as powerful walking out on the floor the first time as I expected it to be.

I was a little disappointed with the way things were organized, at the Olympics, and around the team. We had a lot of external things coming in, and a lot of relatives there. I think that brought us down. Any time we had played well before that, it's been twelve players go here or go there. When we got to the Olympics, it was 3 players here, 3 players there, taking off all the time. We were never really together as a group off the court. The only time we were together was when we had a game or a practice and from there we dispersed. At every other tournament that we'd played in, like in Edmonton when we won in 1983, and in the pre-Olympic tournament, it was always a group going everywhere. I think that had an effect on us.

I think I trained harder than other athletes in my sport. I always have in the past. When we go away, we're away for 2 weeks and then we get a week off. I think I work harder in the week off than I do in the 2 weeks on. The other guys play and shoot but they don't work as hard all the time. I believe in training hard, everyday. There are times when I don't feel like it but to me it's mandatory. Before I can do anything else, I have to train. If I have something to do that night, like going to a show or going out with the guys, I have to finish my training before I go out. It's like a religion.

I'm very organized in the way I set up my training. There are times when I get in the pool and swim, and times when I run, and eat. Everything fits into my training. I'm pretty structured that way. I make sure that I do everything every day. I also chart everything so that I can see where I am going and how I'm progressing. If I miss a day it would throw my chart right off.

I record the number of shots I make every day from certain areas on the floor. I go through a shooting drill I've set up for myself. I record my swimming times, my running times, and also whatever weight training exercise I do and when that tapers off. I wanted to taper that off towards the Olympics.

The only time that I give up my training schedule is if I can play a game. It's a problem finding a game living in Niagara Falls or Vancouver. Our players are all over the country. But if I get a phone call saying, "Come to Toronto and play on Thursday," then I'll train Wednesday, and do something light Thursday. Then I'll go up and play the game because that's the best thing I can do.

182

I think training hard every day helps me mentally. By getting myself to train even when I don't want to, or when my body mentally doesn't feel like it, I become mentally tougher, and that's part of the reason that I do it. I just say to myself, "There are going to be days in the Olympics when we have to play a game and I don't feel like it."

I do a lot of imagery, seeing myself playing and performing well and making shots in my own mind both in training and before a game. I always do it before I play a game, during our afternoon rest, or when I lie in bed at night. I close my eyes and see myself going through motions and making every shot. Sometimes I like to look at it like I am watching it through a T.V. and I also like to watch it from my own eyes so that I can see everything happening from the inside. For example, I see the ball leaving my hands and the follow-through, and the ball going through the net. Even way back in high school when I was high-jumping I used to have that experience of seeing myself going over the bar. I believe in that, as far as my own shot and my own game goes. But I think it's tough for a team to do that when you don't have all the players seeing the same movement of the team and executing an offensive play perfectly from the opening line-up.

In my imagery I do mainly foul shots. That is the only shot that is ever the same in competition as it is in training. I practise that shot 100 times a day. I also do it mentally, seeing the ball go in all the time. When my foul shot is on, I feel better with myself and everything goes well, including my jump shot. I'm left with a good feeling after the imagery of these shots going in, plus in my mind I go through the actual steps that I go through on the court. I bounce the ball 5 times and each bounce represents a specific focus, from the feel of my toes, to the bending of my knees, to my elbow being straight, to my finger tips on the ball, to the last bounce and the follow through. When I go through the imagery I do all those steps again and I do millions of shots in my head.

It used to take me thirty seconds to shoot one foul shot because I'd bounce it once to make sure my toes were right, then I'd bounce it again, my knees, and I'd work up my body, then I'd bounce it again, my elbows are straight, and I'd bounce it again, just my fingertips are on the ball, and then the last bounce is when I'm going to release it. I used to think of all those, but now I just go up there and I bounce it 5 times; it's automatic but each thing is set. Every foul shot is 5 bounces, focus on the rim and shoot. It's always the same. When I'm lying down getting prepared for the game in the afternoon, I do 8 to 10 free throws in my mind, breaking it down nice and slow. Sometimes I like to do it in slow motion just to see the rotation of the ball. During that preparation time a lot of my imagery is just the mesh and seeing the reaction of the mesh, the way it pushes up, and the sound. Often that is the only imagery I have. I don't even follow the shot or my hand, or me. I just focus on the mesh. I do that during warm-ups sometimes, just sitting there watching when other guys are shooting the ball. I watch all the balls going through, just focusing on the mesh. It gives me something to focus on.

Anytime I'm having an off shooting day or couple of days, I just completely forget about everything and go in and focus on the rim. I just stare at the rim. When most players shoot the ball they follow the ball so that they have an idea where the rebound is going. I just focus

I bounce the ball five times and each bounce represents a specific focus, from the feel of my toes, to the bending of my knees, to my elbow being straight, to my finger tips on the ball, to the last bounce and the follow through.

183

on the rim, I don't even look at anything else. A lot of it is focusing, and imagery of seeing the ball going through. I've always focused on the rim. The first thing I do when I step on the court is look at the rim because that's where I'm going to have to be focusing during the game. I think I had always believed in that even before Cal Botterill, our sport psychologist, reinforced it and the positiveness of it.

Coach Donohue has said, "If we can't get in the gym to shoot, we are just going to sit there and put all the lights out. You are going to see yourself doing it well, consistently; all positive, everything is going in." He's been doing that for some time now, but I've expanded on it because I really believe it. When you're in a slump, I think the slump is reinforced because you see your shot miss and then you're thinking about the miss and you see it again and again and that reinforces the miss. That's why you miss all the time, whereas, if you can just think, "It's in, it's in, it's in," it helps you shoot better.

When we are together we work on team things, but often we are not together as a team. When we go home we are expected to work on our own individual games.

I do a lot of imagery every day when I'm practising by myself. There's no-one else in the gym but I have a guy up there in imagery. I'll make a move and, "Oh-oh he's there, he's a big guy, I can't go over him," and then I fake. There's no-one there really. People watching me in the gym must think, "What's he doing?" I'll do it physically, with an image as a defence, and I'll beat the guy. I do stuff like that all the time as far as practice work goes. The imagery of playing against somebody changes so much, because you have to react to them. If they go left, then you have to go right. There's so much instant reaction.

Everyday I shoot one hundred foul shots. Then I shoot twenty shots from 5 different zones on the court. I throw my ball up and catch it like I'm receiving it and make the shot. The next set of one hundred shots is the same thing, only it's man-to-man. I don't just stand and take the shot. I get the ball and then I make the move, and all the time I'm making a move on an imaginary guy. I make 5 different moves. On the first move I beat the guy to the left, on the second I beat him to the right. On the third I go, but he catches me, so I have to pump, fake and get him up there, and then go up for the shot. The next one is the same except I go the opposite way. Then for the final move I make something up. I make some new move on the 5th, every time. The first four are set. I do that so that I get practice going to the left and practice going to the right and one where you beat the guy and hit the jumper, and one where he comes with you and you have to use a fake to get him off.

Everyday I follow the same sequence. I shoot one hundred free shots, 10 at a time. There are 6 baskets in the gym and I shoot 2 at one basket, 2 at another basket all the way around the gym. I do those free shots in between each set of twenty shots where I'm moving with imaginary opponents, so that I'm shooting when I'm tired, when I'm huffing and puffing and it's more like the game situation.

I've shot so many foul shots every day, that now I'm making ninety-six out of one hundred, and I chart that. If I see that going down, I'll slow it right down and take 5 bounces and concentrate on

184

every shot, because some days I find myself not concentrating on every shot when I am shooting so many a day.

Then after a while I can see my score going down by one or two a day until I get down to eighty-eight or ninety, so I say, "Well it's got to get back up. Let's go right back and start again." Then I'll take more time, I'll slow them right down and think about every shot.

We have a pre-game meal 4 hours before the game, and my pre-game plan starts then. We have our pre-game meal with the team, or with individuals when we are in different places, but I always eat with somebody I'm going to be participating with on the team. Then I go for a walk afterwards and then I lie down in bed. I'll read something, try to relax, sleep and then do some imagery. Then it's time to go to the game. Everything is ready, everything is planned. I like to stretch for twenty minutes in the change room before we get onto the floor. Sometimes we're just shoved right onto the floor in different countries, so then I'll do some stretching on the floor, but usually most of the stretching is done in the change room before I get out there. I stretch in the same order, the same muscles every time. Once I get out there I like to run through the lay-ups. I do the same series of things in the lay-ups too. I take a couple of low galloping strides to lay the ball in, early, and then I like to slowly increase my jump, and then slowly increase the speed at which I go. By the time the game comes I'm ready to go as fast as I want.

Before the game starts I think of what we have to do. We have to remember who is going to be guarding the best players on their team, and how are we going to stop them. I'm just focused on the job. I'm thinking about this while I'm stretching, and being the captain I also have to be sure the other guys are thinking about their jobs. So I walk around while I'm stretching saying, "Hey, that guy out there is tough tonight, you've got to do a good job on him," that sort of thing. Very seldom before the game, will I think of the outcome, unless we've played them before and done really well against them.

In the Olympics I didn't start the tournament off well. I played better in the second game. After a while I thought, I'm not as high as I should be. Then I said to myself, "This is the Olympics, this is what I've waited 7 years for, so let's wake up and get out of this dream. If you don't participate the best you can right now, you're going to be pissed off for the rest of your life." Things got better later on in the tournament. I started playing better. I think the fact that we hadn't been together as a team bothered me and being the captain, I felt that it was my job, but at the time I didn't want to cause hard feelings.

When things were going best I was thinking, "Let's not get too excited, just keep on task, keep everything on track. Let's keep on passing the ball, moving the ball up the floor. Let's keep doing that, let's not hold the ball now because we have a lead." During the game so many things go through my mind. When things are going great for me I focus on doing the same things over and over again, like, "Take it again and bury them, you've got them on the line right now, push them over." I think back to the Italy game when we had that lead going in with about 2 or 3 minutes to go and we were playing well. Then we started holding onto the ball. I was going, "Let's go, let's take it at them," and that's what Tony did. He just took it 3 times in a row. He got fouled twice and made us a basket in his foul shot

I do a lot of imagery everyday when I'm practicing by myself. There's no one else in the gym but I have a guy up there in imagery.

and his basket actually won us the game. There are so many things to think about, because offensively everything is going well, and then you have to switch and play defence, which is totally different. You have to be aggressive stopping them without fouling them. You don't want to give them three points. I think a lot of it is experience in learning what to do and when to do it.

I worked hard in each game. When things aren't going well you tend to push. I was really pushing. I was working harder and harder all the time. I never got tired at the Olympics during the competition. I never even noticed it. I was tending to force things a little bit so I just said, "Whoa, just relax and take things the way they come, things will work out, concentrate on something else. My shots aren't going in, let's concentrate on passing the ball, let's concentrate on playing defence and stopping their best player", and that's actually what I did in the second game.

I never got the feeling of the swish in the net in that whole Olympic tournament. We had one practice in the forum where we played and I didn't really get a chance to do a lot of imagery in there, because we were not in there long. I can look at baskets but every basket is different when you really look at it the way I do. I didn't get that chance and it wasn't a shooter's gym. The baskets were tight and the rims were really solid so anything that hit them, rolled. I was hitting them and they were bouncing out. When I look back at the statistics of the whole tournament for all the shooters around the world, no-one really shot well. No one shot consistently well throughout the whole tournament. It could have been the back drop, could have been the rims, could have been the backboard. I had a few games when I shot well such as the Italy game and a couple of other games, but not consistently red hot the way I like to be in a tournament.

Most of the time we get an hour to shoot in the gym where we're going to play the day of the game. That hour I concentrate on the floor and where the bad bounces are, and the backboard and the rim, and the way the ball is going to bounce off the rim and where it's going to go. Then I just focus on the rim and where everything's going to happen. Unfortunately we had only one practice in the forum before the game started and then we practised in another gym the day of the game. I was focusing in those gyms and I was shooting well in practices, but once I got into the games I wasn't absolutely positive about the rims. I did imagery almost every day before the game but I always had this thing in my mind that it wasn't the real game basket that we were practising on. Just changing the mesh can throw off the point I've been concentrating on for the whole day, unless I have time to get used to it. Also we like to practise with the same lights on, the TV lights, so the brightness of the room will be the same as it is when we play because that's what I see in my imagery from the time I practise until I go into the game at night.

Coach Donohue is a believer in knowing what you are going to do and why, even between periods of action, halves of games, or timeouts. This is the same every time. When we go somewhere for a trip, there's a reason behind how many games we're going to play and how many days we're going to stay there. Sometimes we're away for 3 weeks, because he says that when we're at the Olympics we're going

I do those free shots in between each set of twenty shots where I'm moving with imaginary opponents, so that I'm shooting when I'm tired, when I'm huffing and puffing and it's more like the game situation.

186

to be together for 3 weeks, so we're going to be together for 3 weeks at this time.

We go through the same procedures at half time. Some of the guys who didn't get a chance to play are stretching, other are just relaxing and catching their breath. We have time to ourselves to go to the washroom or wash off in the first few minutes and then the coach will come in and explain what went wrong, what went well, what we're going to do.

Before the coach comes in I'm usually thinking about what went well for us and what we should keep doing. We keep a chart and I like to look at the chart at half time and see what happened. Mentally I just look at the chart and see what plays went well and why they went well and then I try to relax and think about the second half, about my job and what I have to do.

The coaches will come in with comments like, "Hey, that guy that we're supposed to shut out has twenty points at the half", and I'll say "Boom; somewhere in that first half I forgot about that guy I was supposed to shut out. The key to the game is going to be shutting him out so, let's concentrate on that again." The coaches remind us and bring up points again of the things that we have to do. We think of stuff too, and most of it's done with everybody talking and throwing in comments and no-one getting mad at each other. I think that's one of the real positive things about our team.

When I go back out on the court for the second half, I have a set procedure which I follow. It depends a lot on how much I played in the first half and how much of a rest I need, but we come out and do our weaves. I like to do two or three and then we throw out the rest of the balls and I shoot. I like to take a few shots if my shot hasn't been going well. I like to shoot and focus on the rim at the other end now. When I sit down I really know what my focus has to be. I just relax.

Coach Donohue has talked about the importance of imagery and mental preparation. He makes you aware of the fact that you are isolated here now but it's taken a lot of work to get to where you are. He makes you think back to all the hard times and all the practices you went through to be where you are now, to have a chance to play in these Games. He brings that up before the Games with each individual and then to the team. Most of what he does is positive. "Hey, these guys can be beaten, we beat these guys two weeks ago in Toronto, now we're going to play them for the bronze medal — these guys can be beaten and you can do it." He's very positive with us and he reviews inventory with us. Sometimes he'll say, "Everybody lie down and see yourself making a shot. Shut your eyes and see 5 guys out there running high post perfectly." We do that. I can shut my eyes right now and think of the game situation, and defensive players out there and running a high post and guys cutting off to the basket. Most of our plays are designed for that.

A lot of what the coach does is reinforcing our belief in ourselves and that we can do it as a team. He is very positive that way. He'll do it individually on the bus on the way to the game, but at the game it's mostly with the whole team. There is never anything negative said before a game.

187

The assistant coaches have input in that way too. I'm always surprised at the way Steve Konchalski is so positive. I'll say something like, "Hey, we can beat these guys," and he'll look at me with a look that says, "There's no doubt: I mean, of course we can beat these guys." He doesn't really say anything but you just know what he's feeling, how confident he is, and that makes you really believe it.

Cal Botterill (sport psychologist) helped us a lot in 1983. He opened our eyes to a lot of things. Filling out the forms made us aware of what the problems were. Whether he did anything with the forms or took the forms and burned them, it made us think of things that could go wrong and things that we should expect. Because of that when we went to Brazil we knew that the food would not be very good. The first day when we had a crappy meal, we just looked at it and thought, "We knew this was going to happen; eat it anyway." Whereas if you hadn't talked about it, you would think, "How are we going to eat here for two weeks?" Right away it is negative. Just by us thinking and knowing about what to expect, they're not hitting us out of nowhere. We had written down everything that we felt was going to happen. We knew the crowd would be a factor, and writing things like that down made us aware of everything before it happened. I think that had a positive effect.

I think Cal really helped a lot of guys, individually, and also at our team meetings. We had key words, like "on task", "on fire," and that really helped us. But, it kind of phased out as we went along. He was mainly the guy behind the bench in Edmonton yelling, "On fire, out there, let's go, on fire", and we were laughing half the time. Then you'd think, "He's right, we are on fire, let's go." We'd think about it and he was right. At the Olympics I missed that. He helped us as a team in 1983, and individually I used him through the year. I talked to him, and corresponded with him about different things and about the way I felt, probably more than most of the other guys. I know we had about half the guys who really felt that it was beneficial, and about half the guys who didn't use it at all. I was on the half that was more receptive.

I think he made the guys aware of what was going on and that's very important, especially when you're travelling in other countries. He'd photocopy different things and we'd read, "It's going to be hot, it is going to be smoggy, and there is going to be a lot of interaction, a lot of cameras, a lot of athletes," etc. It made everyone aware and we had meetings to go over things like that.

Cal gave us constant reminders to go over the imagery. 1983 was the main year, because he taught us a lot of things. Last year he just reminded us of things to do; go through the inventory, relax, think of the key words, concentrate, get your focus point.

Cal had a positive attitude all the time which was beneficial to us. He was always "up", and that's often contagious when you're with the team. He really felt for the team and you could sense that. And we felt for him and accepted him into the group in a short time.

He helped by reinforcing important cues. When we were with the team, he and I would always go out and talk about the way things were going and what to expect. I think by him just being a friend and by me having someone away from the sport and the coaching staff and the players to talk to about their view really helped me. He was

188

almost like a spectator but he knew what was going on, and I think he helped me remain positive by the information he gave me.

In Edmonton, it was mandatory that we filled out the mental readiness form and coach Donohue was right behind it all the way. Last year they weren't mandatory at all. It was, "If you want a form to fill out, go ahead, take one," but no-one took one. If we weren't forced to, it was like kids in high school with homework: if it's not assigned, I'm not doing it. Maybe they should have been assigned at the Olympics so that the coaches could see what was going on. Maybe the point of the players just running off and not being together would have come up on one of the sheets and the coaches would have realized it.

I liked the forms. It was a pain in the neck some of the time and I didn't like filling it out, but I liked what I got out of it. It's the same with training: you don't like it but you enjoy the game and the competition and you don't want to go in unprepared. So you don't like filling in all the forms but you like getting it back and seeing all the results.

The games we played in Canada were very beneficial in helping the Canadian athletes; it brought us to a point where we were high profile, and we should be. The crowds were great for our games and the guys were feeling great about themselves because they got a chance to play in their home town against Yugoslavia, and it was really a powerful feeling.

It would have helped if we could have had all the staff that was with us up to the Olympics continue through the Olympics. We had to drop people because of numbers. I know it's expensive. But those people are important. Doc Ryan wasn't allowed to go, and I think one of the main reasons that we did well in Edmonton was because of his scouting reports of games. He and coach Konchalski did an excellent job videotaping the other teams and breaking it down into pieces so that we knew exactly what they were going to do. At the Olympics that was done but it would have helped to have had his input also, because he had a way of relating to the players. He is a coach but I had played with him and a couple of the other players had played with him. He's kind of in between the players and the coaches. Sometimes the coaches ask too much. He knew what we could do and how to do the different things. I think that would have helped and Cal would have helped. Cal was there but he had problems getting in and out of the village most of the time and it was a pain in the neck for guys to have to go out of the village to see him. I think we needed both those guys because it tore up the team a bit and the good feeling. For the Olympics we should get rid of guys that we don't need and bring those guys.

We had written down everything that we felt was going to happen. We knew the crowd would be a factor, and writing things like that down made us aware of everything before it happened. I think that had a positive effect.

189

NOTES

NOTES

The following books are available for those interested in learning more about the principles underlying some of these success stories:

In Pursuit of Excellence (1980);
Psyching for Sport: Mental Training for Athletes (1986);
Coaches Training Manual to Psyching for Sport (1986);
Mental Training for Coaches and Athletes (1982).

All of these books can be purchased through:
The Coaching Association of Canada
333 River Road
Ottawa, Ontario
Canada
K1L 8H9